F
1500–1715

Alastair Armstrong

Series Editors

Martin Collier
Rosemary Rees

HEINEMANN ADVANCED HISTORY

Heinemann Educational Publishers
Halley Court, Jordan Hill, Oxford OX2 8EJ
Part of Harcourt Education Limited

Heinemann is the registered trademark of Harcourt Education Limited

First published 2003

07 06 05 04 03
10 9 8 7 6 5 4 3 2 1

British Library Cataloguing in Publication Data is available from the British
Library on request.

ISBN 0435327518

Designed, illustrated and typeset by Wyvern 21

Original illustrations © Harcourt Education Limited, 2003

Printed and bound in the UK by Scotprint

Photographic acknowledgements
The author and publisher would like to thank the following for permission to
reproduce photographs: page 4, The Bridgeman; page 7, Corbis; page 8, The
Bridgeman, page 14, The Bridgeman; page 33, Mary Evans; page 35,
Corbis/Charles & Josie Lenars; page 39, The Bridgeman; page 52, Art Archive;
page 56, Art Archive; page 59, Corbis/Bettmann; page 67, Photos12; page 69, Art
Archive; page 74, The Bridgeman; page 93, The Bridgeman; page 96, The
Bridgeman; page 102, Corbis/Bettmann; page 104, The Bridgeman; page 107,
Corbis/Chris Hellier; page 119, The Bridgeman; page 122, The Bridgeman; page
125, Mary Evans Picture Library; page 136, Mary Evans Picture Library; page
139, The Bridgeman; page 140, Corbis/Archivo Iconografico; page 142,
Corbis/Historical Picture Archive; page 150, Photos12; page 212,
The Bridgeman; page 220, The Bridgeman; page 225, The Bridgeman.

Cover photograph: © AKG London

Picture research by: Peter Norris

Author dedication: To Carrie

CONTENTS

HOW TO USE THIS BOOK

This book is divided into two distinct sections.

- The AS section describes and explains the main developments in Renaissance and Reformation France 1498-1610. This section also offers an overview of the reigns of Louis XIII and Louis XIV charting the development of the French monarchy. This narrative aims to give the student in-depth information and some basic analysis. The summary questions at the end of each chapter challenge the student to use the information given to explain, evaluate and analyse important aspects of the topic covered. In this way, students will acquire a clear understanding of the key features of each topic.
- The A2 section focuses on specific themes and concepts concerning the French monarchy and the development of a nation-state during this period, and is more analytical in style. It looks at the main theories which seek to explain the changes that took place in the governing of France, considering theories of centralisation and absolutism. Students who are intending to use this section should refer back to the relevant AS sections that will provide the factual underpinning to the debates.

At the end of each section there are assessment sections based on the requirements of the three Awarding Bodies – AQA, Edexcel and OCR – which give students detailed guidance on how to answer the questions set. The A2 section is based on OCR Module 2590 and AQA module Henry IV. As such, Henry IV is given greater coverage in the A2 section.

The apparent imbalance between the AS and A2 sections, with the AS section being much larger, reflects the emphasis placed by the Awarding Bodies on where, in the specifications, knowledge and understanding of this period of French history is assessed.

The bibliography suggests books that students may wish to consult. Students are strongly advised to broaden their understanding of the period by reading as widely as possible.

AS SECTION: NARRATIVE AND EXPLANATION

INTRODUCTION: SIXTEENTH-CENTURY FRANCE

THE KINGDOM

On 27 May 1498 Louis, Duke of Orleans, was crowned King of France in **Reims Cathedral**. The circumstances of his succession were fortuitous in that his predecessor and cousin, Charles VIII, had stumbled and hit his head on a doorway entrance while on his way to watch a tennis match in the royal château at Amboise. With no immediate male heirs, the crown passed to Louis, thus beginning what many historians have termed a period of **Renaissance monarchy**, in which Louis reformed the legal system, reduced taxes and expanded French territories in Italy. In 1498, when Louis took his coronation oath, in which he promised to defend both church and kingdom, France was some way off being a unified nation-state.

Indeed Frenchmen barely recognised their country as one whole unit, simply because there were few common traits of national identity to bind the kingdom together. French frontiers were vague; no common language existed; and the country's system of law was not unified. European nationalism and the concept of a nation-state developed only fully in the nineteenth century, although we can trace the development of modern France throughout the early modern period. However, it would be foolish to believe that successive French Renaissance monarchs set out to unite the country: there was no grand plan to push France towards a nation-state. Instead, monarchs such as Louis XII and **Francis I** recognised the link between a more centralised government and increased royal authority.

The process of overcoming parochial, provincial barriers was a slow and not entirely successful one during the sixteenth and seventeenth centuries:

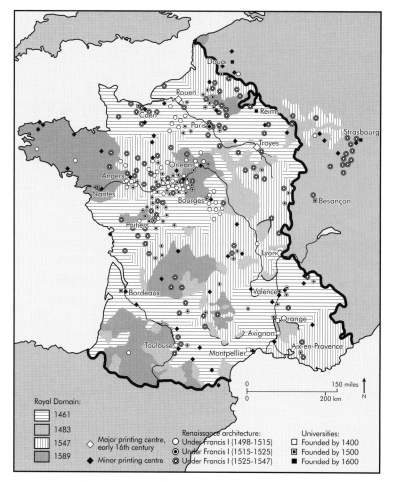

Royal Domain:
- 1461
- 1483
- 1547
- 1589

◇ Major printing centre, early 16th century
◆ Minor printing centre

Renaissance architecture:
- ○ Under Francis I (1498-1515)
- ◉ Under Francis I (1515-1525)
- ◎ Under Francis I (1525-1547)

Universities:
- □ Founded by 1400
- ▣ Founded by 1500
- ■ Founded by 1600

0 ___ 150 miles
0 ___ 200 km   N

Renaissance France

Francis I (1494–1547) The epitome of a Renaissance monarch, Francis succeeded his cousin Louis XII as king of France in 1515, marrying his daughter Claude in the process in order to consolidate the absorption of Brittany into the French kingdom. As a Renaissance prince he naturally welcomed humanists, painters and writers to his court although his admiration for Christian humanists and reform waned after 1534 as his objection to the rise of Protestantism grew. Well known for his rivalry with both Henry VIII (king of England) and Charles V (Holy Roman Emperor and king of Spain), he spent large amounts of money fighting the Habsburg Charles over Italy. Initially successful in Italy with a crushing victory over the Swiss at Marignano in 1515, Francis was later defeated at Pavia in 1525 leading to his capture and imprisonment in Madrid at the hands of Charles. Beaten in Italy Francis is nevertheless remembered as one of the great French monarchs because of his attempts to centralise French government, combat heresy and promote the glory of France abroad. His legacy can still be seen in the Loire Valley where magnificent châteaux such as Chambord bear testament to the grandeur of his reign.

- Of all early modern European kingdoms, France had the greatest area (459,000 square kilometres), the largest population (approximately 15 million) and the richest agriculture, yet government was decentralised and relatively weak.
- The economy was largely rural: over 80 per cent of the population were based in the countryside, although urban populations were on the rise by the sixteenth century. Economic depression in the second half of the sixteenth century, made worse by the French Wars of Religion, hit the rural population hard.
- The three major towns of Paris, Lyons and Rouen had populations over 60,000 and were among the largest towns in western Europe. The cities served as centres of trade, administration and intellect where new ideas could spread through word of mouth or by the newly

developed printing press. Nevertheless, local customs and traditions along with poor internal communications prevented French trade from reaching the levels of its maritime neighbours in this period.

Moreover, the make up of the French kingdom had been altered relatively recently by the assimilation of frontier provinces such as Brittany in 1491. Indeed, in 1500 nearly one-quarter of the kingdom had been acquired in the previous 50 years. Therefore, much of France was new, acquired by diplomacy, conquest or marriage. Metz, Toul and Verdun in 1522 and Calais in 1558 are two more examples of territories that became part of the French kingdom in the sixteenth century. Much of the credit for this unification of France goes to the French king, Francis I.

Yet, to describe France as a nation-state would be false for the following reasons:

KEY TERM

Provincial liberties Many cities, towns and provinces had been granted special conditions by the crown that allowed them to be exempt from taxation or to erect internal trade barriers. Even if such liberties had been granted hundreds of years before the magistrates of the town or local lord guarded them jealously. This would cause problems as French provinces and towns became more interested in protecting their own status and rights rather than those of France as a whole.

- Few Frenchmen regarded their country as a unified whole: **provincial liberties** often overrode central directives.
- The Hundred Years' War had ended only in 1453, and during that conflict much of the realm had been occupied at one time or another by English or Burgundian troops. Only when the English were defeated and removed from the south-west of France did French rule resume for the first time in 300 years.
- Burgundy, Picardy and Provence were all acquisitions made by the French crown since 1470. Clearly the assimilation of such important territories increased the power of the crown and began to form the boundaries of modern France. Renaissance monarchs in France continued this process throughout the sixteenth century, and made efforts to impose the royal will on such provinces. Yet, declaring royal authority and legislation to hold power in such territories was one thing, actually translating that will into practice was another.
- In reality such newly acquired provinces could not easily become part of the French kingdom. They had their own histories, traditions and privileges that were now under threat from the crown.

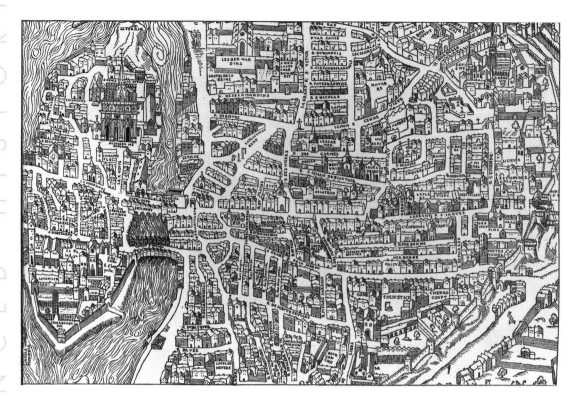

Paris in the mid-sixteenth century

- New *parlements* were established in Dijon, Bordeaux, Rennes and Rouen throughout the sixteenth century in order to ensure that the royal prerogative was carried out. These were provincial replicas of the Paris *parlements*, but they met with mixed success, especially during periods of weak monarchy.

Still, the medieval adage of 'one king, one faith and one law' largely rang true in France. In many ways these were the principles that bound French society together. Despite separate customs and traditions, all Frenchmen in 1500 looked to one rightful king appointed by God, followed the one true faith of Catholicism and abided by the law of the land. Yet it seems impossible to talk of 'Frenchmen': few regarded themselves as such; rather they were Bretons, Normans or such like. While a French monarch existed many provinces ignored royal legislation if they could and avoided paying taxation to the crown if at all possible. The arrival of Protestantism in the sixteenth century shook

Parlements The French *parlements* should not be equated with the English parliament. The *parlements* were sovereign law courts that acted as royal courts of appeal. *Parlements* therefore heard legal grievances involving the king and were expected to uphold the king's will. Royal legislation or edicts were also endorsed and ratified by *parlements* before becoming law. The idea was that royal authority would be extended through *parlements*, and strong monarchs such as Francis I controlled *parlements* effectively. In times of weakness, such as in the second half of the sixteenth century, *parlements* could cause the monarchy problems by refusing to ratify legislation, and opposing royal policies.

French society to the core, challenged the old values and beliefs of Catholicism and fuelled over 30 years of civil war. Royal authority rose under the Renaissance monarchs, fell during the Wars of Religion and recovered again in the seventeenth century, reaching a pinnacle under Louis XIV. Therefore, throughout the period, all three tenets of 'one king, one faith and one law' were challenged and out of turmoil and tragedy emerged the beginnings of the modern state that we recognise as France.

CHAPTER 1

Renaissance monarchy 1: Does Louis XII deserve the title 'Father of the People'?

LOUIS XII, KING OF FRANCE, 1498–1515

Background of Louis XII

Louis was born in 1462 during the reign of his second cousin Louis XI. His father was Charles, Duke of Orleans, head of a branch of the royal house of Valois. Louis XI was succeeded by his son Charles VIII in 1483. Louis of Orleans became heir and got on well with the new king.

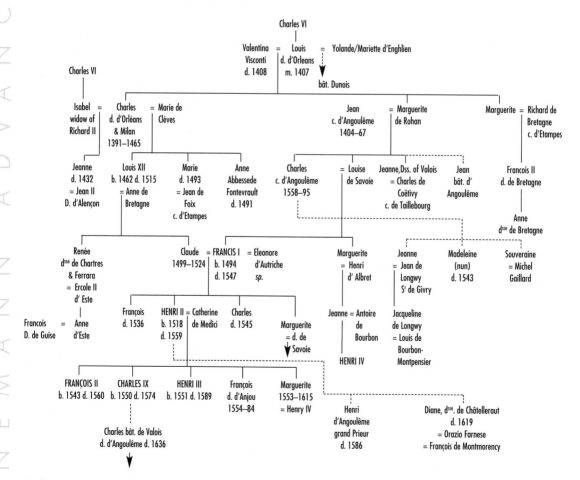

Orleans – Angouléme family tree

Charles VII

Yet, the king's sister Anne of Beaujeau was determined to dominate the king's favour alongside her husband, the Duke of Bourbon. Therefore, in 1485 and again in 1488, Louis was forced to join forces with other discontented nobles, most notably the Duke of Brittany, and rebel against the crown. Captured in 1488, Louis was never charged with treason and by 1491 amicable relations with Charles were restored. So, Louis' background was one of controversy and disorder, and there were even rumours surrounding his legitimacy to rule. However, in May 1498 Louis was crowned king in Reims Cathedral and with little political experience began a rule which lasted nearly seventeen years and did much to set France on the road to legal codification and political centralisation.

CONSOLIDATION OF POWER

Louis' first priority was to secure his position as king and ensure that no opposition to his rule emerged. To this end he ended his first marriage to Jeanne, daughter of Louis XI, and married Anne of Brittany, widow of Charles VIII and eldest daughter of Duke Francis II of Brittany. The marriage served an important political function:

- It consolidated the French absorption of Brittany (although it was not until 1532 that the duchy was formally attached to the French kingdom).
- It allied Louis to a powerful noble family.

Like his contemporary in England, King Henry VII, Louis was wary of noble faction and he was careful not to exclude important nobles from court while also ensuring that they were not able to build up independent power bases. Therefore, Pierre de Rohan, Seigneur de Gie and prominent member of the Bourbon family, became an important royal adviser. Accused of treason in 1504, Rohan fell from power, probably the victim of trumped up charges orchestrated by Cardinal Georges d'Amboise and the queen, both of whom were jealous of Rohan's influence with the king.

Centralisation of government

Louis also made attempts to extend his power and authority into the provinces, thus centralising government and controlling his nobility. In 1499, he issued the **Ordinance of Blois**. This was followed in 1510 by the Ordinance of Lyons. Such edicts may be taken as evidence of Louis XII's willingness to reform and in particular to define clearly the powers of regional officials and make them accountable to the crown. There were other changes that seemingly heralded political and social change:

- Louis set about codifying French law and a new *parlement* was established in Provence.
- Louis' reign also witnessed the beginnings of change in the social hierarchy. Louis' reign marked the emergence of a new noble class, the so-called **nobility of the robe**. Legal reforms created new offices which in turn brought ennoblement for those who were appointed to judicial positions. However, we should not exaggerate the extent of change. In reality the ancient **nobility of the sword** were still the major source of power and prestige within France, and the idea that Louis created legal offices in order to undermine the great magnates is false.

Noble families such as La Trémoille were an important part of Louis XII's regime and in many ways their support was crucial in maintaining law and order in the localities. Louis worked closely with the nobility, and several assemblies of notables reflect the close relationship which existed between the king and this estate. Little noble opposition during the reign of Louis XII bears testament to a relatively consultative and conciliatory approach towards the nobility.

Financial management

Louis had been left a deficit of 1.4 million **livres** by his predecessor and cousin, Charles VIII. In turn, Louis handed on the same deficit to his successor, Francis I. Therefore, while Louis was unable actually to make a profit, he did manage royal finances relatively effectively:

- Louis was also able to reduce the level of the *taille*, a move which was most popular and went some way to

controlling political offices. The debate among historians lies in whether this new administrative noble class actually challenged the social and political standing of the old nobility.

The nobility of the sword
The established nobility in France who were closely related to the crown and inherited their noble title. Many could trace their blood lineage for centuries back and families such as the Condé, Soissons and Guise owned large amounts of land and were extremely powerful. The nobility of the sword did service to the king on the battlefield and raised armies in his name. In return, they were exempted from all taxation.

The *taille* The main direct tax in France levied on those who could afford to pay least, namely the third estate (or peasantry).

Livre This was the currency of the time and is French for pound.

Louis XII, 'Father of the People'

The Italian wars 1494-1553

- - - - - - Territory under French occupation for a period

Novara 1500,1513

Landriano,1529

Bicocco,1522

Ceresole 1544

Agnadello,1509

Turin

Marignano,1515

Susa,1537

Ash

Pavia, 1525

Saluzzo

Genoa

Formovo,1495

Ravenna,1512

Marciano,1554

Siena,1554-5

Adriatic Sea

Garigliano,1503

Naples,1528

Amalfi,1529

Tyrrhenian Sea

N

earning him the title of 'Father of the People'.

- In order to compensate for such a reduction Louis increased the levels of indirect taxation, and exploited church and noble wealth. In 1504 and 1508, Louis introduced financial reforms designed to improve the collection of taxation and the accountancy process.
- Louis made some inroads into levels of corruption in the practice of tax collection through the appointment of eight royal officials, the *gens de finances*, whose job it was to oversee the collection of revenue. Such officers of the crown also increased royal influence in the localities.

KEY TERM

Tax farming Local taxes were collected by individuals who had paid for a contract from the crown to do so. The crown was assured of revenues; the tax farmers could make enormous profits for themselves.

Louis had made a start in the process of effective fiscal management, but given the diversity, size and decentralised nature of the kingdom progress was always likely to be slow and limited. Eight officials would not make a huge difference, and local **tax farmers** were still making vast profits at the expense of the masses.

FOREIGN POLICY

Milan

Louis' fiscal policy was often dictated by an expansionist foreign policy. In particular, Louis inherited the French claim to Naples from Charles VIII and pursued a new claim to Milan. Louis legitimised this claim in his eyes through his grandmother Valentina, the daughter of a Visconti duke of Milan. Both in terms of strategic importance and wealth, Milan was a prize asset and one which Louis was determined to attain. Louis was encouraged in his Italian adventure by d'Amboise, Archbishop of Rouen and a potential candidate for the papacy, as well as by **Pope Alexander VI** himself:

- Alexander was ready to strike a deal with Louis to ensure a papal annulment of Louis' barren and failed marriage to Jeanne and marriage to Anne of Brittany.
- He also promised to make d'Amboise a cardinal in return for French assistance.

The bargain was sealed when Alexander's illegitimate son Cesare travelled to France, delivering the papal dispensation and a cardinal's hat. In 1498, Cesare married the sister of the King of Navarre and then joined the French army which was ready to march into Italy. In contrast, the ruler of Milan, Lodovico Sforza, had few allies; when the French attacked in 1499, Sforza fled allowing Louis to make a triumphant entry into Milan. Sforza turned to the **Holy Roman Emperor**, Maximilian I, and returned in 1500 with 10,000 Swiss mercenaries. However, Sforza could not wrestle control of the duchy away from Louis, and in April 1500 his army surrendered at Novara. Sforza was captured and retired to the French château of Loches where he remained until his death. Milan was now firmly in French control and it remained so for over a decade.

Naples

Louis' next target was Naples and in November 1500 he signed the **Treaty of Granada** with Ferdinand of Aragon. The King of Naples, Federigo, had previously relied upon Spanish aid and he felt betrayed by the treaty. Helpless, Federigo retired to France where he was made Duke of

The Battle of Cerignola
Particularly memorable for
the innovative and effective
use of the recently developed
arquebus which proved too
powerful for the French
cavalry and Swiss pikemen.

Chivalric prince A prince
who followed the rules of
chivalry. This was a code of
behaviour which stressed the
values of courage, honour,
courtesy and justice.

Anjou. However, the allies soon fell out. In 1502, Louis
sought to claim the south through invasion and soon the
Spanish forces led by Cordoba were under siege in Barletta.
Cordoba is widely regarded as one of the finest generals of
the sixteenth century and his two victories over the French
at **Cerignola** and Garigliano in 1503 reflect this. The result
for Louis was the Treaty of Blois in 1505 by which the
French gave up claims to Naples.

Further defeat

Louis' campaigns had met with some success and in many
ways he was fulfilling his role as a **chivalric prince**. Yet,
after 1510, his fortunes changed. The new pope, Julius II,
was more of a soldier than a cleric and he was determined
not only to consolidate the papal states in central Italy but
also to recover papal lands lost by his Borgia predecessors.
A Holy League was formed in 1511 consisting of the
papacy, Spain, Venice and England with the intention of
removing all French influence from Italy. The response of
Louis was to attempt to depose Julius. The attempt failed
and Louis shortly found himself excommunicated by the
pope. Yet the French under their brilliant young general
Gaston de Foix won a great victory at Ravenna in which
the Spanish lost 9,000 men from an army of 16,000.

Unfortunately for Louis, his military leader Gaston de Foix
also perished and without his strategic genius the French
grip on northern Italy gradually slipped:

- The Swiss ousted France from Milan in 1513 and
  installed the son of Lodovico Sforza as duke.
- Louis suffered a humiliating defeat on home soil in 1513
  at the hands of Henry VIII at the Battle of the Spurs. In
  August, the Swiss invaded Burgundy and lay siege to
  Dijon. They withdrew only when Louis promised to
  give up claims to Milan.
- Further problems arose in 1514 when Queen Anne died,
  leaving no male heirs.
- Luckily the instability of alliances in the Italian wars
  prevented France from utter defeat. The Holy League
  was unable to take advantage of Louis' misfortunes and
  separate peace treaties were concluded with France by the
  Swiss, papacy and Spain in 1513 and then the empire in
  1514. Remarkably, England followed suit in 1514, an

alliance bound by the marriage of Henry's sister Mary to Louis in 1514. The marriage did not last long because Louis XII died on New Year's Day 1515. His third marriage provided no son and he was succeeded by Francis of Angoulême who would rule as Francis I.

CONCLUSION

Louis is often regarded as foolish for his attempt to depose Pope Julius II and naive in his military strategy.

- Yet for a good deal of his reign France dominated northern Italy and more than held its own against Maximilian, Ferdinand and the papacy.
- Louis secured the dynasty and made some attempt to centralise French government and increase royal authority in the localities. But there was no overall plan for centralisation and Louis had no vision of a unified nation-state. His actions were largely governed by the political circumstances of his rule and the need to secure his dynasty.
- In the final analysis, Louis governed France effectively using the same measures of control and coercion that his predecessors had relied on. The old nobility were still vital in maintaining royal order and influence both at court and in the provinces.

SUMMARY QUESTIONS

1. In what ways did Louis XII attempt to centralise French government?

2. How successful was Louis XII's foreign policy?

3. Did Louis XII's reign begin Renaissance monarchy in France or was the kingdom still governed along feudal lines?

4. What obstacles existed to effective government in France during the reign of Louis XII?

CHAPTER 2

Renaissance monarchy 2: Francis I

BACKGROUND AND CHARACTER OF FRANCIS I, KING OF FRANCE, 1515–47

Historical interpretations
Interpretations of Francis I's reign have attempted to gauge the extent to which he centralised the French kingdom and whether or not he paved the way for seventeenth century absolutism. In *A History of France 1460–1560*, David Potter sees the rule of Francis in the context of those that preceded him and believes that he continued the gradual erosion of particularism which Louis XI and others before him had begun. In *The Rise and Fall of Renaissance France*, R. J. Knecht sees Francis as a catalyst towards constitutional unity and centralisation, while still recognising the limitations of his rule most notably with regards to foreign policy which contributed to the decline of France in the second half of the sixteenth century.

Francis was fortunate to become king in 1515, in the sense that Louis XII could reasonably have been expected to have fathered a son from one of his three marriages. On his accession to the throne, Francis was 21 years old, and in many ways he fitted the image of a Renaissance monarch perfectly. Tall, strong and athletic, Francis had a passion for war, literature, architecture and art. During his reign, countless châteaux such as that at Chambord in the Loire Valley were constructed, while Francis also built up one of the finest libraries in western Europe. He was no scholar but he was well read in ancient mythology and he was a great conversationalist.

Francis was born on 12 September 1494 in Cognac. His father was Charles, Count of Angoulême, and his mother, Louise, was the daughter of Philip, count of Bresse. Much like his English counterpart, Henry VIII, Francis preferred hunting or jousting to bureaucracy. Still, major decisions especially those concerning foreign affairs were overseen by the king and substantial parts of each morning were spent being briefed on current affairs and proposing policy to be discussed in the *conseil des affaires*. Such routine was regularly disrupted by war, and Francis's character and personality, both positive and negative, are highlighted in the Habsburg–Valois Wars.

KEY TERM

Conseil des affaires The inner cabinet of the king's council made up of his most trusted advisers. It was here that major policy decisions were taken.

FOREIGN POLICY MILAN AND NAPLES

On his accession to the throne in 1515, Francis determined to overturn the humiliation of two years previously when France had been driven out of Milan by the Swiss. Francis once more took up French dynastic claims to Milan and Naples, and the threat to Italy was reflected in the resurrection of the **Anti-French Alliance** in 1515. In August that year, Francis was ready to invade northern Italy and his army consisted of 3000 cavalry and 23,000 German mercenaries. His mother, Louise of Savoy, was left as regent while treaties with Charles of Burgundy and Henry VIII protected his northern boundaries, leaving Francis free to make an aggressive alliance with Venice. The French army eluded the Swiss en route to Milan by taking a rarely used and remote route across the Alps. At Marignano on 14 September 1515, the French won a crushing victory, taking Milan in the process:

- Marignano marked the decline of the Swiss as a major European military power, while the battle also prompted a summit meeting between Francis and Leo X at Bologna which resulted in a concordat (agreement) which reshaped church–state relations in France.
- The victory also marked out the future battle lines in Italy between Francis and the future Charles V.

In 1516, Charles of Burgundy became king of a semi-unified Spain, and his massive inheritance and power base led to his election as Holy Roman Emperor in 1519. For the meantime, the two young monarchs signed the **Treaty of Noyon** in 1516. While this treaty seems heavily in favour of Francis, we must remember that Charles was

KEY TERM

Anti-French Alliance, 1515
Consisted of Massimiliano Sforza (ruler of Milan), Pope Leo X, the Emperor Maximilian and Ferdinand of Aragon.

KEY EVENT

Treaty of Noyon, 1516
Francis and Charles recognised each other's possessions in Milan and Naples, promised neutrality and, rather humiliatingly, Charles agreed a payment of 100,000 ducats annually to the French king as a tribute for Naples, thus recognising the French claim. The treaty was to be sealed with the marriage of Charles to Francis I's daughter Louise who would receive Naples as part of her dowry.

Francis at the Battle of Marignano

ready to travel to Spain to claim his inheritance, and he required neutrality in Italy in order to secure his position as king of Spain.

- In March 1516, the Emperor Maximilian failed to take Milan from the French in an ambitious and flawed attack.
- Francis made peace with the Swiss at Freibourg (November 1516), and in return for an annual pension the Swiss guaranteed neutrality. Such a clause also opened up the possibility of Francis hiring high-quality Swiss mercenaries.
- The threat of the Ottoman Turks to Christendom was reflected in the League of Cambrai (1517) between Francis, Charles and Maximilian which promised an allied crusade against the Turks. Yet, despite Turkish expansion, the great powers remained primarily interested in their own ambitions and possessions.

IMPERIAL ELECTION, 1519

The balance of power had changed after Marignano in favour of France and after the death of Ferdinand it had swung towards the young Charles of Burgundy. The Imperial election of 1519 was crucial not only in deciding upon the next emperor but in dictating the balance of power in Europe. With Charles and Francis the frontrunners for the post, the stakes were extremely high:

- Charles of Burgundy had Habsburg blood, his grandfather Maximilian had just died in January 1519, and whatever Francis could offer in terms of bribes Charles could better. The Fuggers of Augsburg were the foremost banking family in Europe and they offered credit to Charles in the knowledge that they would be well served for their loyalty. Charles was also voted over 600,000 crowns by the Spanish **Cortes** to use in his election campaign. Ultimately, the German princes of the empire were keen to elect another Habsburg, as they knew that their customs and privileges would remain untouched in an empire made up of over 400 relatively autonomous states.

- Despite his great victory at Marignano, the promise of at least two of the electoral votes (Palatine and Cologne) and 400,000 crowns set aside for the purpose of bribing the other four electors, Francis failed to gain the Imperial crown. Really the chances of a French victory had been slim given the influence of the Habsburgs.

On 28 June 1519, Charles was elected as Holy Roman Emperor, and in the process the positions of king of Spain and emperor were unified under one man.

War and defeat
Soon the two young kings were at war. In reaction to French aggression in Navarre and Luxembourg, Charles invaded northern France in 1521. Worse was to follow as Milan fell in November in 1521 and both the pope and Henry VIII of **England** joined Charles. Nevertheless, in October 1524, Francis daringly led an army across the Alps and seized Milan.

The victory was short-lived as the subsequent siege of Pavia during the winter months of 1524–5 sapped French troops and made them easy prey for the resurgent Imperial force in February 1525. Indeed, French casualties may have been as high as 15,000, in comparison to no more than 1500 Imperialists. By the end of the battle Francis was in captivity and his Italian campaign was in pieces. Imprisoned in Spain, Francis was forced to agree to the terms of the **Treaty of Madrid**. When he returned to France, he ignored the treaty. Although this would mean four years of harsh imprisonment for his two sons in Madrid it also freed Francis to put together the **League of Cognac**.

Continuing conflict, 1526–9
With the forces of **Suleiman the Magnificent** rampaging through Hungary in 1526 and threatening Habsburg hereditary lands, Charles V began to exert greater pressure on **Pope Clement VII** for support and loyalty.

- However, this plan was undermined in May 1527 when Imperial forces under the command of Charles of Bourbon marched on Rome, capturing the city and sacking it in the process in an orgy of ill-disciplined

KEY THEME

England Although much smaller and less powerful than France and Spain, England continued to play an important role in the Italian Wars under Henry VIII and his great cardinal minister Thomas Wolsey. England's aim was at various times either to preserve the balance of power, promote peace or gain land/money from allying with the victor. Such contradictory aims meant an opportunistic and reactive foreign policy. England was therefore a potentially important ally to both France and Spain although not indispensable.

KEY EVENT

Treaty of Madrid, 1525
Francis was obliged to hand over Milan to Charles. Francis also handed over his two sons, Francis and Henry (aged 8 and 7 respectively), as hostages to ensure that the terms of the treaty were carried out in full.

KEY TERM

The League of Cognac, 1526 A collection of Italian states, of which Venice, Florence and the papacy were the most prominent, designed to curb Habsburg power in Italy.

chaos. The Pope was left a virtual prisoner of Charles.

- Meanwhile, France turned to Henry VIII of England for support, an alliance being sealed at Amiens in August 1527. That same month, a French army under Marshal Lautrec subdued all of Lombardy with the exception of Milan, and proceeded to lay siege to Naples the following year. Yet the defection of the Genoese admiral Andrea Doria, who was lured onto the Imperial side with a massive bribe, deprived France of crucial naval support and subsequently supplies began to reach the city. The siege had failed and in 1529 the French suffered another crushing defeat at Landriano.
- In June 1529, Pope Clement signed the Treaty of Barcelona with Charles V. Imperial possessions in Naples were recognised in return for papal gains in central Italy while the Pope also promised to crown Charles as emperor.
- This agreement led to peace talks between Francis and Charles at Cambrai, resulting in the so-called **Ladies' Peace**. Essentially the Peace of Cambrai (August 1529) mirrored the terms of Madrid three years previously. Importantly for Francis, Charles renounced all claims to Burgundian lands within France and he reclaimed his sons in return for a cash settlement of 2 million gold crowns.

There was little mistaking where the balance of power lay in Europe as Francis was forced to renounce all territorial claims in Italy and Flanders. The Peace of Cambrai brought to an end the first phase of Francis I's foreign policy, which had yielded little in terms of territory but which had brought some security in terms of Burgundy.

Alliance building

Between 1530 and 1534, Francis replenished the royal coffers and waged war against Charles indirectly through the German princes of the empire:

- Charles V faced the increasing problem of reversing the **Lutheran Reformation** in the empire which undermined Catholicism and threatened to sweep all before it and split the empire.
- Although he was a Catholic, Francis readily financed the

Lutheran **Schmalkaldic League**, eager as he was to create as much havoc for Charles as he could without actually declaring war.

KEY TERMS

Schmalkaldic League, 1531
A military alliance of German princes led by Philip of Hesse, established to defend Lutheranism in the Holy Roman Empire from Catholic oppression.

- In 1534, the French aided the restoration of Duke Ulrich of Württemberg, and Francis made a formal alliance with the leading Lutheran prince, Philip of Hesse.
- Meanwhile in England, Henry VIII's break with Rome and his failure to gain a divorce from Charles V's aunt, Catherine of Aragon, inevitably pushed England closer to France.
- An alliance with the papacy in 1533 resulted in the marriage between Francis's second son, Henry of Orleans, and the pope's niece, Catherine de Medici, and was aimed towards the restoration of French ambitions in Italy.
- Francis even courted Khair ad-Din Barbarossa, the Ottoman, as a potential ally in his struggle against Charles V.

However, in 1534 Francis's alliance building was undermined by two key events:

- Persecution in France against any one suspected of Protestant sympathies damaged relations with the German princes.
- Pope Clement VII died and was replaced by Paul III, thus rendering the marriage between Henry of Orleans and Catherine de Medici politically useless.

Tension in the late 1530s

In November 1535, tension between Francis and Charles increased with the death of Francesco Sforza, Duke of Milan, without a male heir. French dynastic claims to the duchy were revived and Henry of Orleans was put forward as successor. In January 1536, Francis ordered an invasion of Savoy to demonstrate to Charles the seriousness of his intent over Milan. The emperor sprang to the defence of his brother-in-law and ally, Charles III of Savoy, and retaliated by invading Provence (July 1536). Defended admirably by the Duke of Montmorency, Provence did not fall into Imperial Hands. Despite capturing Aix, Imperial forces were unable to take Marseilles and, ravaged by disease and famine, they retreated in September 1536.

Several French garrisons were relieved in Piedmont before stalemate ensued, reflected in the Peace of Monzon (November 1537), which ensured a temporary truce if not a lasting settlement over Milan.

The truce was given greater significance and permanence by the Ten Years' Truce of 1538, negotiated by Pope Paul III. Indeed, Francis and Charles began to operate on more amicable terms between 1538 and 1540:

- The two great leaders met in person at Aigues-Mortes in July 1538.
- Francis allowed Charles to march Spanish troops across France in order to suppress revolt in Ghent.

All the while Francis hoped that Charles would cede Milan to him, but when the emperor made his own son Philip duke of Milan in 1540 it was clear that this would not be the case and in 1541 the Habsburg–Valois struggle was reignited.

War, 1542–4

After the murder of two French diplomats by Imperial troops in Lombardy and Imperial troop movements in Italy, Francis declared war on Charles in July 1542 and attacked Luxembourg in the north and Perpignan in the south. Anglo-French relations also broke down over Scotland and payments of a promised annual French pension. In 1543, Henry VIII and Charles V both declared war on Francis:

- The French king continued to attempt to make alliances with the enemies of Charles, and in 1543 Francis reacted to his increasing diplomatic isolation by allowing **Barbarossa** to make use of the port of Toulon.
- In 1544, both Charles and Henry attacked mainland France, the English laying siege to Boulogne and the emperor targeting Saint-Dizier in the east. Although Saint-Dizier finally fell to Charles as did Meaux, the invasion took longer than expected and, despite being only 75 kilometres from Paris, the decision was taken to retreat.
- On 18 September 1544, Francis and Charles signed the **Peace of Crépy** which proposed marriage alliances with

KEY PERSON

Barbarossa Khair ad-Din was a Turkish pirate who fought for the Ottoman sultan and became admiral of the Ottoman fleet in the Mediterranean. Among his many successes was the defeat of the Spanish in the south Mediterranean and the capture of Algiers.

KEY EVENT

Peace of Crépy, 1544 The peace was not universally popular in France. Many believed that Francis had sold out to Charles at a time when France should have been waging war. The peace was also opposed by Francis's own son Henry, heir to the throne. The settlement appeared to advance the position of his brother Charles and confirmed to Henry the cold relationship that he had with his father. Yet Francis was tired of war and, with little to show for French exertions, he was happy to take advantage of Charles's need to finally address the religious situation in Germany.

major territorial concessions. Either the Duke of Orleans would marry Charles's daughter Maria and receive the Low Countries and Franche-Comte as part of the dowry settlement, or he would marry the emperor's niece Anna and receive Milan. Francis had agreed to support Charles in his desire to have a General Council of the Church summoned in order to act against the growth of Protestantism.

In the end the death of Charles of Orleans in September 1545 negated much of the peace. Henry VIII was pacified by the Treaty of Ardres in June 1546 before Francis himself died in 1547, to be succeeded by his son Henry II.

The foreign policy of Francis I

- Francis I's aims in foreign policy were largely consistent throughout his reign, centring on the acquisition of territory in Italy, particularly the duchy of Milan. Such an expansionist policy was meant to reflect the glory, power and grandeur of Francis I's reign.

- The French victory at Marignano, the capture of Milan and the subsequent Concordat of Bologna were the high points of Francis I's foreign policy. These successes came early in his reign and were short-lived. Milan was briefly recaptured in 1524 but defeat at Pavia in 1525 heralded the beginning of Imperial dominance.

- The accession of Charles V as Holy Roman Emperor, made him the most powerful ruler in western Christendom because he already ruled Spain, the Low Countries, Franche-Comte and Naples. Francis felt encircled by Habsburg territories and wished to demonstrate French power by expanding in Italy.

- Both the Peace of Madrid (1526) and the Peace of Cambrai (1529) should be viewed as failures for Francis as he was forced to surrender his claims to Milan, Naples and Genoa. Moreover, repudiation of Madrid meant that his two sons remained in harsh captivity and relations between Francis and his second son, Henry, remained strained thereafter.

RELIGION AND HUMANISM

Relations with the papacy

When Francis became the king of France in 1515, the relationship between church and state was in theory governed by the Pragmatic Sanction of Bourges of 1438. This was an agreement between the king and the pope allowing cathedral chapters to elect bishops and abbots independently. The relationship between Rome and the French church was called Gallicanism and French clerical liberties were proudly guarded. Yet, the supposed guardian of these liberties, the king, had effectively taken control of the clergy by the beginning of the sixteenth century.

The Concordat of Bologna, 1516 The **Concordat** of Bologna resulted from the political context of the beginning of the sixteenth century. Francis needed papal support in order to consolidate victory at Marignano, while Leo X was eager to restore some semblance of papal authority in France. The Pragmatic Sanction of Bourges was torn apart in 1516, to the horror of the *parlement* of Paris and the Gallican church. By the new agreement the king was legally able to nominate candidates directly for vacant bishoprics and to fill vacancies in abbeys and monasteries. In return, Leo could collect taxation from newly appointed bishops and he had the right to veto any of Francis' nominations. Two issues seem to be important here:

- The Concordat of Bologna gave Francis unprecedented control over the French church.
- *Parlement* was virtually forced to agree to the concordat despite bitterly opposing the extension of royal authority. Through threats and intimidation Francis exerted his will upon the *parlement* of Paris.

Impact of the concordat One of the unfortunate effects of the Concordat was the way in which Francis used his powers of appointment as a means of patronage, rewarding leading nobles with clerical positions. Of the 129 men appointed by Francis nearly 100 were related to leading aristocratic families. Few had any theological training and the extension in royal authority over the church contributed to the declining standards of the French church. Moreover, Henry II continued the practice of his father in appointing Italians to leading positions in the church as a source of political patronage in order to advance the French position in Italy. Absenteeism, **pluralism**, **simony** and **nepotism** were rife and it is hardly surprising that calls for reform were heard in the early sixteenth century.

French Christian humanism

In the early sixteenth century, a movement emerged which answered contemporary calls for reform of the church. This movement existed at a high academic level and became known as Christian humanism.

- Humanists sought to improve Christian life and worship through a return to the original scriptures and a better understanding of how God wishes us to live.
- Men such as **Desiderius Erasmus** believed that the simple gospel message, the word of God, had been obscured by scholarly interpretation and indeed clerical ignorance.
- The humanist agenda was a spiritual renewal based around retranslation of the scriptures and moral reform of clerical practice.
- Some historians have described the humanist movement as pre-reform in that much of what these men put forward was carried one stage further by more radical Protestant reformers. The difference is that the humanists wanted reform from within the Catholic Church and had no wish for a split.

Jacques Lefèvre d'Étaples The foremost Christian humanist in France at the beginning of the sixteenth century was Jacques Lefèvre d'Étaples from Picardy:

- Lefèvre returned to the original scriptures, editing and writing commentaries on the Latin **Vulgate Bible**, starting with the Psalms in 1509 before publishing an edition of St Paul's Epistles in 1512.
- Some scholastic theologians attacked Lefèvre for questioning the authority of the Vulgate, but his

Pluralism is holding a number of posts at once.

Simony is the buying and selling of Church privileges.

Nepotism is getting jobs for one's family.

Desiderius Erasmus (1466–1536) The most prominent and famous of the Christian humanists. Born in Rotterdam, Erasmus spent six years in an Augustinian monastery before becoming private secretary to the bishop of Cambrai and a priest (1492). He moved to England, where he became professor of divinity and Greek at Cambridge. In 1509, he wrote a satirical attack on the wealth and corruption of the church entitled *In Praise of Folly* and in 1516 he produced a translation of the Greek New Testament. Reform from within and the revival of learning were the principles by which Erasmus worked. He and others like him laid the intellectual foundations for the Reformation by heightening awareness of scripture. Nevertheless, Lutheran doctrine such as justification by faith alone was too radical for Erasmus and his split from Luther was marked by the work *On the Freedom of the Will*, 1525.

response was that he was merely revealing the true meaning of the scriptures as God had meant.

- Lefèvre became increasingly significant in France, especially after 1516 when he joined with Guillaume Briçonnet in the latter's bishopric at Meaux.
- An intellectual circle developed around Lefèvre and Briçonnet which included like-minded clerics and scholars. An emphasis was placed upon the scriptures and preaching, while devotional superstition was rejected.
- Travelling preachers endorsed the evangelical message across the diocese, led by Briçonnet and his vicar-general Lefèvre. In 1523, Lefèvre published a French translation of the Gospels and the entire New Testament.

In reality, the intellectual Circle of Meaux was no threat to the church; men such as Lefèvre were trying to reinvigorate Catholicism.

Lutheranism

On the whole, Lutheranism made little impact in France but from 1518 Luther's books were being smuggled into the country and were read eagerly by scholars, humanists and clerics. In 1521, the **Sorbonne** believed Lutheran influence strong enough to have his books outlawed and his doctrines condemned. From this point on the Circle of Meaux came under suspicion as even the most moderate of reformers risked being labelled heretics, or Lutherans:

- First charged with heresy in 1523, Briçonnet responded with a traditional explanation of Catholic doctrine and instructed his preachers to be conservative in their sermons.
- At court, the king's sister, Marguerite of Angoulême, had one of the circle, Michel d'Arande, preach in her territories in Alençon and Bourges.
- Certainly some members of the circle were more radical than others and most were critical of popular devotional practices such as the cult of saints or indulgences.
- Royal protection preserved the circle until 1525 when the king was held captive after the French defeat at Pavia. The Sorbonne and *parlements* of Paris dissolved the group, and Lefèvre was forced to flee to Strasbourg.

- Briçonnet stood trial, but was saved by the return of Francis I in 1526. Francis promptly put an end to proceedings and allowed his sister to recall the exiles, Lefèvre being made tutor to the royal children.

The problem in religious policy was that Francis and the Sorbonne differed in their outlook on what constituted heresy. Francis's toleration of humanism marks him out as enlightened. Francis was no Protestant sympathiser, and not even a convinced evangelical, but he was not going to allow the Sorbonne to dictate religious policy and he was determined to protect the humanist circle.

Francis's power

The powers given to Francis by the Concordat of Bologna meant that the king's decision mattered most and, as long as the humanists did not openly attack Catholicism or hold views that were clearly heretical, he was unlikely to act against them. Yet, as religious dissenters became more common and radical throughout France, the conservatives became more vigilant and active:

In 1528, Duprat, Archbishop of Sens, proposed a harsh series of penalties for convicted heretics. In the same year, a statue of the Virgin Mary was deliberately damaged by radical iconoclasts in Paris. The number of Protestants in France was low, but sporadic events such as this kept the authorities on their guard. Francis himself paid for a new statue in silver and heeded warnings that such events signalled a radicalisation and popularisation of the reform movement. Many humanists such as **Guillaume Farel** turned to Zwingli, the Zurich reformer who denied entirely the real presence of Christ in the eucharist and saw the mass as purely commemorative. However, as Protestant sympathisers became more extreme Francis still sought to protect the intellectual, moderate reform movement which he had patronised throughout the 1520s. Tensions between *parlement*, Sorbonne and Francis continued to grow, as the two former institutions attempted to clean up the court of those suspected of heresy. Attention turned once again to Berquin, who was tried in 1528 before a jury which ought to have been sympathetic towards him, appointed as it was by the Pope under orders from Francis.

KEY PERSON

Guillaume Farel An original member of the Circle of Meaux. In 1528, he rejected Lefèvre and Luther in favour of Zwingli and headed to Switzerland. Working from Neuchâtel, Farel made it his goal to convert his homeland to the reforms of Zwingli.

Yet with the king out of Paris the Sorbonne bullied Clement VII into removing the commissioners and a new, more conservative group was appointed. With the Italian Wars going badly, Francis was in no position to act and Berquin was found guilty of heresy. When Berquin appealed to the *parlement* he was once again found guilty and burned on the Place de Grève.

Heresy

Another member of the original Circle of Meaux, namely Gerard Roussel, was targeted in 1533, and accused by the Sorbonne of preaching heresy. Indeed, Roussel had preached a number of sermons in Paris during Lent which had attracted over 5000 listeners, and some of the content had caused alarm among conservatives. Once more, royal protection was at hand for Roussel as Francis set up his own commission of enquiry and silenced those who wanted to see Roussel stand trial. Altogether, there was little to suggest that Francis had altered his rather ambiguous policy on heresy in 1533, and the protection of men such as Roussel encouraged more radical strains to develop.

One instigator of reform, Nicholas Cop, was moved to act on All Saints' Day 1533. Cop was the new rector of the University of Paris, and he used his traditional address to criticise the persecution of evangelicals and endorse the simple preaching of the gospel. **Cop's sermon** caused a great stir among the Sorbonne who likened Cop's doctrine not only to that of Lefèvre but also to that of Luther. Cop, fearing for his life, was forced to flee to Switzerland. The sermon set off a wave of persecution in Paris sponsored by the Sorbonne; there were more than 50 arrests. On his return to the capital, Francis took a more measured approach, ordering the Bishop of Paris to stop the persecution. It was clear that it was Francis who controlled religious policy.

The Affair of the Placards Once more the **evangelicals** were confident that if they progressed at a slow pace and maintained royal support they could survive and prosper. Yet the situation changed on the night of 17–18 October 1534 when placards (posters) were put up all over Paris attacking the mass and in particular the Catholic doctrine of transubstantiation:

- The placards were crude and violently offensive, attacking the Catholic mass.
- They attacked priests as the antichrist and transubstantiation as the doctrine of devils.

Such abuse played straight into the hands of the conservatives who used the affair to push the king towards taking a harsher line on heresy. Cop's sermon had been evangelical and humanist in nature; the placards were blatantly heretical. The author of the placards was Antoine Marcourt, a Frenchman living in Neuchâtel, Switzerland. The immediate consequence of the placards was a severe period of repression driven by the Sorbonne and this time backed by Francis I. Marcourt and his supporters represented a small minority in their views but the consequences of their actions severely dented the ambitions of a larger minority of evangelicals. The period of repression saw 24 executions and the passing of numerous edicts encouraging citizens to inform upon heretics in the community. Informers would receive one-quarter of their victim's property and possessions. Massive religious processions were staged in Paris to demonstrate the orthodoxy and commitment of the Most Christian King, while all book printing was banned. The persecution did not end until 16 July 1535 when the king proposed the **Edict of Coucy** which released religious prisoners and offered amnesty to exiles (except supporters of the placards) if they promised to admit their errors within six months.

There are three main points to make about the Affair of the Placards and its consequences:

- The placards did not necessarily harden Francis's line on heresy as he had never tolerated such a doctrine, but they did move him to act against radicals, and in some ways clarified the division between reform and heresy.
- Protestant and evangelical reformers were in a very small minority in France in the 1520s and early 1530s, operating in secret and underground. Cop's sermon and the placards were exceptions to this, but because they

Edict of Coucy, 1535
Francis was eager to consolidate his alliance with the Schmalkaldic League and the fierce repression did not look good to men such as Philip of Hesse. An alliance was not forthcoming in 1535 yet despite this Francis opened up the pardon to Zwinglian sacramentarians in 1536.

were such high-profile cases the consequences were far-reaching. Protestantism became seen as the religion of rebels and a threat to the national order which had to be eradicated.

- By 1536, Francis had offered a pardon to all heretics provided they abjured within six months, thus demonstrating that his position had not been greatly altered by the placards. He still wished to pursue a middle line if possible, although he had become more aware of radical elements within the reform movement which threatened to undermine his rule.

Repression

The Truce of Nice (1538) freed Francis from the need to court the German princes, and Francis recognised that greater powers over heresy needed to be given to the *parlement* in order to isolate French Protestants at home and prevent them from contacting those in exile:

- The Edict of Fontainebleau in June 1540 gave the *parlement* overall control of heresy jurisdiction, reflecting just how much headway Protestantism was beginning to make in France.
- In 1543, ecclesiastical authorities were given more powers to search and arrest subjects.
- Also in 1543, Francis ordered the Sorbonne to draw up a Catholic Confession of Faith, defining Catholic doctrine so that no one was in any doubt about how to worship and the doctrine to follow. The 25 articles of faith became law in 1543. In 1544 a **list of condemned books** was published.

KEY EVENT

List of condemned books
The list drawn up by the Sorbonne contained 65 titles with works from Luther and Melanchthon featuring, as well as those by John Calvin.

John Calvin was slowly emerging as the main influence in French Protestantism, reinforced by the publication of his *Institutes* in French in 1541. The first edition had been dedicated to Francis, evidence perhaps that Calvin believed the king sympathetic towards reform, and also a statement to his co-reformers and supporters in his native France that French Protestants were not the rebels that they were being made out to be. The *Institutes* were banned one year later, and a heretic in Rouen was burned at the stake for quoting from them. As evidence of heresy increased, Francis became more active in his repression. Heretical ideas and doctrine permeated French society in the 1540s and the number of heresy cases brought before the *parlement* of Paris increased because of this growth and the increasing vigilance of the authorities.

DOMESTIC POLICY

Taxation

The primary issue concerning the domestic policies of Francis I appears to be the extent to which he was able to centralise French government and lay the foundations for absolutism. The ability of Francis to collect taxation and maintain law and order effectively is a marker as to how strong and centralised his royal authority became between 1515 and 1547:

Francis I and religion

- Francis took a consistently hard line on heresy, and, while sympathetic towards the moderate reform of Lefèvre and willing to patronise humanism at court, he never tolerated attacks on Catholic doctrine.

- The Affair of the Placards clarified the religious problem for Francis and he inevitably became more active in promoting persecution as the threat from Protestantism increased.

- Protestantism made little impact in France during the 1520s and early 1530s but under the influence of Calvin made real headway in the 1540s.

- Francis was reluctant to cede power to the Sorbonne and the *parlement* in the 1530s, but was forced to recognise the growing threat of Protestantism in French society in the 1540s and give these institutions more authority to search, arrest and try heretics.

- Heresy and attacks on Catholicism fundamentally undermined the rule of the French king, as his authority was based on the will of God and the one true faith. Francis had to uphold his image as the Most Christian King and heretics were seditious and dangerous rebels who contaminated society. They had to be eradicated.

HISTORIANS' VIEWS

The historian **Georges Pagès**, writing in the 1940s, saw the reign of Francis I as a triumph for absolutism, and believed that Francis did manage to centralise the institutions of French government. More recently, historians such as **R. J. Knecht** have been more sceptical of Francis I's achievements in this area, stressing that limitations still existed on his power and particularism still prevailed in the provinces. However, even Knecht suggests that the king's actions and informal pronouncements pointed towards absolutism.

The Estates General A national representative body made up of elected representatives from the clergy, nobility and third estate. Called by the king, usually to discuss and debate matters of critical importance.

The Assembly of Notables It was not elected and therefore the king was able to select its participants. The principal purpose of the assembly in 1527 was to ratify the king's demand for 2 million gold crowns with which he proposed to pay the ransom for his two sons, still held captive in Madrid.

The third estate All those who did not belong to the clergy and the nobility. At the top end of the third estate were wealthy merchants and landowners who may have held ambitions to become noble. The majority of the third estate were peasants living off the land.

Gabelle A tax levied on salt in five areas out of six within France. The tax is an example of French kings attempting to alleviate the strain caused by the *taille* by increasing income through other means. Yet unrest was just as likely to occur as a consequence of the *gabelle* as it was from the *taille*, especially in the western salt marshes where the effect of the *gabelle* was felt most acutely.

- Francis never felt vulnerable or weak enough to summon the **Estates General** and only in 1527 did he call an **Assembly of Notables** which comprised leading clerics, nobles and *parlementaires*. The assembly therefore acted as an extension of the king's council and was summoned, and to a great extent controlled, by the king himself.
- Taxation demands were high throughout the reign of Francis I, but there was a surprising lack of resistance from the **third estate** in the face of such fiscal pressure.
- Outbreaks of popular revolt were few, although a serious revolt did occur in western France in 1542. In response to the king's attempts to reform the *gabelle*, salt tax, through the Edict of Chatellerault, the people of the salt marshes took up arms. In 1542, over 10,000 men took advantage of the king's absence fighting Charles V to take up arms and force the royal commissioners out of the localities. Only the personal intervention of Francis I quashed the revolt and the king himself arrived at La Rochelle to pass judgement on the rebels. In the end they were pardoned, although they were made to deliver a quantity of salt to the royal warehouse in Rouen, which was subsequently used to pay off debts. Francis did ultimately get his way over the reform of the salt tax two years later.
- More typical of his attitude towards dissenters was perhaps the manner in which he ordered the town of Lagny-sur-Marne to be sacked in 1544 following revolt over the *gabelle*.

The *parlement* of Rouen

In many ways the *parlement* were the most significant guarantors of provincial liberties and privilege, and their twin roles of acting as courts of law and ratifying royal legislation made them potentially important checks on royal authority. Francis believed that the *parlement* should automatically pass royal laws, but he knew that they could stand in the way of his increasing demands for taxation or the creation of more royal offices for sale. In 1539, Francis vented his anger towards the provincial *parlement* of Rouen:

- The *parlement* at Rouen delayed the passing of an important law, the Ordinance of Villers-Cotterêts.

When it was eventually passed in 1540 it left out the points which it found unacceptable. Francis told the *parlement* that he was preparing to travel to Rouen and sort out the problem personally. He went to Rouen anyway, closed the court down and took the seals.

- Some of the Rouen magistrats whom Francis believed were loyal stayed on to judge criminal cases in Normandy and others held Grand Jours in Bayeaux which served as a travelling court of session to try criminal cases throughout the province. The *parlement* of Rouen was reopened in 1541 after Francis was satisfied with the loyalty of its members and the work of the Grand Jours.

Provincial estates

Provincial estates continued to operate along traditional lines, and in theory they were representative of provincial rights. Yet the estates were not democratic and the king decided where and when they met as well as fixing the agenda and choosing the president.

- The estates had the right to make complaints to the king through royal commissioners and in theory their requests were supposed to be addressed before any form of taxation or subsidy was granted to the crown.
- However, Francis often ran roughshod over such provincial rights, especially when he urgently needed a subsidy to finance the Italian Wars. In 1538, Francis told his commissioners at Albi to take the subsidy first and hear the grievances later.
- In 1537, the *gabelle* was extended to Languedoc and then Normandy in 1546 despite the fact that both were exempt from the salt tax.
- Fiscal pressures increased and Francis often imposed his will at the expense of local rights and privileges. Yet Francis still needed the support of central government and local institutions to maintain law and order and run the country. At a local level, Francis still relied upon his **provincial governors**, and *baillis*. Leading nobles fulfilled the roles of provincial governors and acted as local representatives of central authority.

KEY TERMS

Provincial estates
Representative assemblies held in some areas throughout France that guarded the particular rights and privileges of those areas. Such estates existed in Languedoc, Brittany and Burgundy where taxation was levied by local magistrates rather than the crown.

Bailli A local royal official whose job it was to ensure that the royal decree was carried out in that area (*bailliage*).

KEY PEOPLE

Provincial governors
Despite being effectively royal viceroys, they held much power in their own right controlling military levies and overseeing the collection of taxation. Their clientele network was great and potentially the governors were a threat to the crown, as in 1542 when Francis removed the power of all governors stating that they had become too great.

Royal bureaucracy

In terms of central government, Francis ruled through the king's council and it was in his reign that the *conseil des affaires* developed into an important decision-making body. Moreover royal bureaucracy also increased with one royal administrator existing for every 60 square kilometres in 1515, and growing to one for every 45 by 1547. Francis came increasingly to rely upon the *maîtres des requêtes de l'hôtel* who were officials trained in the law who worked in the chancery and served as a link between various departments of state. Such men were ennobled for their efforts, and we might argue that their increased responsibility and the complex nature of royal government served to sideline the aristocracy.

Venality Francis knowingly created more offices and sold them to increase revenue, a practice known as venality. The short-term financial rewards for Francis were substantial, and, while the major councillors of the realm remained princes of the blood and leading nobles, the systematic creation and sale of offices did create a new noble class, the nobility of the robe, who over time challenged the political power of the old nobility. The number of offices or government posts rose from 4000 in 1515 to over 46,000 in 1665: there is little doubt that this trend began under Francis I.

The market for offices was huge, with many seeing their purchase as a way of bettering their social standing. Yet such practice did create problems for Francis and his successors:

- Important royal offices tended to become the property of a small group of families although Francis did try to counter this with the 40-day rule which declared resignations invalid unless the owner survived 40 days after making the act of resignation. The penalty was forfeiture of the office back to the crown, and so anyone dying on the job produced a windfall for the king's coffers. On the whole, however, offices were often handed down to relatives or friends.
- In an attempt to increase revenue, offices were often divided into two or three thus creating more layers of bureaucracy and in the long run creating more salaries to be paid.

- While venality often meant that the king could choose his office holders carefully and expect loyalty from them, it also created a political power base which in some ways diluted the king's authority and power. Certainly a king who had aspirations of absolutism should not have to depend upon venality for fiscal security.

Trends in domestic policy

While there were few innovations in the reign of Francis I with regard to administration we do see a number of trends developing:

- Royal government was becoming increasingly centralised through the effective use of provincial governors, *baillis* and *maîtres des requêtes de l'hôtel*. Royal control over the provinces was increasing.

- Although royal legislation was still subject to the ratification of the *parlement* and taxation was in theory granted by provincial estates, the king's will often trampled on local traditions and privileges.

- Popular resistance to royal policy under Francis I was rare and easily subdued.

- Through the systematic use of venality more royal offices were created. Financial rewards must be balanced against the long-term problems of hereditary offices and reliance upon such practice.

- A by-product of venality was the creation of a new noble class, the nobility of the robe, and it could be argued that Francis began to sideline the old nobility and relied more upon trained professionals who specialised in certain areas of royal administration.

- Limitations on royal authority continued to exist. The *parlement* still had to ratify legislation; provincial estates had to grant subsidies; tax collection was haphazard; and maintaining law and order in the frontier regions was still a problem.

- Francis was not an absolutist monarch, but he did bring a greater sense of centralisation and uniformity to French government and ultimately his word held sway over provincial liberties.

Francis I at a meeting of the *parlement*

IMAGE SYMBOLIQUE DE LA COUR DU ROI FRANÇOIS I.

THE ARTS AND ARCHITECTURE

Francis I's court

Artistic styles and architecture were used by Francis to reflect not only the enlightened nature of his kingship but also the power of his authority and the grandeur of his monarchy:

- To begin with the court of Francis I was much larger than that of his predecessors. The court was generally made up of the **royal household** and nobles who were eager to attain the king's ear and his patronage.
- The court also included departments concerned with the military to guard the king, law and order, finance, the queen's household as well as foreign ambassadors and dignitaries. Francis created a new group, namely the gentlemen of the chamber, which encompassed his closest male companions who provided companionship and carried out a variety of tasks such as signing contracts for building work, or looking after the king's private purse.
- The chamber also served an important political function in that ideas could be discussed and disseminated, while,

by exchanging gentlemen with those from foreign courts such as that in England, the king could display his friendship and trust to foreign monarchs.

The size of the royal court had been on the increase since the early fifteenth century, and by 1535 Francis employed over 600 household officials on a permanent basis. The actual size of the court was much greater, totalling nearly 10,000 people depending upon its location and the political circumstances.

A Renaissance court

Importantly, the court was **nomadic**, which allowed the king to undertake relatively frequent royal progresses to visit the outlying provinces. Thus the king's subjects saw their monarch while Francis also used such opportunities to patronise local nobles and allow them to join the court. In short, the nomadic nature of the court contributed to the centralisation of royal authority. The makeup of the court under Francis also reflected his Renaissance aspirations in that more Italians were present in the royal entourage. Primarily this came about because Francis was looking to attain further political influence and potential military allies south of the Alps, and often Italian princes looked to Francis for protection from Habsburg oppression. Moreover, the marriage of Henry of Orleans, second son of Francis, to Catherine de Medici in 1533 brought a significant number of Florentines to the French court. Frenchmen also served in Italian courts and the consequence of such interaction was that a greater refinement and extravagance was brought to the French court in terms of the arts and literature. Clothes, entertainment, food, dress and jewels were all supposed to demonstrate the grandeur and status of the court and the monarch.

Italian influence

The Italian influence at court can be seen in the changing architectural styles that typified the reign of Francis I. Classical architecture, typically incorporating columns, pilasters and medallions, gradually permeated into French buildings:

• Francis himself oversaw the construction of a new wing

KEY TERM

Nomadic This means that the court travelled around rather than remaining in one place.

Chateau de Blois

KEY TERM

Loggia The Italian for lodge; refers to a gallery behind an open arcade facing onto a garden or square.

at his château in Blois which featured Italianate galleries and **loggias**, the inspiration for which came from Bramante's loggias at the Vatican Palace in Rome.

- At Chambord, the Italian influence was even more obvious as the architect was probably Domenico da Cortona, himself a pupil of Giuliano da Sangallo.
- Perhaps the two most significant architectural developments during Francis's reign were the transformations of the châteaux at Saint Germain-en-Laye and Fontainebleau. The former was rebuilt in 1539, under the watchful eye of the king and with the expertise of the Parisian master-mason Pierre

Chambiges. More important was the palace at Fontainebleau which became Francis's favourite residence. Francis expended large amounts of money to transform it from a hunting lodge into one of the most beautiful palaces in Europe. The Parisian master-mason Gilles Le Breton, along with Italian artists Giovanni Batista Rosso and Francesco Primaticcio, were responsible for Fontainebleau, a château which more than any other mirrored the glory of Francis's reign and projected his Renaissance kingship onto the rest of Europe. The Emperor Charles V visited the palace in 1539, and was given a tour of the gallery on the first floor, the walls of which were adorned with frescoes displaying the classical and triumphal nature of the French king's rule.

Visual arts

In painting and sculpture Francis employed a number of Italian artists. Early in his reign after the conquest of Milan in 1515, he invited **Leonardo da Vinci** to France, and slightly later Andrea del Sarto. Both enjoyed the king's patronage and company and there is little doubt that Francis was an enthusiastic and knowledgeable patron of the arts. Later, in 1531, Rosso's art and in particular his murals characterised Fontainebleau. Francis also collected art, avidly acquiring work by the artists Raphael and Aretino. **Benvenuto Cellini** visited France in 1537 and 1540, producing a silver statue of Jupiter for the king and a bronze relief of the Nymph of Fontainebleau. Non-Italian painters of note were Jean Clouet and his son François, both leading portait painters. Although born in the Netherlands, Jean Clouet was trained in France and his portraits of the king and his family were much admired.

Francis was also regarded as a great patron of humanism, a fact reinforced by the establishment of four royal lectureships in Greek and Hebrew in 1530. Although their significance has perhaps been overestimated by some who would like to see the *lecteurs royaux* as a symbol of the king's support of the humanists against the conservative Sorbonne, they were still an indication of the enlightened nature of Francis I. The king was also noted as a keen collector of literature, as the libraries at Blois and Fontainebleau bear witness. In 1537, the king even passed

KEY TERM

Ordinance of Montpellier
Law which required all printers and booksellers to deliver a copy of every new book to the royal librarian at Blois.

the **Ordinance of Montpellier.** Poetry and literature played an important role in the sixteenth century as forms of propaganda, glorifying military victories and reinforcing the power and authority of the crown. The foremost court poet was Clement Marot, whose career was disrupted by the fact that he held evangelical sympathies which forced him into exile. The leading literary figure of the period in France was François Rabelais whose *Chronicles* were typical of his satirical humour which amused the king and offended the authorities, most notably the Sorbonne.

Francis I and the Renaissance

- The Renaissance monarchy of Francis I was bolstered and underpinned by the arts and architecture which served to project the necessary image and prestige of the crown onto its subjects and the other powers of Europe.
- Francis was a keen patron of the arts and architecture, recognising their aesthetic and political value. The châteaux, frescoes, literature, music and the court itself all played a crucial function in emphasising and displaying the authority of the crown.
- The nobility imitated their monarch and consequently the palaces of Lorraine at Meudon and of Montmorency at Chantilly took their inspiration from Blois and Fontainebleau.
- The growth of the royal household and the king's architectural passions were expensive and such grandeur did evoke criticism from those who regarded the court as immoral and debauched.

SUMMARY QUESTIONS

1. To what extent was the foreign policy of Francis I a success?

2. In what respects did the Affair of the Placards mark a turning point in the religious outlook of Francis I?

3. Was Francis consultative in his domestic policies or authoritarian?

4. How important were the arts and architecture in projecting the image of a powerful monarch in the sixteenth century?

CHAPTER 3

Henry II and the origins of the French Wars of Religion

THE NEW KING, 1547–59

Court reshuffle

Immediately after the death of Francis I and coronation of Henry II, there was an inevitable court reshuffle as Francis's favourites were replaced by those close to Henry, especially **Diane de Poitiers**:

- Also returning to court and favour was Anne de Montmorency who had fallen from power in 1541. Restored in 1547 as president of the king's council, four years later he was made a duke.
- One noble family of great importance which also benefited from Henry's patronage was the Guise family, especially François and Charles, sons of Claude, duke of Guise. Soon Charles, already Archbishop of Reims, was made a cardinal and his brother a duke. Their five brothers and four sisters all married into influential families, most notably Mary who had married James V of Scotland in 1538 with whom she had a daughter, the future Mary, Queen of Scots.

FOREIGN POLICY

Boulogne

Henry II's first move in diplomacy was to recapture Boulogne which had been lost to the English in 1544. Unprepared at first to go to war with England, Henry set about forging a dynastic alliance with Scotland, conveniently ruled over by the Scottish **dowager** Mary of Guise. Henry saw the advantage of **marriage between his son, the dauphin Francis, and the infant queen of Scots** (James had died in 1542). Having relieved Scotland, Henry attacked Boulogne in 1549, retaking the city in

KEY PERSON

Diane de Poitiers, mistress of Henry II
Francis's mistress Anne, duchess of Étampes (who had become deeply unpopular), was overthrown and effectively replaced by Henry's mistress, Diane de Poitiers, who became very influential in policy decisions. She was 21 years older than Henry and shortly she amassed a huge fortune and distributed her patronage widely, her son-in-law Robert de la Marck being one beneficiary as he was made marshal of France.

KEY TERM

Dowager A widow with a dowry, in this case Mary of Guise who had been married to James V of Scotland until his death in 1542.

KEY EVENT

The pledging of Mary, Queen of Scots, to Dauphin Francis. In 1547, the English defeated the Scots at Pinkie so the Scots looked to their old allies in France for protection. The Scottish Earl of Arran struck a deal with Henry which secured French aid in return for the marriage of Mary to the dauphin. So Mary, queen of Scots, who was also in line to the English succession was taken to France and pledged to the young Francis.

Diane de Poitiers, mistress of Henry II, portrayed as the Roman goddess of the hunt

Luigi's assassination, 1547
Charles had objected to Luigi being given the titles of duke of Parma and Piacenza by Paul III, as he felt that they were part of the duchy of Milan.

1550. France paid England 400,000 crowns for the surrender of the city and thereafter relations between Henry and the English king, Edward VI, became extremely friendly with a marriage alliance signed in 1551 between Henry's daughter Elizabeth and the English king.

Italy and war Henry now turned his attentions towards Italy and the ancient French claim to Milan:

- Stronger relations with the papacy were forged as Paul III had recently fallen out with Charles V, after the **assassination of the pope's son Pier Luigi** in 1547 by Charles's agents. Seven French cardinals were sent to Rome and Charles of Lorraine was instructed to negotiate an alliance.
- In 1548, Henry travelled to Italy and met some influential Italian princes, particularly the duke of Ferrara who married off his daughter Anne to François de Guise.
- In 1551, Henry again intervened in Italian affairs, this time on behalf of the pope's grandson Ottavio Farnese, who had been declared rightful heir to Parma and Piacenza by Paul III on his deathbed. The new pope, Julius III, disapproved of the succession wanting instead to ally with Emperor Charles V. Isolated, Ottavio turned to Henry II who set up camp along the Piedmont–Milan border and made an alliance with the German princes, both Catholic and Protestant, who were increasingly disgruntled at the heavy-handed and overbearing rule of their emperor. In return for substantial financial aid, Henry was to administer the towns of Cambrai, Metz, Toul and Verdun.
- In 1552, with the security of this German alliance still intact and 50,000 men in total, Henry invaded the empire and occupied Toul, Metz and Verdun with little cost in terms of lives or money. Three important strategic towns had been acquired on the north-east border of France and the garrison in Metz under the command of François de Guise was strong enough to resist an Imperial bombardment and siege in the last months of 1551.

War with Spain
French relations with England took a step backwards in 1554 following the death of Edward VI, and the succession

of Mary Tudor. Charles V married off his son Philip to the new English queen thus ruining any hopes which Henry harboured of unifying Scotland, England and France through Mary, Queen of Scots:

- In October 1555, Charles V abdicated responsibility of the Low Countries to Philip and three months later Spain and Italy went the same way. Charles's brother Ferdinand became Holy Roman Emperor.
- In 1555, Paul IV was elected pope. He was known to oppose Spain and the empire, on the grounds that both Naples and Piacenza were under the control of Philip and Charles respectively. He wanted his nephew Carlo Carafa to become bishop of Naples and by December 1555 an **alliance between France and the papacy** was struck.
- A Spanish army led by the duke of Savoy invaded France and laid siege to Saint Quentin defeating Montmorency's army in the process. Montmorency was captured and replaced by Guise who was appointed lieutenant-general by the king. In 1558, Guise became a hero overnight when the French captured Calais from the English. However, the growing costs of war and the spread of heresy in France meant that Henry had to seek peace.
- At Cateau-Cambrésis in April 1559 two separate peace treaties were signed, one with England and the other with Spain. In the agreement with England, France held Calais for eight years after which compensation would be paid or it would be handed back to England. The Spanish settlement was more significant allowing Henry to hold on to Metz, Toul and Verdun, but all French acquisitions in Italy were lost and Philip II was to marry Elizabeth, daughter of Henry II.

While the peace appeared to be a disaster for France, particularly with regard to Italy, there were redeeming features. After all, France managed to hold on to Calais and the three northern bishoprics as well as prevent Philip from pursuing a marriage with the new queen of England. Henry could now concentrate on domestic issues and, in particular, the growth of Calvinism.

Centralisation

Like Francis, Henry continued to centralise French government and end the **liberties of the provinces** whenever possible: neither king called an Estates General. Thus, as with Francis the consent of the provincial estates often came second to the king's interests:

- In terms of centralisation Henry passed an important piece of legislation in 1552 which created a new law court called the *siège présidial* to judge certain criminal and civil cases. Sixty of these courts were put into operation; they were overseen by two lieutenants, seven councillors and, from 1557, a president and a chancery.
- *Bailliages* tended to be absorbed into *présidiaux* and the courts tended to judge local land disputes, acting as an appeal court on property under the value of 250 livres. In some ways they increased royal authority in the localities and brought uniformity in lesser provincial land cases, but their real worth to the king was the creation of further new offices which could be sold for profit. In this respect, Henry carried on the trend established by his father.
- In a similar respect to Francis I, Henry II faced little popular opposition to his rule, although there was the continuing issue of the *gabelle* (salt tax), which Francis had attempted to reform in 1542, a policy met with resistance in western France. In 1548, Henry II ordered the plan for a single salt tax levied at the salt marsh and a system of royal warehouses. Once more trouble ensued in the west, particularly in Angoumois, Perigord and Saintonge where over 20,000 rebels took up arms against tax officials, destroying warehouses and murdering royal commissioners. The revolt grew in size throughout August 1548 spreading to **Bordeaux** and Cognac. Soon the rebels began targeting the homes of the rich and the nature of the uprising became more generally based on class. After the uprising had been crushed, Henry was wise enough to recognise what had caused the problem in the first place and by 1553 the salt tax had been abolished in the west and an amnesty offered to the rebels.

Henry and the provinces

Henry was just as capable of enforcing royal authority at the expense of the provinces as Francis had been. In June 1549, Henry was granted a supplement to the *taille*, known as the *taillon*, by the estates of Normandy to pay for the French army garrisoned there and relieve some of the pressures associated with billeting from the local populace. Henry continued to collect the *taillon* for years afterwards and still billeted troops in Normandy.

Violence in Bordeaux

Particularly acute: a leading royal official was lynched and salt tax collectors murdered and their bodies covered in salt. In October, Henry sent Montmorency and Aumale to Bordeaux with 10,000 troops to put down the revolt. The *parlement* was dissolved and the authorities were punished for failing to subdue the rebellion and maintain order. The city was stripped of its privileges and fined accordingly. Over 150 rebels were executed in Bordeaux.

Finance

Financially there were few innovations during the reign of Henry II, and generally he subjected the third estate to the same fiscal pressures as his father had done in order to finance foreign affairs:

- The *taillon* served to support the military in 1549, while in 1552 a new clerical tax raised an additional 1.4 million livres per annum.
- Traditional sources of revenue were tapped, but initially with greater success. In his first year, Henry collected 8.4 million livres from taxation, an increase of 25 per cent on his father's haul in 1515. Such an increase may well be an indication of the extent to which father and son had managed to bring some uniformity and centralisation to fiscal machinery.
- Venality continued to be a short-term moneyspinner for the crown aided not only by the presidial courts but also by the formation of a new *parlement* at Rennes in 1552.
- Like his father, Henry relied on bankers' loans to subsidise his foreign policy, borrowing 1.2 million livres from the Lyons bankers in 1552 and a further 1.8 million a year later. Francis had pursued a similar policy, but Henry was able to gain a favourable credit rating with the bankers of Lyons because he instituted a systematic way of repaying debt.
- In 1555, he introduced the *grand parti de Lyons* (a special treasury) which promised four annual repayments, instilling a confidence among the bankers which allowed Henry to negotiate further loans amounting to over 10 million livres in 1555–6.

Yet ultimately Henry's legacy, like his father's, was one of debt and fiscal insecurity.

RELIGION UNDER HENRY II

Relations with Rome

Henry followed a harsh policy of repression towards French Protestants but also relations between the monarchy and the papacy were strained because of:

- the papal alliance with Charles V in the war over Parma
- the decision of Pope Julius III to reconvene the General Council to the Imperial city of Trent.

Henry rightly concluded that papal sympathies now lay with the emperor so he ordered all French bishops away from the council, cutting the payment of annates to Rome and proposing the establishment of a French council as a national alternative to the **Council of Trent**. Julius threatened to excommunicate Henry II, while the latter hinted that a complete break with Rome was imminent. With relations at their worst a compromise was found and an agreement made between Henry and Julius in 1552:

- Henry promised not to call a Gallican council.
- Julius in return allowed Henry to continue collecting annates (the payments made by clerics on their appointment to benefices).

Ultimately, Henry was unwilling to go the same way as Henry VIII of England and break with Rome. He realised how important his role was as guardian of the church and how unpopular a split with Rome would be among French conservatives in the Sorbonne. Julius too saw how damaging a split with France would be to the Catholic cause just as the General Council was attempting to address the second wave of Protestant reform. The whole episode demonstrates that Henry was willing to protect Gallican interests against Rome, and fulfil his duties as protector of the French church.

Heresy

Henry was steadfastly orthodox and conservative in his religious outlook, a fact reflected in the creation of the *chambre ardente* (burning chamber) in 1547. Henry followed up the creation of the *chambre ardente* with the Edict of Châteaubriand in 1551:

- The edict banned the printing, sale or possession of Protestant literature while also prohibiting any gatherings or secret assemblies of heretics.
- Rewards and incentives were offered for informers who would receive one-third of the confiscated property of

any one they named who was successfully prosecuted for heresy.

- Magistrates were also given the right to actively search out Protestants, raiding homes of suspected heretics or those in which they might be sheltered. Interestingly, the edict made little reference to Calvinism, instead still incorrectly talking of the Lutheran heresy, yet the message of the legislation was a clear one. Heretics were dangerous and seditious rebels, who undermined the natural social order and hierarchy. Even the magistrates of the *parlements* were to be examined every three months in order to ensure their dogmatic orthodoxy.

Yet, Henry was distracted during this period by events elsewhere, most notably in Italy. While he was preoccupied, heresy continued to progress. Indeed, Calvinism was not just finding support among the artisans and lower classes, as the king himself believed, but it was finding favour among some of the nobility.

The Rise of Calvinism

As the French crown was devising means to destroy heresy, so John Calvin, Pierre Viret and Guillaume Farel were promoting their doctrine from Geneva. Calvin's *French Institutes* (1541) had made a huge impact, and were accordingly banned by the authorities in 1542. Calvin's works also featured prominently on the list of prohibited books drawn up in 1544, yet the amount of Calvinist literature and propaganda arriving from abroad continued to increase. The Edict of Châteaubriand created more French exiles who settled in Geneva, creating a base from which further literature and strategies emerged to galvanise the Reformed cause in France. The success of **urban-based Calvinism** in France during the 1550s and 1560s can be attributed to many factors:

- Geneva was geographically close to the French trade centre of Lyons, and much literature was smuggled into France and disseminated throughout the kingdom via Lyons.
- Calvin was French, and he took a special interest in the progress of the Reformed movement in his homeland. He still had an extensive network of contacts and friends

The French Institutes
Written by Calvin in 1536 and first published in Basel, although the final edition did not appear until 1559. The *Institutes* offered a clear and systematic exposition of the Reformed doctrine, instructing people not only in doctrine but also on how to worship in order to lead a more spiritually fulfilling Christian life.

Urban-based Calvinism
Trial records tend to show a disproportionate number of the clergy and urban elites indicted for heresy and these are the social groups which we would normally associate with Calvinism. The fact that the majority of missionaries were sent to urban centres such as Poitiers or Orleans reinforces this point.

within the kingdom and, with no figure emerging to lead the movement from within France, Calvin established himself as the natural figurehead for French Protestants.

- Calvin himself was very active in terms of writing polemics which attacked the Catholic church and offered guidance for his co-religionaries in France. Works such as *Little Treatise on the Lord's Supper, What a Faithful Man should do among the Papists* and *Apology to the Nicodemites* all contributed to the success of the movement.

- Small, secret underground groups called conventicles (which sprang up during the 1520s) were spiritually nourished by the works of Calvin emanating from Geneva during the 1540s. For the first time, those who did not conform to Catholicism were given direction and advice.

- During times of harsh repression, Calvin's letters to those under persecution offered solace and a sense of belonging. Calvin tied his French contacts closely to his church in Geneva, and the increasing number of refugees in that city also strengthened the bond with France. In time Calvin would oversee the training of ministers and pastors in Geneva and send them back to France as Calvinist missionaries. Of the 88 missionaries sent to France between 1555 and 1562, 62 were French by birth. After the establishment of the Genevan Academy in 1559, under Theodore de Beza, the number of missionaries increased.

Calvin and the nobility

Calvinism's success in France came from the support not only of the artisans but also of the nobility who offered the movement protection, finance and status. The period 1555–62 witnessed the recruitment of influential nobles in Guyenne, Gascony, Normandy, Dauphine and Languedoc. Calvin deliberately targeted the nobility, knowing the benefits of their support. Noble missionaries were sent back to France well versed in the gospel and the organisation of the Calvinist church.

- Several leading members of the Bourbon family, themselves princes of the blood, were early converts, among them Antoine de Bourbon, **King of Navarre**, who had vast holdings in the south-west around Gascony and Guyenne. Calvin set up a personal correspondence with Navarre and it is no surprise that the earliest Calvinist congregations emerged in the relative security of the south-west.

- Other leading **noble converts** in this period were Louis de Bourbon, Prince of Condé, the younger brother of Antoine who had actually visited Geneva in person in 1555. Condé played a crucial role as the military leader of the Huguenots during the initial years of the Wars of Religion.
- The Châtillon family also provided noble converts, most notably Gaspard de Coligny who owned much land in Normandy. He and his two brothers became fervent supporters of Calvin despite the fact that they were nephews of Anne de Montmorency, the Constable of France (France's military leader). Other lesser nobles converted for political or personal gain, but during the 1550s as Calvinism sought to extend its feelers throughout France it mattered not. Noble support enabled Calvinism to spread from the cities into the countryside, and congregations could worship in relative safety on the estates of the nobility.

The survival of Calvinism

Throughout the 1550s French Calvinists became not only more numerous but also better organised and more unified:

- The church of Paris was established in 1555 by Jean le Macon along with François de Morel and Antoine de La Roche Chandieu. The danger of detection and persecution was real, as was shown in September 1557 when an angry mob **attacked a Calvinist congregation** in the rue Saint Jacques. The congregation reflected the wide social spectrum which was attracted to the Reformed faith as nobles worshipped alongside artisans.
- Despite such setbacks, the Reformed movement continued to survive and expand at a **local level**. In 1558, Calvinists staged a mass demonstration in Paris when over 4000 gathered to sing psalms on the left bank of the Seine, in clear defiance of the *parlement*.

KEY THEMES

Navarre and Calvinism
Antoine de Bourbon, king of Navarre, was never fully committed to the cause, unlike his wife Jeanne d'Albret, herself the daughter of Francis I's sister Marguerite who had been such a leading supporter of the Circle of Meaux. Navarre's son Henry became the military and political leader of the Huguenot cause before returning to Catholicism in 1593 in order to become king of France.

The nobility and Calvinism
For Coligny and Louis de Bourbon the attraction of the new faith was theological and in that respect genuine. In short, they were committed adherents of the gospel and believed in Calvin's view of the eucharist.

KEY EVENT

Attack on the Paris congregation, 1557 More than 100 people were arrested and three were consequently burned in the Place Maubert. Worse still, Catholic propaganda purported that the congregation was taking part in lewd sexual acts, material which did the movement no favours.

KEY THEME

Calvinism at a local level
A whole network of provincial synods, consistories and colloquies existed throughout France; it bound local churches and provinces together.

- In 1559, French Calvinists held their first National Synod in Paris under the leadership of Morel. Pastors from ten other French Calvinist churches attended to discuss matters of organisation and doctrine. The outcome was a Confession of Faith and Ecclesiastical Discipline which were both closely modelled on Calvin's own works. For the first time Calvinism in France was organised and unified, something which was crucial if the movement was going to survive and prosper.
- A minority of Calvinist supporters in the *parlements* of Paris also helped to delay legislation unfavourable to Calvinism. Most notably **Anne du Bourg** had clear Protestant sympathies and, after personally insulting

How successful was Calvinism?

- Even at its peak, between 1555 and 1562, perhaps only 10 per cent of the population were Calvinist, which equates to 1.8 million people: a large number certainly, but still a significant minority. 1200 churches distributed throughout the kingdom was a major success in the face of such harsh repression, but many relied upon the protection and patronage of the nobility.
- In north-east France, where the Guises held much property, Calvinism made little headway and no missionaries ventured into Picardy, Flanders or Burgundy. Calvinism was never going to sweep all before it.
- To many of Calvin's adherents in France, their leader and figurehead was a rather distant figure who asked too much of their loyalty and commitment at times. For example, in his *Letter to the Nicodemites* written in 1544 Calvin urged his followers in France who still worshipped in secret while maintaining a façade of orthodoxy to come out into the open and face persecution or flee the country. Some found this too severe, and in 1544 Antoine Fumee protested on behalf of French evangelicals stating that Calvin demanded the ultimate sacrifice. The issue of resistance to royal authority was raised by Anne du Bourg. Such action was too revolutionary for Calvin at this stage, but demonstrated the extremes to which some were taking the Reformed faith.

Henry II in 1559, was imprisoned along with six of his supporters and ordered to reject his religion.
• Calvinist doctrine also gave encouragement and determination to those under threat of persecution. Calvinist theories of divine providence and predestination offered the converted self-belief that they were God's elect and that ultimately they would triumph over the forces of Catholicism.

SUMMARY QUESTIONS

1. To what extent did the Treaty of Cateau-Cambrésis symbolise French failure in the Italian Wars?

2. How far did Henry II continue the policies of Francis I?

3. Explain the rise of Calvinism in France.

4. Why was Protestantism regarded as such a threat in France?

CHAPTER 4

The French Wars of Religion, 1562–72

CIVIL WAR BETWEEN CATHOLICS AND PROTESTANTS

KEY THEME

Belief The historian Mack Holt emphasises the significance of religion in a social context rather than a doctrinal one, that is to say that France was made up of a vast community of believers each believing that they were the godly and the other community were misfits.

The French Wars of Religion began in 1562 with the massacre at Vassy; continued until the Edict of Nantes in 1598; and then erupted again briefly in the 1620s. This civil conflict was between two communities of **belief**, namely Catholics and Protestants (or Huguenots as French Calvinists were known). The French Wars of Religion served to divide the populace along confessional lines as well as politically and socially. We must not underestimate the importance of religion in the Wars of Religion. Political, social and economic issues were intertwined around the issue of religion.

Huguenots rejected transubstantiation and, similarly, Catholics objected to the singing of psalms in the vernacular, but it is the social backdrop to such doctrinal rejection which sets the scene for over 30 years of internal strife:

- Neither side could accept the presence of the other, so any compromise was going to be short-lived.
- Each side viewed the other as having broken God's will and, in particular, the Catholics viewed the Huguenots as dangerous and seditious rebels threatening the accepted social and political order which had existed for centuries.

Bearing this in mind it is no surprise that there were specific acts of violent cleansing and purification, nor that the conflict lasted for so long. Religion was at the heart of the troubles but the premature death of Henry II in 1559 was the immediate cause of the problems.

THE DEATH OF HENRY II, 1559

The unexpected death of Henry II took place at a festival in celebration of the recently concluded peace treaty of Cateau-Cambrésis in July 1559. The king died as a consequence of head wounds received in a jousting accident. His death created a power vacuum at court which coincided with increased religious tensions (in part due to increasing Huguenot strength). Henry was succeeded on the throne by his 15-year-old son Francis II. Recently married to Mary Stuart, queen of Scots, Francis was clearly inexperienced and vulnerable to political faction:

- In particular, the **Guise family** looked to dominate court, as Mary's mother was a sister of Francis, duke of Guise, and Charles, cardinal of Lorraine.
- Opposed to the Guises were the mainly Huguenot Bourbon family, princes of the blood, and led by the

KEY PERSON

Guise family Staunch Catholics, the wealthiest and principle noble family in France. As the Guise family eased into power after the death of Henry II, prospects for the Huguenots looked bleak.

Protestant churches in 1562

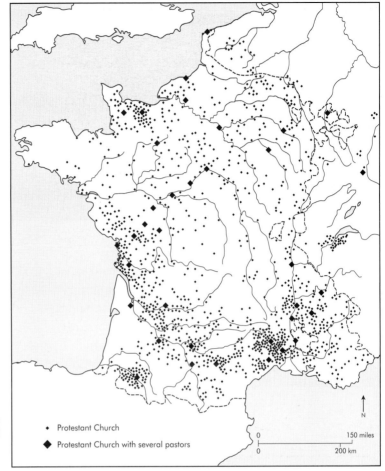

- Protestant Church
- Protestant Church with several pastors

0   150 miles
0   200 km

N

KEY PEOPLE

Antoine de Bourbon Some Protestants believed that because Francis had not yet reached the age of 21 he was a minor and that the King of Navarre, namely Antoine de Bourbon, should become regent.

Catherine de Medici (1519–89) The death of Henry II in 1559 began a power struggle between his widow, Catherine de Medici, and the followers of the duke of Guise over who should control the successive boy kings, Francis II and Charles IX. Catherine lost out over Francis but regained the regency of Charles and proceeded to pursue a policy of religious toleration towards the Huguenots.

vacillating **Antoine de Bourbon** and his more committed wife (in terms of Huguenot allegiance) Jeanne d'Albret. Louis de Bourbon, Prince of Condé and younger brother of Antoine, was also dismayed by the Guise dominance of the young king and proposed military means to counter such activity.

- The ruling house of Valois, overseen by Henry's widow, **Catherine de Medici,** objected to the domination of Francis II for other reasons. While unquestionably Catholic, Catherine wanted what was best for all four of her sons, and she was convinced that the Guise family would only look after their own interests. Catherine was a thoughtful and pragmatic lady who did not wish to see the crown under the stranglehold of a noble family as powerful and influential as the Guises; but at first Francis himself seemed to pay more attention to his uncle, the Duke of Guise, than his mother.

The three Guise brothers, leaders of the Catholic cause: left to right, cardinal of Lorraine, Henry of Lorraine and Duke of Mayenne

- The Montmorency family was a mixture of confessional and political loyalties. Anne de Montmorency, Constable of France, was head of the family and had been a loyal and close adviser to Henry II. Steadfastly Catholic, Anne viewed heresy as a cancer which had to be taken out of French society. Yet his sister Louise de Châtillon favoured the Huguenots, and her three sons all became prominent members of the Reformed cause.

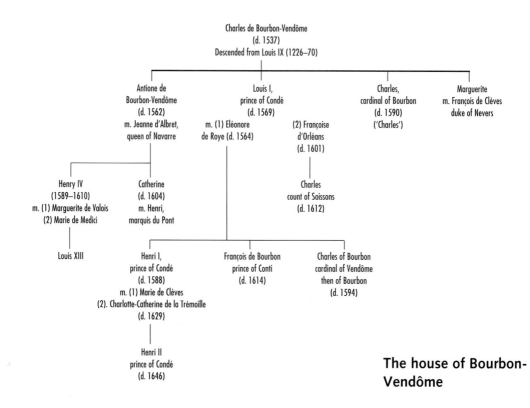

Charles de Bourbon-Vendôme
(d. 1537)
Descended from Louis IX (1226–70)

Antione de
Bourbon-Vendôme
(d. 1562)
m. Jeanne d'Albret,
queen of Navarre

Louis I,
prince of Condé
(d. 1569)

m. (1) Eléonore
de Roye (d. 1564)

(2) Françoise
d'Orléans
(d. 1601)

Charles,
cardinal of Bourbon
(d. 1590)
('Charles')

Marguerite
m. François de Clèves
duke of Nevers

Henry IV
(1589–1610)
m. (1) Marguerite de Valois
(2) Marie de Medici

Catherine
(d. 1604)
m. Henri,
marquis du Pont

Charles
count of Soissons
(d. 1612)

Louis XIII

Henri I,
prince of Condé
(d. 1588)
m. (1) Marie de Clèves
(2). Charlotte-Catherine de la Trémoille
(d. 1629)

François de Bourbon
prince of Conti
(d. 1614)

Charles of Bourbon
cardinal of Vendôme
then of Bourbon
(d. 1594)

Henri II
prince of Condé
(d. 1646)

The house of Bourbon-Vendôme

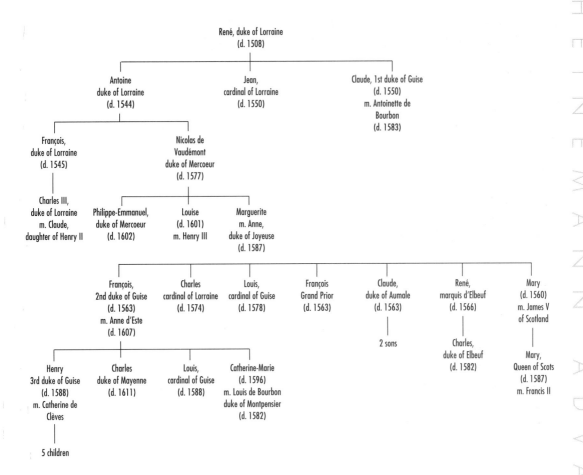

The house of Guise-Lorraine

Two of Montmorency's sons Francis and Henry de Damville also joined the Huguenot movement when their own needs dictated that they do so, and when political and financial rewards were offered. Both were opportunists who looked to further their own ambitions amid monarchical weakness and religious tension.

Conspiracy of Amboise

The drift to war began in March 1560, when a group of Huguenot nobles attempted to capture Francis II while the royal court wintered at the Château of Amboise; they wanted to liberate him from the clutches of the Guise family. The leader of the plot was Jean du Barry, Seigneur de la Renaudie. La Renaudie had consulted Louis de Bourbon and Calvin, although the latter was not willing to endorse the conspiracy. The plot was leaked to the Guises who were ready and waiting in March 1560 as the conspirators prepared to ride on the royal château. With the element of surprise lost the conspirators had little chance against the royal troops under Guise's command. Several hundred Huguenots were captured and summarily hanged from the château walls as traitors. The so-called Conspiracy of Amboise had failed, but more than this it re-emphasised to Catholics all over France that the Huguenots were dangerous and seditious rebels who sought to overthrow the established order and perhaps even the crown itself.

Charles IX

Condé was also arrested for his links with the conspirators and would have faced execution had Francis II not died in December 1560 from an ear infection. Francis was immediately succeeded by his 9-year-old brother, Charles IX, and Guise influence at court was lost, as Catherine de Medici assumed the position of regent with Antoine de Bourbon as lieutenant-general and the overtly Protestant Gaspard de Coligny on the council. Here are the first signs of the middle course which Catherine de Medici pursued in religious policy, tolerating known Huguenots in order to create political stability. In the long term she recognised that toleration could never create stability because the bulk of the French population believed the Huguenots to be heretical rebels who undermined the monarchy and the kingdom. Nevertheless, Catherine released Condé and pursued her policy of compromise and toleration under the watchful eye of the new chancellor, Michel de l'Hopital. Both believed that a policy of toleration would restore order.

Poissy

Two meetings of the Estates General in 1560 and 1561 had failed to find a solution to the religious problem, so in September 1561 Catherine took matters into her own hands and invited religious leaders from both sides to a meeting at Poissy in order to see if a middle ground could be found to reunite all Frenchmen under the Gallican church. Yet reconciliation was impossible as neither side was willing to compromise with the other:

- Theological matters of doctrine such as disagreement over the eucharist were insurmountable.
- The popular and political strength of Calvinism had perhaps hardened the Huguenots' resolve to stand their ground.

Ultra-Catholics, for their part, were entirely disillusioned with a regime which sat around the negotiating table with heretics and those such as the Guises began to make more militant noises. In late 1561, Duke Francis of Guise, Constable Montmorency and Marshal Saint André formed a military triumvirate to destroy heresy in France with Spanish aid from Philip II. France was moving closer to civil war by the day, and the threat to obliterate all Protestants merely hastened its advance.

Toleration and backlash

In January 1562, Catherine de Medici issued the Edict of Saint Germain (the Edict of January) which proclaimed the limited but legal recognition of the Huguenots:

- Huguenots were allowed to assemble for worship outside town walls during the daytime, although they were not allowed to arm themselves, sing the psalms in public or worship freely without fear of persecution.
- Protestant nobles could organise and protect Calvinist congregations on their own estates, thus recognising the support that the Reformed faith had among sections of the aristocracy.

The government had stuck to its policy of toleration in order to maintain order but, in offering legal recognition to the Huguenots, Catherine de Medici had gone too far. The edict aroused anger and resentment in the *parlement* of Paris which predictably refused to register the edict until ordered to do so by Catherine herself. A formal **remonstrance** was sent to the queen mother emphasising the king's duty to defend the one true faith, Catholicism, as outlined in his coronation oath, an oath which Charles was yet to take. The *parlement* finally registered the edict on 6 March 1562, but with an amendment attached stating that it was against its will and only because the king had expressly commanded that it do so. Yet by this time such objections were insignificant because the edict had already proved to be unenforcable.

On 1 March 1562, the duke of Guise and a group of armed followers had come upon a group of Huguenots worshipping within the town walls of Vassy, in Champagne, a contravention of the January Edict. Guise and his followers killed the unarmed worshippers and marched on Paris in order to raise a Catholic army. In response to the massacre, the Protestants held a National Synod at Orleans where it was agreed that troops should be mobilised under the leadership of Louis de Bourbon, Prince of Condé. Two opposing camps, both armed, now faced each other, and France was on the brink of a civil war which would span three generations and result in political and economic ruin.

Catherine de Medici

THE EARLY WARS OF RELIGION, 1562–70

The first three Wars of Religion are characterised by local tension, stalemate on the battlefield and inadequate peace settlements which served to spark off further violence. As the wars progressed in this period we see the steady decline of central authority and the growing hostilities in local communities which would ultimately result in the St Bartholomew's Day Massacre of 1572.

First War of Religion, 1563

Call to arms The initial conflict which began in 1562 saw a number of powerful nobles take up the military leadership of the Reformed cause. Condé and Coligny were the leading lights and their large clientele network throughout Picardy and Normandy respectively ensured further aristocratic support. The third National Synod met at Orleans in April 1562: Condé was proclaimed protector of all the Calvinist churches in France and of the house and crown of France. Armed resistance to the Guise family was proclaimed, and significantly little mention was made of pastors, ministers or even Geneva. The fate of Protestantism in France appeared to be in the hands of the rural nobility.

Edict of Amboise, 1563 Catherine de Medici was helpless in the face of military mobilisation on both sides, and she could only watch as Guise was given a hero's welcome into Paris after Vassy:

- The Catholic military **triumvirate** which had orchestrated the massacre was able to recruit Antoine de Bourbon, King of Navarre, who gave up his mild Protestant sympathies and threw in his lot with the Guise faction.
- From his base in Orleans, Condé directed operations, and the Huguenots built fortified strongholds throughout Guyenne, Languedoc and Dauphine either through military conquest or genuine conversion of the municipal magistrates. With Orleans, Rouen, Lyons and Tours in Huguenot hands in 1563 control of the major waterways and land routes became a priority. The queen mother now had little option but to back the triumvirate and endorse religious war.
- Guise dispatched Catholic forces to lay siege to Huguenot towns in the north in an attempt to split Condé's forces in two and disrupt communications. Eventually, towns such as Rouen, Blois and Tours were won back by Guise but at a cost. Antoine de Bourbon was fatally wounded during the siege of Rouen while the three months it had taken for that city to submit demonstrated to the triumvirate how difficult it would be to overturn all of the fortified strongholds which the Huguenots possessed.

KEY EVENT

Edict of Amboise, March 1563 As with the earlier Edict of January, this new settlement allowed for limited freedom of worship for Huguenots. Worship was restricted to the suburbs of one town in each *bailliage* rather than outside any town. Huguenot nobles were still allowed to worship on their estates, a telling recognition of their continued importance. Again, little mention is made of Calvinist ministers or pastors, and the towns, especially in the south, remained torn by religious differences.

- In December 1562, the only major engagement of the first war was fought at Dreux, and although the Catholics were victorious Marshal Saint André was killed while rival commanders Condé and Montmorency were captured. Worse was to follow for the Catholics as Duke Francis of Guise was assassinated while besieging Orleans in February 1563. Two of the original triumvirate were dead and the other was being held captive. Stalemate now ensued on the battlefield.
- Outright victory for the Catholics was impossible and Catherine de Medici took this opportunity to draw up a peace settlement. Having secured the release of Montmorency and Condé, the peace process began and resulted in the **Edict of Amboise** (March 1563).

The first war set a trend which was followed until 1598 and the Edict of Nantes. Neither side was capable of gaining outright victory over the other and, with resources expended, a compromise peace settlement was concluded which was unenforceable and entirely inadequate. It was only a matter of time before the conflict was resumed, and both sides knew it. The personnel might be slightly different, especially on the Catholic side, but the roots of the problem and the nature of the conflict remained the same.

Failure of the edict Once again the *parlement* of Paris led the way in refusing to ratify the Edict of Amboise because it offered legal recognition to Calvinism. Registration was provisional upon the king reaching his age of majority; attached to the ratification was an explicit remonstrance. In reply, Catherine took a swipe at the perceived arrogance of the *parlement* of Paris by proclaiming the majority of Charles IX in the *parlement* of Rouen. The declaration was in the form of a *lit de justice*, a rare event which typified Catherine's desire to reimpose order through the crown. Between 1564 and 1566 Charles IX and his mother along with the chancellor l'Hopital and the rest of the household undertook a royal progress through the provinces to display the king in his year of majority to his subjects as well as ensure that all the *parlements* ratified the peace edict. Catherine also hoped for the support of moderate nobles who shared her vision of peace through toleration. Yet while acknowledged as a success the progress also demonstrated to Catherine how unpopular her edict was and how unenforceable it was in practice. Local tensions were made worse by the clauses offering toleration; in particular, Catholic violence towards Huguenots became more common.

Second War of Religion, 1567

War restarts At court the dominant faction was still the Guise family despite the assassination of Duke Francis. The deceased duke's two brothers, Claude, duke of Aumale, and Charles, cardinal of Lorraine, continued to press for a resumption of hostilities; the family issued a vendetta against Admiral Coligny whom they suspected of organising the assassination of Francis. Worryingly for

KEY TERM

Lit de justice The personal attendance by the king in *parlement* in order that an unpopular edict, in this case Amboise, be registered. On the one hand it was symbolic of the king's majority but on the other it demonstrated the unwillingness of *parlement* to ratify any legislation that offered toleration to Huguenots.

Gaspard de Coligny

Catherine, Henry, Duke of Anjou, younger brother of Charles and heir to the throne, was heavily influenced by Charles, Cardinal of Lorraine, while Condé and Coligny had stopped attending council meetings altogether. Once again, Catherine's vision of peace was slowly disintegrating and a second war that lasted almost six months broke out in September 1567.

The war began over Huguenot fears that a Spanish army marching along France's eastern frontier to get to **the Netherlands** was going to change course and confront the Huguenots on the battlefield. Such suspicions were not unreasonable given the political circumstances. The Catholics had received aid from Philip II in the form of troops to fight in Guyenne during the first war. Also, in June 1565, Catherine herself had met with her daughter, the queen of Spain, and the **Duke of Alva** at Bayonne, and there is little doubt that Alva attempted to persuade her to take a more aggressive and hard line towards the Protestants in France. The same Alva led the Spanish troops across eastern France in 1567.

Although we now know that Catherine had no intention of attacking the Protestant leadership in 1567, the rumours and fears were enough to prompt Coligny and Condé to organise another plot to kidnap the king and free him from the clutches of the Guise faction. The coup was nearly a success as Huguenot forces mobilised rapidly and a number of local risings took Catholic leaders by surprise. However, the main event, like the previous attempt at Amboise in 1560, was not a success, and war effectively broke out when the royal court at Meaux heard that Condé's troops had mobilised in September 1567:

- The king fled to Paris under the protection of his Swiss guards, and the cardinal of Lorraine prepared for war, confirming the worst fears of the Huguenots by sending out an invitation to Alva to intervene and join the fight.
- Once more the Huguenots were able to seize a number of fortified towns, namely Orleans, Nîmes, Valence, Auxerre and Montpellier.

Stalemate Militarily the second war mirrored the first, with neither side able to inflict outright defeat on the other. **Condé's superior army** laid siege to Paris in another attempt to capture the king. As the siege progressed, the Catholics were able to put together a royal army and a major confrontation occurred at Saint Denis in November 1567. The result was a draw:

- Condé was forced to call off the siege of Paris.
- Anne de Montmorency, the Constable of France and last remaining member of the original triumvirate, was killed.

Lacking leadership the Catholics looked for peace; lacking further foreign aid the Huguenots did likewise. The result was the **Edict of Longjumeau** (26 March 1568) which confirmed the previous edict drawn up at Amboise. The edict was sent directly to the royal governors in the provinces, thus preventing the predictable procrastination and protest from the *parlements*. Yet the fundamental problem still existed, namely toleration of the Huguenots was seen as a violation of Gallican principles by the majority of the population; if Amboise had failed as a consequence of this fact then it was more than likely that Longjumeau would also fail to uphold a lasting peace.

A plot against the Huguenots Hostility to the peace was greatest in Paris and right from the start the cardinal of Lorraine worked to overturn the peace settlement. The cardinal outlined a plot to seize a number of Huguenot towns such as Orleans and La Rochelle and in the process capture Condé and Coligny. The plot was forced through the royal council in August 1568, an indication of how the Guise faction now dominated affairs. Moderates like l'Hopital were sidelined and the queen mother along with Charles IX himself were little more than bystanders. Henry, Duke of Anjou, on the other hand had been appointed lieutenant-general of the army, effectively taking on the role left vacant by Montmorency. The loyalties of Anjou were clear, and his own political advancement rode on the back of his affiliation to the cardinal of Lorraine rather than his mother. The plot to strike at the heart of Huguenot power predictably failed, and the Protestant leaders fled to La Rochelle.

KEY THEME

The superiority of Condé's army The army was strengthened by German mercenaries provided by Frederick III, elector of the Palatinate, and led by his son John of Casimir.

KEY EVENT

Edict of Longjumeau (March 1568) Allowed for the legal worship of Calvinism in the suburbs of one town in each *bailliage*, as well as on noble estates.

KEY PERSON

William of Orange (1533–84) The father of Dutch independence and hero of the Dutch struggle against the Catholic Spanish. A failure in 1566 and again in 1568, Orange led a more successful revolt in 1572 leading to the Pacification of Ghent in which all seventeen Dutch provinces were united against Spain. However, the alliance was short-lived as the southern provinces returned to the Spanish fold. William continued to campaign for religious toleration and conciliation. He courted the French duke of Anjou as a sovereign figurehead for the northern provinces in revolt with limited success. In 1584, Orange was assassinated leaving the United Provinces of the north leaderless.

KEY THEME

Ties between Huguenots and Elizabeth I Mary Stuart, queen of Scots (niece of the cardinal of Lorraine), had been forced to flee Scotland in 1568 as a consequence of a Calvinist, noble revolution and she threw herself upon the mercy of Elizabeth. Mary was next in line to the throne as long as Elizabeth remained childless. For this reason Elizabeth had her imprisoned, fearful of the scheming of Lorraine. Lorraine's plan was to marry off Anjou to Mary and unite the two crowns under Catholicism. Such thoughts naturally pushed Elizabeth closer to Condé and Coligny.

The Third War, 1568–70

A longer war The peace of Longjumeau proved to be the most short-lived of the Wars of Religion, and the Third War was the most destructive, thus demonstrating the rise in tension and hostility between the faiths and the increasing strength and organisation of both sides on the battlefield. The Third War was also longer than the previous two, probably as a consequence of increased foreign support for the Huguenots:

- In August 1568, Condé and Coligny signed a formal treaty of mutual support with the Dutch nobleman in exile **William of Orange.** Both had a common enemy in Philip II – Orange had narrowly escaped execution in June 1568 after a failed revolt against Spanish power in the Netherlands while the Spanish king had encouraged the cardinal of Lorraine to violate the peace of Longjumeau and renew hostilities. Orange could not offer the Huguenots a great deal of aid given his own precarious situation in 1568 but the German states and England were a different story.
- Wolfgang Wilhelm of Zweibrucken offered 8000 reiters and 40 ensigns of foot which were paid for by Elizabeth I. **Ties between the Huguenots and the English queen** were growing ever stronger.

The fighting in the Third Civil War was mainly concentrated around the south, which made life difficult for the crown in terms of concentrating its forces. The fortified towns at Cognac, Castres and Montpellier were going to be difficult to overcome for Anjou and his more seasoned Catholic general Tavannes:

- The first encounter at Jarnac in March 1569 was a resounding victory for the Catholics, a defeat which was made all the worse by the capture and probable execution of Condé.
- Coligny now took control of the Huguenot forces and retreated further into the Huguenot heartland of the south-west, pulling the Catholics ever further away from Paris.
- As help arrived from Zweibrucken, the Huguenots pressed forward crossing the Loire and taking La Charité

in May. A rare Huguenot victory then followed at La
Roche-l'Abeille in June as the royal army suffered from a
lack of pay and supplies.

- Up to this point, however, Coligny had wisely avoided a
  pitched encounter, in recognition of superior royal
  numbers. Yet at Moncontour in October the Huguenots
  were drawn into open battle and soundly defeated by
  Anjou's mercenaries. The Huguenot army staggered
  back to Languedoc to regroup
- Instead of following them and inflicting total defeat, the
  duke of Anjou made the disastrous decision to lay siege
  to the Huguenot stronghold of St Jean d'Angély. The
  operation cost him time and men. By the time the siege
  was called off the opportunity to strike against Coligny
  was lost, and the Huguenots had recovered.
- Coligny had recruited successfully from local Calvinist
  lords in Languedoc and on 25–26 June 1570 the
  Huguenot army defeated the Catholics at Arnay-le-Duc.
  Such a reversal for the royal army allowed Coligny to
  take up a powerful bargaining position at the resulting
  peace talks. A new peace settlement was agreed at Saint
  Germain in August 1570 which was labelled permanent.

The Peace of Saint Germain The peace edict reflected
Huguenot strength on the battlefield and the victory at
Arnay-le-Duc, and the terms were the most favourable yet
to the Huguenots. With the Cardinal of Lorraine disgraced
and out of favour, the council agreed on more specific
terms:

- Protestant worship was permitted inside two towns per
  government region and the towns were actually specified
  to avoid dispute or ambiguity.
- The Protestants were also allowed to occupy four
  fortified towns for a two-year period, namely La
  Rochelle, Cognac, Montauban and La Charité.
- Provisions were also made to reintegrate Huguenots into
  French society such as equality in taxation and the right
  to hold offices. All property seized from Huguenots from
  1562 onwards was to be returned. On the whole, the
  edict reflected major royal concessions of toleration. Not
  only could Protestants worship freely inside the walls of
  certain towns for the first time, but they were able to

consolidate their military position in the south-west through the creation of fortified towns. After three civil wars and eight years of bloodshed, the Catholic forces seemed no nearer to eliminating heresy.

KEY THEME

Foreign Aid Both sides relied heavily on Swiss and German mercenaries, but the Huguenots desperately needed the financial and logistical support given to them by Elector Frederick III, the duke of Zweibrucken, Elizabeth I and William of Orange. Foreign support served to internationalise the conflict and prolong the wars.

Civil war, 1562–70

The pattern of military stalemate, unenforceable peace edicts and renewed conflict created a vicious circle of civil violence which continued until 1598.

- **Foreign aid** for both Huguenots and Catholics was crucial in supplementing the respective armies.
- Catherine de Medici, Charles IX and chancellor l'Hôpital pursued a middle course to restore peace and order through toleration. Yet, in undermining the Gallican principles which bound French society together, they misjudged the intensity of belief within French society. Catholics in particular could not tolerate living alongside seditious heretics, and events such as the conspiracy of Amboise reinforced their view of Protestants as traitors. Any peace settlement that offered toleration to the Huguenots was unlikely to last for any length of time.
- Outright military victory on the battlefield was unachievable for either side during this period although we might have expected the royal army to triumph, given its superior resources and personnel. Indeed Anjou had his chance after Moncontour in 1569 but chose instead to lay siege to St Jean d'Angély. In general, however, such opportunities were few and far between. The royal forces found it difficult to mobilise quickly, and to get troops into the south-west in order to launch an effective strike. Foreign mercenaries made up the bulk of the royal army and they were costly and had to be recruited from abroad. Also, if they were not paid regularly they became disgruntled and dissatisfied. Huguenot strongholds were difficult to breach and they were well dispersed throughout the kingdom. The royal forces were not able to target one particular town, and sieges were costly both in terms of money and lives. During the 1560s, the crown spent an average 4.6 million livres per annum to maintain its army in the field. The war was taking up nearly half of the royal revenue and was rapidly sapping royal finances.

- The Huguenots were in a minority (only 10 per cent of the population) but they were well organised, disciplined and committed. The religious environment elsewhere in Europe, such as in the Netherlands or in the Palatinate, ensured foreign aid while the hierarchical structure of the Calvinist church in France allowed funds to be raised with relative ease. Strong fortified towns along the Loire and in the south-west were easy to defend and did not put vast numbers of lives at risk.

- Condé and Coligny managed their armies and resources more effectively than Anjou or even Tavennes. The Huguenot leaders avoided pitched battles wherever possible and settled for a more defensive strategy until Coligny was able to take advantage of a weak royal force in 1570, and thus put the Huguenots in a relatively strong position.

SUMMARY QUESTIONS

1. Why did Catherine de Medici's policies of conciliation at Poissy fail?

2. Who supported Calvinism in French society?

3. Why did civil war break out in 1562?

4. Why were the royal forces unable to defeat the Huguenots in the first eight years of the conflict?

CHAPTER 5

The French Wars of Religion: St Bartholomew's Day, 1572

THE ST BARTHOLOMEW'S DAY MASSACRE, 1572

Historical controversy surrounds the St Bartholomew's Day Massacre and our understanding of the events is not helped by the unreliability of most of the contemporary material. Two sequences of events are crucial which together make up the massacre.

- The first is the attempted assassination of Coligny that took place on 22 August, along with the murder of several dozen Huguenot leaders, on the morning of 24 August.
- The second sequence is inextricably linked to the first: the popular wave of killings which broke out in Paris between 24 and 27 August and which were mimicked across the provinces throughout September and October.

The situation in France following the edict of Saint Germain was more favourable to the Protestants than at any previous time, and prospects for a lasting peace appeared to be good. Provisions had been made for the reintegration of Huguenots into French society and Catherine de Medici was arranging two marriage alliances to strengthen her peace policy:

- The first was between Henry, Duke of Anjou, and Queen Elizabeth of England. It fell through when Anjou came under predictable pressure from the Guise faction to denounce the heretical queen of England. Catherine then put forward her youngest son, Francis, duke of Alençon, as a potential suitor for Elizabeth but with similar results.
- The second marriage was probably more contentious but easier to arrange. Catherine wanted to marry her daughter, Marguerite, to the Protestant king of Navarre.

In the eyes of the Queen Mother this Huguenot–
Catholic matrimonial bond would be symbolic of the
new era of peace of Saint Germain.

Tension and violence

The numbers of conversions to Protestantism were
beginning to fall and Huguenot numbers had reached their
pinnacle in the late 1560s. But there were serious
outbreaks of violence on both sides:

- Yet Protestant attitudes were becoming more extreme
  and several Protestant texts **attacked the Gallican
  monarchy** and the authority of the king. These texts
  served to polarise attitudes and horrified Catholics who
  held the monarchy to be at the core of French society.
- Moreover, religious tensions among the community at
  large were on the increase after Saint Germain. Catholic
  mob violence in Paris and in the provinces became more
  common. In November 1571, the removal of the **Croix**

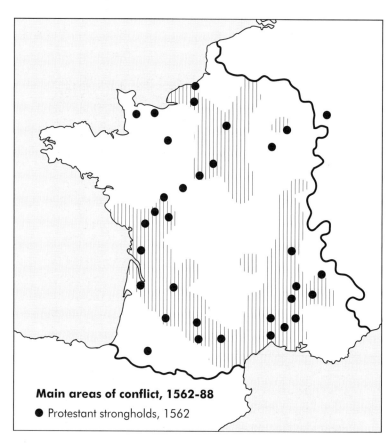

Main areas of conflict, 1562-88
● Protestant strongholds, 1562

KEY THEME

**Attack on the Gallican
monarchy** The *Declaration
and Protestation of those of the
Reformed Religion in La
Rochelle* went so far as to
suggest that kings had no
right to command the
consciences of their subjects.
Kings such as Charles IX
could rule by God's will only
if they followed God's will,
and such pamphlets advocated
popular sovereignty.

KEY EVENT

Croix de Gastines This
large cross was erected in Paris
in 1569 to symbolise the just
execution of two Huguenots.
The Peace of Saint Germain
(1570) specified that all such
monuments to the
persecution of Huguenots be
torn down. The order
provoked riots among the
Catholic Parisian mob.

**Protestant strongholds,
1562**

de Gastines to another location under a clause in the edict of Saint Germain, sparked off rioting which led to over 40 deaths. In Rouen, armed Catholics massacred another 40 Huguenots after an earlier altercation over the Corpus Christi.

Religious tensions were ready to boil over at a popular level and communities, especially Catholic ones, were willing and ready to take matters into their own hands in order to preserve the 'one true faith'.

POWER OF COLIGNY

Between 1570 and 1572 Coligny's power on the royal council increased, at the expense of the Guise family. Coligny was eager to persuade Catherine that a **renewed war against the Habsburgs** over the Netherlands might reunite the country. Yet Coligny was in a minority on the royal council in wanting war and even he could not promise to control the French Huguenots who wanted to join the fight in the Netherlands against Philip II. Charles was rapidly going off the idea of war by August 1572

Henry, king of Navarre, and Marguerite of Valois

although Coligny's warmongering policy should not be seen as a reason for Catherine wanting him dead. Indeed, if her marriage alliance between Marguerite and Navarre was to be a success, she would require Coligny's support. Therefore, it appears difficult to argue that Catherine was the driving force behind the plot to assassinate Coligny. Yet, it was the royal wedding, orchestrated by Catherine, on 18 August 1572 which provided the backdrop for the St Bartholomew's Day Massacre.

ATTEMPTED ASSASSINATION OF COLIGNY, 22 AUGUST 1572

The series of killings collectively known as the St Bartholomew's Day Massacre began on 22 August 1572 with the attempted assassination of Gaspard de Coligny. The admiral had remained in Paris with several other Huguenot leaders after the royal wedding in order to discuss recent violations of the edict of Saint Germain with Charles IX. While returning from a meeting with the king in the Louvre, Coligny was shot in the arm and hand. The attempt to assassinate Coligny failed, and the wounded admiral along with the other Huguenot leaders took the decision to remain in Paris. Had **Sieur de Maurevert** been successful in killing Coligny it is likely that the other leaders would have fled the capital and simply regrouped and prepared for a fourth war. As it was, their fateful decision to stay allowed the ensuing massacre to take place. Charles IX promised to apprehend the assassin, but most Huguenots were talking of revenge rather than justice. As for who arranged the assassination, it is unlikely to have been the work of Catherine and more likely to have been arranged by Guise.

REVENGE, 24 AUGUST 1572

The assassination attempt on Coligny's life was an attempt to kill the Huguenot leader, rather than the first part of a plan to massacre all Huguenots in Paris. Yet a massacre did occur and just how this came to be and who was responsible are still shrouded in mystery:

KEY PERSON

Sieur de Maurevert Just who Maurevert was working for has been the topic of much debate over the centuries. The most likely suspects were the Guises, especially because they owned the house from which the shots were fired. Moreover, the Guises remained convinced that Coligny had orchestrated the assassination of Duke Francis of Guise in 1563, and the cardinal of Lorraine was jealous of Coligny's influence at court.

- A royal council meeting was held on 23 August to discuss the attempt on Coligny's life and the increasing tensions within the capital. Fears abounded of a Protestant revenge attack and Catherine was panicked into making the decision to remove the Huguenot leaders.
- Rumours were circulating of the 4000 Huguenot troops commanded by Coligny's brother-in-law Teligny which were stationed just outside Paris. Many Catholics believed that the Huguenots were ready to strike against the Guises and all other Catholics in Paris.
- A decision was therefore taken at the council meeting to carry out a strike against the Huguenot leaders.

Between three and four in the morning of Sunday 24 August 1572, 100 Swiss guards led by Duke Henry of Guise carried out a series of murders with Coligny being one of the first victims. The admiral was slain by Guise himself and then his body was thrown out of the window onto the street below. The **murder of Coligny** was followed by several dozen others, but the killing did not stop there.

MASSACRE, 24–27 AUGUST 1572

The general massacre of Huguenots began on Sunday 24 August and lasted for three days. Fanatical Catholics

KEY EVENT

Coligny's murder Coligny was murdered at 4 am on 24 August 1572 in the Hotel de Bethisy by members of the king's guard led by Guise. His body was thrown out of the window. Coligny's head was then hacked off and taken to the royal palace in order that the queen mother and Charles could be satisfied that the deed was done. A mob which had gathered outside the Hotel de Bethisy further mutilated the headless corpse and dragged it through the city for three days before it was hung up at the gibbet of Mautfaucon.

The massacre of St Bartholomew's Day

among the city militia led the way but ordinary Parisians driven to a collective zeal joined in the carnage. Among the first non-noble victims of the general massacre were wealthy Huguenot merchants, perhaps suggesting long-term popular resentment and jealousy. Other victims included Nicolas Le Mercier who had been attacked before during the Gastines affair. The manner in which the Huguenots were murdered tells us much about Catholic hatred towards Protestantism:

- The youngest daughter of Nicolas Le Mercier was dipped naked in the blood of her massacred father and mother and baptised with threats that she would follow her family into hell if she ever became a Huguenot.
- Antoine Mulenchon, with a sword held to his throat, was told to invoke the Virgin Mary and the saints and renounce Calvinism. He refused to be reconverted and was slaughtered.
- The corpse of the wife of Mathurin Lussault was turned on a spit like a wild boar before being dragged through the streets of Paris and dumped in the Seine.

By Wednesday 27 August over 2000 Huguenots had been murdered in Paris.

ROLE OF CHARLES IX

In seeking to explain such bloodshed we must understand that many Catholic citizens believed they were acting with **royal approval**. Ultimately, Charles would take responsibility for the massacre although he did state that the crown was faced with a Protestant coup on Saturday night and was forced to act. One immediate consequence of the king's admission of guilt was that he gained credibility among the ultra-Catholics within Paris, and attention was momentarily taken away from Duke Henry of Guise. In reality, the king probably agreed to a plot to murder the Huguenot leaders, but Guise's words were overheard by Catholic militants and the royal authorisation for massacre spread rapidly throughout the city. There is even evidence to suggest that Charles tried to halt the general massacre once it broke out.

Some Catholics in Paris on St Bartholomew's Day believed that they were carrying out **God's will** in the slaughter of Huguenots. Catholic preachers and literature had become more violent after the edict of Saint Germain in the belief that God was becoming angry with the citizens of Paris for living alongside heretics. Parisians feared God's wrath for their sins and this community of believers acted on divine authority as they set about purifying the city of heretics.

Nevertheless, only a minority of Parisians took part in the violence, although the majority approved of the cleansing. There was **Catholic compassion** towards Huguenot neighbours. Protestant propaganda which lays the blame for the general massacre upon Guise, Anjou and the queen mother is therefore suspect. Certainly the court ought to have foreseen the violence which would follow Coligny's murder and the court might have prevented the massacre, but there is nothing to suggest that they specifically planned or ordered it.

VIOLENCE IN THE PROVINCES

The violence in Paris spread to the provinces, specifically the urban centres of Bordeaux, Lyons, Orleans, Rouen and Toulouse:

- These were towns which were controlled by Catholics but which contained a significant Protestant minority.
- Some of these towns, such as Rouen and Orleans, had even been taken over during the first three conflicts by a Huguenot minority, so feelings and tension ran high.
- Solely Huguenot or Catholic strongholds did not witness violence in the wake of the Parisian slaughter; instead it was those towns with sizeable Huguenot minorities that saw bloodshed.

Over 3000 Huguenots were killed in the provinces by Catholics encouraged by the events in Paris, and equally certain that they were carrying out the will of God and king.

The consequences of St Bartholomew's Day, 1572

- More than 5000 Huguenots were killed. Confessional violence had occurred before, but previous bloodshed had built up fervour which overspilled on St Bartholomew's Day, 1572. The massacre in Paris and subsequently in the provinces was the most dramatic and extensive in a line of confessional hatred and violence.

- The Huguenot leadership was devastated by the massacre, and with Coligny dead most Calvinists looked to **Henry of Navarre** as their figurehead. Thousands of Huguenots reconverted to Catholicism after the massacre.

- The majority of Huguenots were disillusioned with their religion and believed God had deserted them and that Catholicism was after all the one true faith. Others abandoned Calvinism to preserve their lives. Over 3000 Huguenots in Rouen became Catholics. Many left France altogether and went into exile in Geneva and London. Numerically Calvinism would never recover from the St Bartholomew's Day Massacre and those who remained felt isolated and vulnerable.

- The massacre was a crucial turning point in the Wars of Religion because the Huguenots were now openly at war with the crown. Between 1562 and 1570 the Huguenots had fought to overturn the policies of the crown and gain toleration in the process. After 1572, the Huguenots fought against the very existence of the crown and political theories of resistance to the crown became more radical and extreme.

- The most immediate consequence of the massacres was the resumption of war. The Fourth War of Religion began in November 1572 after the Huguenot stronghold of La Rochelle refused to admit the royal governor or pay allegiance to the king.

KEY PERSON

Henry of Navarre
Unfortunately for the Huguenots, Navarre was forced to give up his Calvinism and return to the Catholic fold in 1572, being put under house arrest in the process. News of Navarre's abjuration was a further blow to the Huguenot contingent in France, but by 1576 he had escaped from court to lead the Huguenot cause once more.

WAR CONTINUES

Fourth War of Religion, 1572–3

Although many Catholics hoped that the St Bartholomew's Day Massacre and its aftermath would signal an end to

Protestantism in France, they were wrong. Huguenot strongholds across the south-west ensured not only the survival of their faith, but also the continuation of the wars. La Rochelle on the west coast of Poitou became the centre of the Fourth War after its Huguenot magistrates refused to admit entry to the Catholic royal governor Armand de Gontaut, Marshall Biron.

On 6 November 1572, Charles IX declared war on La Rochelle, determined to make the city submit to the royal will. Hampered by logistical problems, the siege of La Rochelle directed by Biron did not begin until February 1573. The siege appeared doomed through a combination of factors:

KEY PEOPLE

Henry of Anjou and Francis of Alençon Alençon was jealous of his elder brother's status and military record, while it was also suggested that members of Alençon's entourage were in league with the Huguenots and were conspiring to stage a coup headed by the count of Montgomery, who was at this time still in exile in England.

KEY EVENTS

Death of Sigismund Augustus Sigismund died leaving no male heirs. Catherine de Medici was determined to secure the Polish throne for her son Henry of Anjou. On 29 May 1573, Henry learned of his election to the Polish throne.

The Peace of la Rochelle, 1573 When contrasted with that of Saint Germain in 1570, La Rochelle effectively demonstrates the extent to which the Huguenot position had changed in those three years, primarily as a consequence of the massacres.

- Huguenot resistance was firm. The commitment of the population of La Rochelle should not be underestimated in repelling Biron's forces. The town withstood the siege for five months, bolstered by the arrival of refugees in exile after the horrific events of 1572.
- Rumours of discontent and treason abounded among the Catholic forces especially between the king's two brothers, **Henry of Anjou and Francis of Alençon**.
- The location of La Rochelle on the Atlantic coast also made it easy for supplies to be shipped in to the city, and close relations had built up between the Huguenot fortress and Protestant governments in England and the Netherlands.

In the end the peace settlement came about in May 1573 as a consequence of the **death of Sigismund Augustus**, king of Poland and Henry of Anjou's election as his successor:

- One of the regulations drawn up by the leader of the Polish church called for freedom of worship in Poland and Henry felt that a show of good will in France would do no harm.
- The siege at La Rochelle was draining royal finances, costing as it was over 500,000 livres per month.
- There were over 12,000 royal casualties and munition stocks were depleted. peace was a necessity for the crown.

PEACE OF LA ROCHELLE

On 2 July 1573, the **peace of La Rochelle** was signed allowing Huguenot worship in the private homes of La Rochelle, Montauban and Nîmes. Everywhere else in the kingdom, Protestant worship was banned outright. Yet the Huguenots had not been exterminated, and throughout the Midi royal ordinances were being ignored including the latest peace settlement. Catholic suspicions increased after the Huguenots attempted to free the still captive Navarre along with Alençon in the spring of 1574. Shortly afterwards in May 1574, Charles IX died and was succeeded by his brother Henry of Anjou, King of Poland. Henry returned from Cracow to rule over a kingdom which was becoming increasingly polarised along confessional lines.

Charles IX

Huguenot resistance

Deprived of leadership after 1572, Huguenot policy became increasingly directed by local leaders in the south. Huguenot leaders of the Reformed faith assembled in late 1572 in Languedoc to draw up a defensive alliance and, more significantly, the **Huguenot constitution** of an independent state.

In some respects a state within a state had been formed although it should be noted that the delegates at the meeting at Millau in 1574 denied that they wanted to remove the king as their lord and protector:

- The constitution was inherently anti-monarchical because it was now the federal assemblies who appointed the protector rather than the king.
- Taxes would be set and raised locally and powers of legislation were similarly self-governed.

By 1574, the Huguenot leaders from the Midi had also allied themselves to the governor of Languedoc, **Henry of Damville**, son of Anne de Montmorency. Disillusioned with royal policy he became protector of the Huguenot constitution, thus emphasising the depths of division that existed within French society.

KEY CONCEPTS

Resistance theories directly opposed the crown and the very nature and origins of the French monarchy. Such resistance theories as those emerging after 1572 advocated a Huguenot republic and an elective monarchy.

Huguenot attitudes The concept of a United Provinces in the Midi combined with a calls to arms against the Valois dynasty were a severe attack on Gallican values, and represented a more radical stance than that of pre-1572. Huguenot strength may have been severely curtailed by the massacres but the movement was also radicalised by the carnage.

Resistance theories

Other more radical **resistance theories** began to emerge in the wake of the St Bartholomew's Day Massacre:

- In *Francogallia* (1573) Francis Hotman argued that the French monarchy was elective not hereditary. Theodore de Beza took Hotman's views one step further with his *Du Droit des Magistrats* (1574) which took the line that not only were subjects not required to obey a tyrannical king but also that it was the duty of the magistrates to overthrow such a monarch. Both authors called upon the Estates General to resist the French king and represent the rights of the people.
- More influential was the *French Alarm Bell* (1574) by Nicolas Barnaud which attacked the crown over its authorisation of the St Bartholomew's Day Massacre. It urged princes and peers to overthrow tyrannical monarchs, and included a draft of the Huguenot constitution endorsing popular sovereignty.
- *The Defence of Liberty against Tyrants* (1579), written by Philippe Duplessis Mornay, argued that it was lawful to resist a tyrannical monarch.

Such resistance theories underscore the point that the St Bartholomew's Day Massacre changed the nature of the conflict and in particular moved **Huguenot attitudes** to a more radical position.

Catholic response

In response to such revolutionary literature came Jean Bodin's principles of absolute sovereignty. In *The Six Books of the Commonwealth* (1576) Bodin stated that:

- all political authority came from God and therefore kings were answerable to God alone
- the king was an instrument of God's will
- in order for a government to be efficient the king required a council of advisers, to make laws to provide a link between master and subjects
- although the king was not a law unto himself he could not be deposed by his subjects.

Thus Bodin, a political theorist from Angers, led the way in defending the sacred nature of the monarchy.

SUMMARY QUESTIONS

1. Who was to blame for the St Bartholomew's Day Massacre?

2. What does the way in which Huguenots were killed on St Bartholomew's Day reveal about popular Catholic attitudes towards Huguenots?

3. How did St Bartholomew's Day change the nature of the Protestant movement in France?

4. What was the significance of resistance theories?

CHAPTER 6

The French Wars of Religion: The reign of Henry III, 1574–84

ACCESSION OF HENRY III

Henry of Anjou, the military hero of Jarnac and Moncontour, but with little political experience, became king at a time when France was on the verge of political and social collapse. France required a strong and resourceful monarch to see the kingdom through such turmoil, but Henry was ostentatious and weak. Between 1574 and 1584 France suffered from three more religious wars and Henry III oversaw a disintegration of monarchical authority.

Alençon

Huguenot nobles were always likely to target Navarre's independence as a priority for continued survival of the Huguenot cause. Alençon was a different matter. Although young and inexperienced, Alençon was beginning to attract the attention of influential and ambitious princes, known as the *politiques*, such as Navarre, Condé and de la Mole. In fact, many of these princes at court were motivated by their own ambitions to advance their careers. **Alençon's opposition** was rooted in his jealousy of Henry. He fled court in September 1575. He then issued a political manifesto from Dreux which announced his armed opposition to his brother's tyranny. Alençon then marched his small band of Catholic princes southwards to link up with the forces being assembled by Condé and **John of Casimir**. Such an alliance was extremely serious for Henry III on two counts:

- Casimir's father, Elector Frederick III of the Palatinate, had recently provided 20,000 German mercenaries for an invasion of France. Added to the Huguenot forces commanded by Condé, Damville and the recently

KEY TERM

Politiques Describes those in favour of religious coexistence in order to ensure stability. The term was only really used after 1584, but these princes were certainly moderates and were not necessarily bound together along confessional lines.

KEY THEME

Alençon's opposition Alençon claimed that he opposed the king's advisers such as the Guises, not the king, but this did not ring true. Alençon also called for a religious peace in order that a church council could be held and for a meeting of the Estates General.

KEY PERSON

John of Casimir Son of Frederick III of the Palatinate, John of Casimir led a German mercenary army into France in 1576 to fight on behalf of the Huguenots.

escaped Navarre the overall Protestant army in the field outnumbered the royal forces.

- Alençon was heir to the throne and this offered the coalition rebel forces status and legality.

Fifth War of Religion, 1576

The Remonstance, 1576 Alençon was put at the forefront of negotiations with the king, and he presented a remonstrance of 93 articles to Henry III in March 1576. Alençon, Navarre, Damville and Condé demanded:

- the free exercise of the Reformed religion
- the creation of unbiased courts where Huguenots could get justice
- a number of fortified towns as well as payment of the German mercenaries under Casimir
- individual requests, for example Alençon asked for the title of **Duke of Anjou.**

The demands of the Huguenot princes led by the Catholic Alençon were overwhelming and almost unbelievable coming as they did only four years after St Bartholomew's Day. Yet, Henry III and Catherine de Medici were hardly in a position to refuse the remonstrance because the royal forces could not match those mustered by Condé, Navarre and Damville. With the German mercenaries under Casimir closing in on the towns of the Loire Valley, Henry III decided to give in to the demands of his brother and with barely a shot being fired the Fifth War of Religion was brought to an end with the Edict of Beaulieu on 6 May 1576. Known as the Peace of Monsieur, as it was seen to have been forced upon the king by his brother, it represented a massive turnaround in Huguenot fortunes.

Peace of Monsieur, 1576 The treaty comprised 63 articles and concessions to the Huguenots were considerable:

- All French Protestants were given the right of a free, public and general exercise of religion everywhere in France except Paris. This meant that Protestant churches could be built.
- Special law courts were established guaranteeing equality in cases involving litigants of different faiths.

> ### KEY TERM
>
> **Duke of Anjou** The title Duke of Anjou had been his brother's before Henry's succession and was considered by Alençon to be adequate recognition of his position as heir to the throne.

- The king was to call a meeting of the Estates General within six months and the Huguenots were granted eight surety towns, mainly in the south.
- Alençon was granted the duchies and revenue of Anjou, Touraine and Berry along with an annual pension of over 300,000 livres.

The peace was met with predictable hostility from Catholics all over France. Henry had reconciled with Alençon and there were clauses in the peace which required Huguenots to restore Catholic worship in towns where it had been abolished and Protestants to observe Catholic feast days, but to many Catholics Henry appeared to have given in to Huguenot force.

Yet although the concessions were unprecedented it is crucial to remember that this treaty was dictated in arms and the long-term policies of Henry and Catherine towards the Huguenots did not change. Also, Huguenot strength was boosted by the mercenaries and financial aid of Elector Frederick, and their actual number on the ground remained less than 8 per cent of the population. Finally, the leadership of Alençon and other Catholic princes gave the Huguenots greater legitimacy and ensured that Henry took their demands seriously.

Formation of the Catholic League

At the Estates General which opened at Blois in November 1576, the assembly was dominated by Catholic deputies opposed to the peace of Monsieur:

- Most of the Catholic deputies were in favour of a return to war although few were willing to bear the financial burden demand by Henry III.
- The clergy voted unanimously for the suppression of Protestantism and granted the king subsidies for this purpose.
- The nobility also decided in favour of religious uniformity but were eager to stress their right to be exempt from taxation.
- The third estate included a minority of moderates who wished for a negotiated peace and religious tolerance. Among the moderates was the legist and political

theorist **Jean Bodin,** whose *Six Books of the Commonwealth* had just appeared. In the end the third estate voted for the suppression of Protestantism but hoped that it could be achieved without war.

In February 1577, each estate handed over its own *cahier de doléances* which demanded the eradication of Protestantism and the restoration of Catholicism as the one true faith. Yet Henry had been granted little additional income in order to carry out this aim, and the unwillingness of the nobility and the third estate to assist the king financially severely undermined his position.

As the Huguenots were already mobilised and making ground in the regions of Provence and Dauphine, the Catholic militants at Blois became frustrated at the king's lack of action. Many of these Catholics, including Duke Henry of Guise, had already realised that their aims and ambitions would be better served through the formation of their own party designed to defend the Catholic cause, and thus the Catholic League was born. Guise issued a manifesto proclaiming the Holy Catholic League which aimed to:

• implement the law of God in its entirety
• uphold Catholic worship
• maintain the king in the authority and obedience owed to him by his subjects.

Ultimately, the League undermined Henry's authority – a fact which he recognised in December 1576 when he tried unsuccessfully to put himself at the head of the League. Henry's aim was to deny leadership to the Guises, but as he had no money to wage a war which he had been put under pressure to renew and had subsequently started, the League lost faith in the king and his advisers whom the militants branded *mignons* (or pretty ones). Henry had managed to win back Damville from the Huguenot cause in 1577 luring him with the marquisate of Saluzzo.

Sixth War of Religion, 1576–7
The Sixth War of Religion was always likely to be brief and inconclusive given the king's lack of funding. Fighting

Jean Bodin (1529–96)
Argued in favour of a lasting peace that would restore order to the kingdom, and he opposed the king's demands for an increase in taxation. Although an advocate of monarchical absolutism, Bodin did not believe that a rise in taxation was in the best interests of the crown because the populace had already been forced to endure fiscal strain.

Cahier de doléances
Complaints presented to the king by each estate at a meeting of the Estates General.

began in December 1576 and the royal army under Anjou and the Duke of Nevers struggled from the outset, hampered by inadequate supplies and equipment. Although both La Charité and Issoire fell to the royalist army in May and June 1577, the king's lack of finances prevented these victories from being consolidated. Nevers wanted to make further inroads into the fortified towns given to the Huguenots at the peace of Monsieur, but royal troops were increasingly being billeted on the local population and, with the Huguenots receiving aid from Elizabeth I of England, Henry III had little choice but to conclude another peace settlement in September 1577.

Peace of Bergerac, 1577 The Peace of Bergerac halted the fighting but like all the previous settlements made little impact on the long-term prospects of peace. It limited the concessions given to the Huguenots at the Peace of Monsieur: freedom of worship was restricted to the suburbs of only one town per *bailliage* and to towns held by the Huguenots on 17 September. Catholic worship was to be restored throughout the kingdom and all leagues and confraternities were to be banned. The Peace of Bergerac was very much Henry III's peace; a belated attempt to restore royal authority.

Seventh War of Religion, 1577–80

Between 1577 and 1580, the Peace of Bergerac was threatened by continuing tensions in the Low Countries. Moreover, Henry III's credibility as king of France continued to be eroded as both Protestants and Catholics openly flouted the recent peace edict:

- **Unrest at court** continued between Henry's supporters and other courtiers such as Guise and Anjou.
- Amid peasant uprisings in the south-east over increased fiscal burdens, and the ambitious foreign policy of Anjou in the Netherlands the seventh and shortest war of religion, nicknamed the **Lovers' War**, broke out in the north.
- Most Huguenots in the Midi were not in favour of a costly and long war, and Anjou was more interested in furthering his own cause in the Netherlands.

KEY THEME

Unrest at court Brawls and duels at court were commonplace, and while Henry's reputation among militant Catholics dwindled that of Guise was daily enhanced.

KEY EVENT

The Lovers' War The Seventh War of Religion was nicknamed the Lovers' War because of the tension and hatred which existed between Henry of Navarre and his wife, Marguerite. Neither side was able to launch a sustained offensive. Condé took La Frère in the north in November 1579, a success shortly followed by the capture of the Catholic bastion of Cahors in May by Navarre.

Peace of Félix, 1580 Another compromise peace settlement was arranged in November 1580. Existing Protestant political and religious privileges were acknowledged between Navarre and Anjou, and the Huguenots were allowed to keep their surety towns for a further six years. Such a settlement was equally doomed to failure just as the previous six edicts had been. Henry had once more lacked adequate funds and resources to defeat the Huguenots and his situation was made worse by the increasing popularity of Guise and the actions of his brother Anjou, who proved a complete liability both in life and in death.

Peasant revolts, 1579

ANJOU'S CONTINUING THREAT

KEY THEME

Anjou's activities Their importance in the Netherlands and his marriage negotiations with Elizabeth should not be underestimated. Militant Catholics were suspicious of Anjou after the Peace of Monsieur and his alliances with foreign Protestant governments in the late 1570s and early 1580s heightened the tension at court. Henry III had no male heirs and Anjou was heir-apparent. To many Catholics, Anjou was undermining the sacred nature of French monarchy by colluding with heretics.

Though he had abandoned the Huguenots after the peace of Monsieur, **Anjou's activities** still commanded attention from Protestant governments' abroad:

- He was again being touted as a potential husband for the English queen, Elizabeth I, in 1577.
- More worrying for Henry III was his brother's contacts with the Dutch rebels. The Dutch Calvinist provinces of Holland and Zeeland were interested in using Anjou as a sovereign figurehead to replace Philip II of Spain as their prince.

Assistance to Dutch rebels

Henry III was eager to see a decline in Spanish domination of the Netherlands, but he was anxious not to go to war with Philip. Anjou's blatant support for the Dutch rebels in July 1578 when he arrived in Mons and offered his assistance to William of Orange threatened Franco-Spanish neutrality. Fears of a Spanish reprisal were temporarily put on hold, however, as Anjou's aid vanished amid the ill discipline and disorganisation of his troops. Nevertheless, in 1580 Anjou signed another agreement with the Dutch rebels at Plessis les Tours:

- It installed the duke as successor to Philip II as sovereign prince in the seven northern provinces which were revolting against Spanish rule.
- Anjou was to receive a sizeable annual pension as well as various titles in return for French military aid and leadership.
- The Dutch States-General were vigilant, however, in terms of placing limitations on Anjou's power. Anjou had no authority over the army or in deciding the religion of each province. Even with such checks on his power the fact remained that Anjou was openly assisting the Dutch rebels in their fight against Spain.

In 1582, Anjou was installed as prince and lord of the Dutch provinces in the north, a title which he held for only one year. Reliant upon funding from his brother and Elizabeth I, Anjou made little impact upon the Spanish army in the Netherlands. Frustrated by checks on his sovereign power and with the Dutch falling behind on his annual stipend, Anjou became disillusioned with his role in the northern provinces. In 1583, he lost the support of the Dutch after his army tried to seize Antwerp by force and he was forced to return to France.

Death of Anjou

On 10 June 1584, the Duke of Anjou died of tuberculosis at his estate in Château Thierry. The implications of his death for the French crown were enormous because Henry III had no son. For some time most Catholics had believed that Anjou would succeed his elder brother. The death of Anjou left Henry of Navarre as heir under **Salic law**. The implications of the Huguenot leader Navarre becoming king of France were unthinkable for most Frenchmen, who believed in the **Catholicity of the crown**, and opposition from militant Catholics was inevitable and fierce. Navarre refused an invitation from Henry III to abjure his faith for a second time, possibly fearing for his life if he came to court. With Navarre next in line to the throne, the intensity and bloodshed of the French Wars of Religion grew worse throughout the remainder of the 1580s.

REVIVAL OF THE CATHOLIC LEAGUE, 1584–93

Henry of Navarre's proximity to the throne filled most Catholics with sheer horror and prompted Duke Henry of Guise to revitalise the Catholic Holy Union established at the Estates General at Blois in 1576. The stakes now were very much higher, and Guise relished the opportunity to take the limelight and advance his own status as leader of the League. In September 1584, Guise and his two brothers, the Duke of Mayenne and the Cardinal of Guise, along with two other nobles founded an institution specifically designed to keep Navarre off the French throne.

In December 1584, the Catholic League signed a treaty with Philip II at Joinville which agreed on the aim of defending the Catholic faith, removing Protestantism from France and the Netherlands and recognising that a heretic could not become king. The agreement suited both parties:

> ### KEY TERM
>
> **Salic law** The fundamental laws of the French monarchy dictating succession. Heretics and women were excluded from the succession by Salic law.

> ### KEY THEME
>
> **Catholicity of the Crown** For many Catholics, the idea of the succession to the throne of a Protestant was out of the question as it threatened the very fabric of French society and the sacred nature of Gallican monarchy.

- For the Guises it brought power and wealth to the League because Philip agreed to pay a monthly subsidy of 50,000 escudos in order for it to wage war against the Huguenots.
- For Philip it brought the opportunity to interfere in French affairs, undermine Henry III and promote and publish the decrees of the Council of Trent which the French crown had refused to register. Potential territorial gains for Philip at Cambrai and along the Spanish border were relatively unimportant in comparison with the chance to dictate League policy in France.

Support for the League

The League itself existed on a number of levels and accordingly drew on a range of social classes for support:

- At the top came the Guises who had a vast clientele network among the aristocracy throughout Lorraine, Champagne, Burgundy and Brittany where their interests were strongly represented. Together this noble group provided military and political direction.
- The popular arm of the organisation existed in urban centres where merchants, the urban gentry and artisans provided the membership. Predictably the urban leagues were more fundamental and intense in their policies. This was especially true in Paris where the revolutionary committee known as the **Sixteen,** after the sixteen *quartiers* of the city, was established.

The League was a complex institution which was only loosely under Guise control. The one issue which bound it together was protection of the Catholic faith. At Reims in March 1585, the League issued a public manifesto outlining its **aims and objectives.** The tone of the manifesto was a highly critical one towards Henry III and Catherine de Medici for having tolerated Protestantism for so long, and having placed a huge fiscal burden on the populace. In 1576, Henry III had sought wisely to put himself at the head of the League, but he was in no position to sideline Guise. Instead Henry III was forced to submit to the League through the **Treaty of Nemours** in July 1585. All Huguenot gains since the start of the Wars of Religion were essentially revoked, and two months later

KEY THEMES

The Sixteen Founded by a group of urban notables, in the beginning it was the domain of the middle classes. Yet even at this early stage the Sixteen enjoyed widespread popular support because of its commitment to eradicate Protestantism and keep the crown Catholic. The Sixteen soon evolved to become a powerful political body, independent of Guise control and revolutionary in nature.

Aims of the Catholic League Armed opposition to Navarre and the recognition of his ageing uncle the Catholic Charles, cardinal of Bourbon, as rightful heir were the major points made by the League.

KEY EVENT

Treaty of Nemours, 1585 Overturned all former edicts of pacification. Protestantism was banned everywhere in the kingdom. Pastors were to be banished and all Huguenots were to abjure within six months or go into exile. Duke Henry of Guise was awarded the governorships of Verdun, Toul, Saint Dizier and Châlons sur Marne.

Pope Sixtus V excommunicated Navarre and Condé. Both were now barred from the succession in French Catholic eyes. Nemours demonstrates how low royal authority had become, as Henry III had little option but to capitulate before the League at Nemours given his precarious financial position.

Eighth War of Religion

Unsurprisingly, the terms of Nemours and the League's alliance with Spain sparked a renewal of violence in late 1585 and early 1586, as Catholic nobles set about enforcing Nemours. The death of Anjou had initiated the War of the Three Henrys – king, Navarre and Guise. The Eighth War lasted for more than a decade and witnessed more bloodshed than any of the previous conflicts.

- The initiative for the Catholic attack in northern and eastern France came from the League rather than the king. With Philip II's subsidy and the full backing of the Guises along with popular support, the League found itself in a stronger situation than the crown to deal with Protestantism.
- The Huguenots, appalled by the Treaty of Nemours (apparently half of Navarre's moustache turned white on hearing of its terms), looked once more to Germany and Queen Elizabeth for support. The queen of England gave 100,000 crowns to the Reformed cause and Casimir once more mobilised mercenaries in the Palatinate.

Henry III momentarily placated Catholic opinion by registering a series of anti-Huguenot edicts, but in the long term the militants demanded action and Henry was unable to offer his generals sufficient resources to crush Condé and Navarre. Catholic opinion was further intensified by news of the **execution of Mary, Queen of Scots**, and many Frenchmen wanted Henry to avenge her death. Henry's control of the kingdom was slowly slipping away, and rumours of League-inspired plots to kidnap the king and seize power were commonplace throughout the spring of 1586.

KEY EVENT

Execution of Mary, Queen of Scots Having fled to England in 1568 after defeat at the Battle of Langside, Mary was imprisoned by Elizabeth. Her presence in England gave rise to countless plots to depose Elizabeth and restore Catholicism. Finally, after the Babington Conspiracy in 1586, she was brought to trial for treason and executed at Fotheringhay Castle, Northamptonshire.

On the battlefield, the Catholic aim was to repel the German mercenaries under Casimir which had crossed the border into eastern France.

- A leaguer army under Guise confronted the Germans while a royal force under the Duke of Joyeuse marched south to meet Navarre's forces and prevent them from linking up with the mercenaries.
- The Huguenots defeated the royal forces at Coutras in October 1587 and killed Joyeuse in the process. The victory was offset however by a crushing defeat inflicted by Guise on the Germans outside Chartres.
- In early 1588, two of Navarre's allies, Henry, Prince of Condé, and Robert de la Marck, Duke of Bouillon, died leaving Navarre as sole leader of the Huguenot forces.
- Catholic forces seemed to be on top, but disunity between leaguers and royalists prevented an outright victory. Henry III further angered Duke Henry of Guise by awarding his royal favourite, the **Duke of Epernon,** with offices previously held by Joyeuse. Moreover those who supported Henry III were now labelled in a rather derisory fashion as *politiques*. Soon the minority of *politiques* became bitter enemies of the Sixteen, who increasingly looked to Guise for inspiration.

KEY PERSON

Duke of Epernon Became governor of Normandy and admiral of France, while Guise, the conqueror of Casimir's mercenaries, received nothing. Leaguer propaganda tore into Epernon who was accused of building up his own fortune at the expense of the kingdom.

Guise defies Henry III

In early 1588, tension between Guise and the king increased as the League made a series of demands to Henry III which included the dismissal of Epernon, the acceptance of Guise's policy in exterminating heresy and publication of the decrees of the Council of Trent. Attempts were made on Epernon's life by those leaguers who resented his political influence on the king and his fortune. In April 1588, Henry III prohibited Duke Henry of Guise from entering Paris. When Guise defied the ban and entered the capital in May to a tumultuous welcome from the Sixteen and other Parisian Catholics, a showdown between two of the three Henrys was inevitable.

KEY EVENT

The Day of the Barricades According to Mack Holt, the events in Paris on 12 May 1588 marked the nadir of royal authority in Henry III's reign. The king was no longer resident in his capital.

Guise had defied the king in entering Paris in the first place, but tried to justify his conduct in terms of meeting the king and possibly negotiating a settlement. On the **Day of the Barricades**, Henry III chose not to have Guise arrested but instead posted over 4000 Swiss guards in strategic positions around the city. Parisians objected to the presence of the Swiss and rumours spread of another royal massacre but this time with Catholics as the victims. Parisians from every social level took up arms against the royal troops while streets and neighbourhoods were cordoned off and protected with barricades formed by stretching chains across street corners:

- With the capital clearly behind the League, Henry had little option but to leave Paris. On 13 May, he fled to Chartres and on the following day the Bastille surrendered to Guise.
- The king's supporters fled the city and were replaced in official posts by more radical officers loyal to the League and **the Sixteen**. Effectively a *coup d'état* had occurred and as a result Henry III had lost control of his capital. With the gates of the city secure and the militia purged much power had actually passed over to the ordinary populace. A new revolutionary government may have provisionally been in place in 1588, but just how much control the Sixteen and Guise exercised in the absence of the king is questionable. Certainly the capital was about to experience a period of radical government.

Edict of Union, 1588

Meanwhile, Henry III's humiliation was completed in a new **Edict of Union** (July 1588) which reflected his loss of authority in France. Henry looked to play for time, all the while plotting revenge on his rivals. Buoyed by news of the failure of Philip II's Armada against England, Henry sacked his ministers and replaced them with younger, more independent-minded men who importantly owed nothing to Catherine de Medici. Men such as Francois d'O and Montholon entered the king's service and Catherine's influence in political affairs dwindled until her death in 1589. Although Henry could control appointments to his own council he could not influence elections for the Estates General and all three presidents were leading leaguers. The financial problems of the king left him vulnerable and exposed to criticism. Salaries of office holders remained unpaid while annuities were also outstanding. Henry had to agree to the creation of a financial tribunal to oversee fiscal

Advancement of the Sixteen Thirteen of the sixteen colonels of the city militia were replaced while the leader of the Sixteen, La Chapelle Marteau, was elected as mayor and in the process swore an oath of loyalty to Guise and the cardinal of Bourbon.

The Edict of Union, 1588 Henry was forced to dismiss Epernon, reaffirm the Treaty of Nemours, recognise the cardinal of Bourbon as heir to the throne, appoint Guise lieutenant-general of the realm (commander-in-chief of the army) and call a meeting of the Estates General for the autumn in order to prepare for all-out war against the Huguenots.

affairs while the third estate took this opportunity to question the nature of royal authority. No doubt the third estate were being encouraged by aristocratic leaguers to undermine the position of the king further, but for once Henry III was ready to respond in ruthless fashion.

Murder of Guise

In an act of calculated desperation, Henry III decided to strike at the heart of the League and avenge his recent disgrace:

- On 23 December 1588, he summoned the Duke and Cardinal of Guise to his apartments in the Château of Blois, where the royal guards immediately murdered the duke and arrested his brother the cardinal.
- The following day, as the king was in mass to celebrate Christmas, the Cardinal of Guise was killed while other prominent leaguers were imprisoned, including the cardinal of Bourbon.

Resistance to Henry in Paris intensified. A Guise cousin, the Duke of Aumale, became governor of Paris and the League's Council of Forty named the youngest Guise brother – Charles, Duke of Mayenne – lieutenant-general of the realm. The new council denounced Henry III as tyrannical and the Sorbonne declared the king deposed and called upon all Frenchmen to rise against him in defence of the Catholic faith. If the death of Anjou had sparked a debate on the Catholicity of the crown the murder of the Guise brothers provoked an explosion of League radicalism.

Murder of Henry III On 5 January 1589, Catherine de Medici died removing the one person who may have been able to negotiate with the Catholic militants. Subsequently, Henry was more vulnerable and isolated than ever. Henry controlled much of the Loire as well as Bordeaux; to the north the League was dominant; to the south the Huguenots were in command. Henry desperately needed an ally for both military and financial purposes. In reality, he had only one remaining option and that was to seek an alliance with Navarre.

KEY EVENT

The murder of Guise
Henry claimed that he acted in self-defence and that the Guises were plotting to murder and depose him. However, few believed him and news of the murders spread quickly, sparking off feelings of grief, resentment and anger in the towns loyal to the League.

KEY THEME

Resistance to Henry
The most persuasive and powerful advocate of authorised regicide was Jean Boucher, a parish priest of Saint Benoît and a leading light in the administration of Paris from 1589. Boucher published his views in a tract *De Justa Henrici tertii abdicatione* (Just Deposition of Henry III) in which Henry was charged with ten major crimes. Boucher called upon the pope to release Henry's subjects from their obedience and, failing this, the people must depose and kill the despot.

- On 30 April, Henry III and Henry of Navarre signed an alliance at Plessis les Tours which involved the king recognising Navarre as his rightful successor.
- The two combined armies marched on the capital capturing Senlis and Pontoise on the way. A major clash with the Catholic forces seemed inevitable and within Paris anti-Valois passions reached fever pitch. Henry was portrayed as the antichrist in **League propaganda** and calls for his extermination grew louder.
- As the king's forces besieged Paris in August 1589, a young Dominican lay brother named Jacques Clément made his way into the royal camp intent on carrying out his duty to God and kill Henry. Clément bluffed his way in on the grounds that he carried a message of support from some of the king's supporters still in Paris. The king beckoned him nearer at which point Clément stabbed Henry in the abdomen. The king died the following day and the Valois dynasty was over.
- Before he died, Henry had declared Navarre to be his heir on the condition that he converted to Catholicism. Salic law endorsed the late king's proclamation yet with no conversion imminent and Navarre being a convinced Huguenot the troubles were far from over.

News of the king's assassination prompted rejoicing in the capital and Clément was subsequently canonised by the League convinced as they were that outright Catholic triumph was close at hand.

KEY THEME

League propaganda
Catholic propagandists advocated murdering Henry, arguing that kingship was a human institution created by the people for their own convenience. Sovereignty had been transferred to the king in a contract between God and the people. The people retained power over the king in order to ensure that the contract was observed and fulfilled. In short, the monarchy was elective, the people held sovereign power and tyrannical kings could be deposed legitimately by force.

SUMMARY QUESTIONS

1. Why did successive peace edicts fail to keep the peace?

2. How were the Huguenots able to wage war effectively after St Bartholomew's Day?

3. In what ways did the Catholic League undermine the authority of the crown?

4. To what extent was Henry III a failure as king of France?

CHAPTER 7

The triumph of Henry IV

A DIVIDED NATION

The assassination of Henry III and the resulting power vacuum polarised opinion in France and divided the realm:

- The *parlements* under pressure from the League immediately recognised the Cardinal of Bourbon (still imprisoned) as King Charles X.
- The Protestants recognised Navarre as Henry IV.
- The Catholic army at Saint Cloud, which had been part of the unlikely alliance between the late king and Navarre, was split. Many decided to join the League,

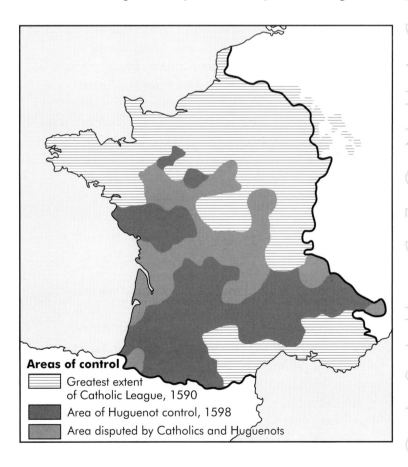

Areas of control
- Greatest extent of Catholic League, 1590
- Area of Huguenot control, 1598
- Area disputed by Catholics and Huguenots

Areas of League and Huguenot control

and radicals such as La Trémoille immediately withdrew their forces from the camp at Meudon. The royal army besieging Paris halved in number as many refused to serve a heretical king thus ensuring that the siege failed. However, Catholic captains led by François d'O recognised Navarre as king on his acceptance of an accord in which Navarre promised to protect the Catholic faith, and place towns and fortresses seized from the rebels under Catholic control while still guaranteeing Protestant rights in areas that they held.

Henry and appeasement

Already it was clear that the new king-elect faced a daunting task. On the one hand, he recognised that if he was to succeed to the throne he required the support of the moderate Catholic majority who were becoming increasingly tired of civil war. Such support would only come at the price of his rejection of Protestantism. On the other hand, this move would upset the Huguenots. Henry did his best to satisfy both camps:

- An immediate religious conversion was out of the question but he obtained the support of royal Catholic officials both secular and clerical with his broad commitment to a Catholic monarchy and realm.
- To many moderate Catholics support for Henry was preferable to that for the League because at least this would keep Gallican independence from Rome alive.

Military action

Alongside the policy of appeasement Henry recognised the need for effective military action and force in order to defeat the League on the battlefield.

- In September 1589, Henry was victorious over the duke of Mayenne at **Arques** near Dieppe.
- Henry followed up victory at Arques with further successes throughout Normandy. In the winter of 1589, all major towns except Rouen and Le Havre were taken and, in March 1590, Mayenne's army was routed once again at Ivry.
- Paris, however, proved to be a real obstacle for Henry, galvanised as it was by the duke of Nemours who had

KEY EVENT

Arques, 1589 The victory was hugely important as many provincial leaders of the League began to reject Mayenne's leadership while Pope Sixtus V, always keen to back a winner, became more receptive to the idea of Henry; fully reinstructed as a Catholic; becoming king.

supplanted the hapless Mayenne as commander of the League. Henry's siege brought great hardship and death to the citizens of the capital between May and September 1590 with Henry himself well aware that his activities might unite Catholic opinion against him. However, as Henry called off the siege in September, events conspired to work in his favour.

- In May 1590, the cardinal of Bourbon had died and in September Mayenne claimed the throne for himself. Most leaguers preferred Mayenne's younger nephew Charles, Duke of Guise, while others advocated the accession of Philip II in order to save the faith.

In short, the extreme Catholic faction was disunited in their views over who should become king, and to the majority of France Henry was gradually emerging as the only reasonable claimant.

Support for the Sixteen and the League wanes

Furthermore, the group of Sixteen was becoming too powerful, resulting in division between the noble League led by Mayenne and the revolutionary government in the capital:

- In late 1590, the Sixteen embarked upon a campaign of terror directed against anyone suspected of moderate or *politiques* views.

A parade of supporters of the Catholic League in Paris, 1590

- The *parlement* protested and several members of the Sixteen resigned. The new more radical Sixteen made up of La Chapelle-Marteau, Acarie and Bussy-Leclerc were determined to stamp out any royalist sympathisers.
- Paranoia took over and *parlement* was accused of being too lenient over its action towards a royal agent Brigard.
- On 15 November 1591, the Sixteen purged the *parlement* executing its president Barnabé Brisson in the process. Two other magistrates suffered the same fate and it appeared that the capital was being governed by fear and terror. Mayenne was forced to march back into Paris and restore order by force, with the result that four of the Sixteen were hanged at the Louvre.

Whether the Sixteen was representative of the lower classes and popular opinion is highly debatable. However, it is clear that divisions between those who opposed Henry of Navarre were widening.

Support for the League and the Sixteen had reached its pinnacle during the Day of the Barricades when opposition to Henry III had united Parisians. In 1591, other issues such as Spanish intervention, the succession, the nature of royal authority and the fear of social disorder served to polarise opinion and the role of the Sixteen waned considerably, much to the advantage of Henry of Navarre.

Stalemate

Henry IV's sieges of Paris (1590) and Rouen (1592) failed because of one of Philip II's leading generals, the Duke of Parma. Despite numerical and financial advantages, Parma was unable to inflict an outright defeat on Henry IV. Moreover, just before the siege of Rouen Henry had audaciously launched an offensive with some 7000 cavalry against the 23,000-strong Spanish force led by Parma at Aumale. Parma ordered his men to withdraw certain that Henry must have reserves capable of inflicting a serious defeat on the Spanish. Henry had no such reserves and clearly risked disaster at Aumale. Yet his gamble paid off and thereafter he avoided open warfare. A period of stalemate ensued in which divisions within the League became more apparent and a combination of the presence of Spanish troops on French soil, tiredness with war, pillaging troops and poor harvests combined to present strong government under Henry IV as an attractive option.

HENRY CONVERTS

In 1593, Mayenne summoned an Estates General to Paris in order to resolve the question of succession:

- The Spanish ambassador proposed a **Spanish succession** of Philip II's daughter – the Infanta Isabella Clara Eugenia, grand-daughter of Henry II, but barred from succession by Salic law which prevented a woman succeeding to the throne.
- It was Henry IV who broke the deadlock when he announced his decision to abandon the Reformed faith. On 25 July 1593, he solemnly abjured in the abbey at Saint Denis. Henry's conversion was a critical turning point in the French Wars of Religion because at once Henry removed the League's main reason for excluding him from the succession. While he may not have been a genuine Catholic to the extremists; Henry's conversion was what many of the more moderate *politiques* Catholics had been waiting for.
- Town governors now saw it appropriate to declare their loyalty to Henry although such capitulation did not come cheaply and **bribes** were used to win over leaguer towns and nobles. Agreements included clauses forbidding Protestant worship and leaguer office holders retained their positions. Thus, Henry continued his policy of appeasement towards towns of the League, a far cheaper and more attractive alternative to war.
- On 27 February 1594, Henry was crowned at Chartres rather than the customary Reims, which was still in the hands of the League. Nevertheless, the usual pomp and ceremony accompanied his coronation and, importantly, Henry swore the coronation oath promising to expel all heretics from his kingdom. On 22 March, Henry entered Paris, meeting with little resistance, and symbolically, heard Mass at Notre Dame.
- In September 1595, he reached an agreement with Pope Clement VIII promising to publish the decrees of the Council of Trent in return for absolution. With the

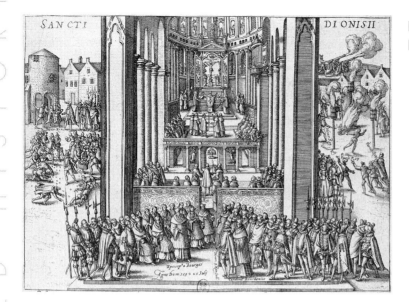

SANCTI   DIONISII

Sorbonne, *parlements*, papacy and most importantly the majority of the populace behind him Henry could now turn his attentions towards ridding France of the Spanish.

War against Spain

War was declared on Spain in January 1595 and in June of that year a royalist force led by Henry himself defeated the numerically superior Spanish at Fontaine-Française. Henry had won Burgundy and subsequently entered Lyons. Mayenne was disillusioned with his Spanish allies and came over to the king. Guise, Epernon and Joyeuse followed in early 1596 and only the Duke of Mercoeur of the influential, great nobles remained aloof:

- By September 1596, Amiens had fallen to Henry and by the end of the year Mercoeur had submitted to the king's authority also.
- All the great nobles were suitably compensated for their actions and by the spring of 1598 the situation was considerably better for Henry than a year previously.
- Despite inevitable discontent and resentment from the Protestant minority which manifested itself in assemblies at Sainte-Foy (1594), Saumur (1595) and Loudun (1596) all factions were ready to listen to the peace terms at Nantes in 1598.

THE EDICT OF NANTES, 13 APRIL 1598

The Edict of Nantes provided a legal and political structure for ending the Wars of Religion although the actual process was never going to be quick or easy. The edict consisted of four separate documents: the 92 general articles, the 56 secret articles and two royal **brevets**. The 92 articles generally reaffirmed the provisions of earlier edicts:

- They recognised the legal existence of the French Reformed churches and granted Protestants the same civil rights as Catholics.
- Huguenots were free to acquire or inherit office and bipartisan courts (*chambres mi parties*) were established in the *parlements* to judge lawsuits involving Protestants.
- However, Huguenots were still not allowed to impose taxes, build fortifications, levy troops or hold political assemblies.
- Moreover, Protestant worship was still a contentious issue; to be allowed in two places in each *bailliage* and wherever the Huguenots could prove it had been openly practised in 1596 and 1597.

KEY THEME

Henry's pragmatism was shown in his conversion to Catholicism and in the Edict of Nantes. Many saw the brevets of the edict as too liberal towards the Huguenots although the guiding principle behind the edict was the re-establishment of the celebration of the mass throughout the kingdom. Huguenot liberties were temporary in the eyes of Henry IV as he recognised the need for unity behind the principles of Gallicanism. Yet he was also a realist recognising that an end to religious schism was unachievable and in the meantime a lasting truce had to be put into place.

Henry's pragmatism was displayed in the edict in which Catholics and Protestants could live together in peace despite the fact that Protestantism had not been given full parity with Catholicism:

- The 56 secret articles appeased certain towns with specific promises to ensure the safe passage of the edict through the *parlements*. Paris and Toulouse for example were exempted from Protestant worship within their walls while commissioners were also appointed to ensure that the edict was carried out on the ground.
- The two brevets were the most significant part of the edict in many ways. In them Protestants were granted a degree of military and political independence establishing surety towns garrisoned by troops where Protestants could worship freely. Moreover the payment of stipends to Protestant pastors from public funds was provided and Huguenots were allowed to hold for eight years all towns which they occupied in August 1597. Annual royal payments were to be made to garrisons.

Reactions

Opposition to the Edict of Nantes was stiff among *parlementaires* and it required much pressure from Henry himself to have the edict ratified by the *parlements*. The edict was not innovative in any respect: it was based on toleration and conciliation. However, Henry IV had made it clear that the state's well-being rested on religious unity in the long term, a promise which was readily accepted by the *parlements*. Moreover, the context of the edict was very different to its predecessors in that war-weariness encouraged both sides to accept it as a lasting truce. In some respects the provisions of the edict contained the seeds of future conflict:

- The brevets had effectively created a Huguenot state within a state funded by the crown. The Huguenots were bound by royal favour but also had time, space and money to build churches and fortify towns.
- Naturally, tensions between the crown and the Huguenots came to the fore again after the death of Henry IV in 1610 (see page 114).

ECONOMIC AND SOCIAL CONSEQUENCES OF THE FRENCH WARS OF RELIGION

In general, the French Wars of Religion caused great distress throughout the kingdom: the wars between 1585 and 1596 inflicted particularly harsh suffering on millions. Yet throughout Europe people were experiencing economic depression brought about by population growth, land shortage and inflation. Harvest failures throughout the 1580s and 1590s caused famine across France and indeed Europe. So France would have suffered economic changes whether civil war had broken out or not. The wars made the economic crisis worse and also brought the threat of war and disorder to French civilians:

- Mortality figures were high throughout France in the 1580s and 1590s because of harvest failure, famine and plague. Yet in areas such as Rouen it was long sieges and open warfare that raised the death toll. Moreover, while poor harvests could send prices rocketing skywards it should not be forgotten that sieges and billeting could also lead to a scarcity of resources. Paris, Rouen and La Rochelle all suffered siege warfare during this period and prices reflected this disruption. Rural economies were also affected during the civil wars as peasants suffered at the hands of billeted troops. Livestock was seized, crops requisitioned and agricultural output dropped.

- The tax demands of the crown increased throughout the period, and it was the third estate that bore the burden of the king's demands. Discontent at the increase in the level of the *taille* occasionally manifested itself in open revolt as was the case in Provence (1578), the Rhône Valley (1579) and **Normandy**. For the desperate peasant oppressed by the local landlord economic concerns and the instinct for survival surpassed confessional allegiance. As the wars of the League took their toll, more open revolts occurred. Peasants in Brittany also revolted in 1589, targeting châteaux and other symbols of aristocratic oppression. Only in November 1590 were the peasants crushed by royalist forces at Cahaix. Even more serious uprisings occurred in Burgundy (1594 and 1597) and most famously in the south-west (by the *croquants*, 1593–5).

The Dordogne

The Dordogne Valley regions of Limousin and Périgord suffered more than most during the Wars of Religion through billeting and bloodshed. It was here that peasants joined together in hatred of oppression. As many as 40,000 peasants assembled in Perigord in May 1594 and they appealed to the new king Henry IV to redress their grievances. The king took a sympathetic line towards them and the arrears that they owed in taxes were reduced while future levies were significantly curtailed. Henry also called for no aristocratic reprisal killings and it is likely that the *croquants* made the king aware of the need for peace at all costs. Therefore, fiscal pressures on the third estate caused many to borrow heavily from local nobles who charged exorbitant rates of interest. Economic distress and suffering were commonplace and the economic effects of the wars lasted long after the Edict of Nantes.

KEY EVENT

Unrest in Normandy, 1589
The Gautiers of Normandy attacked the Château of La Tour near Falaise, wrecking and pillaging as they went. Ultimately, over 3000 were slaughtered by the duke of Montpensier as order was restored by the sword.

KEY TERM

Croquants Dubbed *croquants* (or country bumpkins) by their socially superior opponents the peasants laid out their grievances in written manifestos and it became clear that noble administration had been grossly abused during the chaotic period of civil strife.

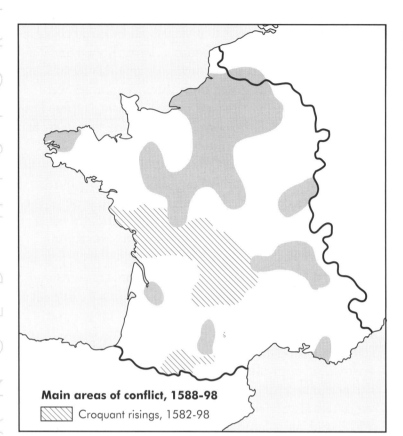

Croquant risings, 1582–98

Main areas of conflict, 1588-98

▨ Croquant risings, 1582-98

The nobility

Land sale figures seem to display a **decline in the power and status of the rural nobility**, a change which some have chosen to interpret as the beginning of a decline in the political power of the nobility in France. However,

- great nobles benefited from Henry IV's generous policy. The powerful landowning nobles became richer and more powerful at the expense of some lesser rural nobles – hardly a fundamental shift in the makeup of society
- venality continued to enlarge the nobility of the robe and, while real political power and influence tended to lie with the great nobles, more individuals claiming to be of noble birth existed in France by 1600
- intermarriage between new and old nobility further integrated the new additions and the nobility as an institution remained a healthy and vibrant political force.

Decline in the power and status of the rural nobility
The historian M.P. Holt has shown in his book *The French Wars of Religion, 1562–1629* (1995) that we must be careful with figures detailing the demise of the rural nobility. While many lesser nobles were hit hard by fiscal pressures and rapid inflation other larger landowners actually profited from the wars and it was this latter group that bought much of the available land.

If anything, the gap between rich and poor grew ever wider during the Wars of Religion and it continued to be the third estate that suffered most.

France and the Wars of Religion 1562–98

- Calvinism never really fulfilled the promise of the 1550s and 1560s in terms of expansion and numbers of adherents. At no time did Calvinists exceed 10 per cent of the population and, while a skeletal framework of national and regional synods was constructed, the notion of a national church remained vague.

- The survival of the Reformed faith through disasters such as St Bartholomew's Day and the formation of the Spanish-backed League illustrates the importance of noble protection as well as the discipline and organisation of a committed minority.

- Religion permeated every aspect of the wars. At the highest level, it shaped the peace settlements and provided the rationale for the Catholic League. At a popular level, religion incited the massacres of 1572 and ensured that the peace edicts would fail. Throughout the period the majority of the French population stuck to the Gallican principles of one king, one faith and one law. This bond explains why toleration of a Huguenot minority was unacceptable.

- The economic impact of over 40 years of warfare was great, but ought to be viewed in the context of a general Europe-wide depression. France suffered more than most due to the cost of war although the social framework remained largely unchanged. The financial weakness of the crown undermined the rule of Henry III and explains why he was unable to defeat the Huguenots on the battlefield and subsequently became a puppet of the League.

- Political considerations were never far from the surface during the Wars of Religion as we can see from the actions of Alençon, the featuring of the Huguenot nobility in all of the peace edicts and the appeasement of major League nobles by Henry IV. Nevertheless we could argue that politics may have guided the course of the wars at times but it was religion that formed the basis of the conflict.

- The Edict of Nantes brought lasting peace partly through the policy of unity and appeasement employed by Henry IV and partly through the weariness of the French with war. The edict did not end confessional strife and the royal brevets in particular sowed the seeds of future discontent by creating a Huguenot state within a state.

Marie de Medici

SUCCESSION OF LOUIS XIII

Regency of Marie de Medici

After the relative peace and order of Henry IV's reign, France was faced with the prospect of a royal minority. On the death of Henry IV in February 1610, his son and successor, Louis XIII, was not yet 9 years old. Henry had not formally nominated a regent, but at the request of *parlements* this office was assumed by his widow, the 37-year-old **Marie de Medici**. Marie de Medici's cause had been bolstered by two prominent events:

- her belated coronation in 1600
- the power given to her by Henry IV when he had led his troops to capture Julich and Cleves.

All who believed in the stability of the state now needed to support her regency and, for those at the heart of Parisian politics in 1610, the immediate need was to attach themselves to her regime. Marie believed in peace with the Austrians and it is in this context that we should view the regency of Marie de Medici, a regency which lasted seven years, and created much resentment and jealousy among the leading magnates. Where possible Marie de Medici looked to continue the policies of Henry IV and at first her late husband's ministers and system of government were maintained. However, change swiftly became apparent both in terms of personnel at court and administration. Two interrelated factors need to be highlighted:

- Marie adopted a pro-Spanish policy in line with her zealous Catholicism. Such an alliance was to be underpinned by a marriage between Louis and Anne of Austria, the Infanta of Spain.

- A court clique emerged centring upon an old friend and half sister of Medici, Leonora Galigai, and Leonara's husband Concino Concini. Both were Italian and their favoured position at court was reinforced by Concini's elevation to Marshal d'Ancre. Among those who were now surplus to requirements was **Sully**, who was forced to resign in 1611, albeit with a massive golden handshake.

KEY PERSON

Maximilien de Béthune, duke of Sully (1560–1641)
Held the post of *surintendant des finances*, 1598–1611, and was the most important minister on Henry IV's royal council.

Concino Concini

Concini's meteoric rise to prominence created resentment at court that was only dampened in the years 1610–14 by the generosity of Marie de Medici. In those four years, Marie spent over 10 million livres in bribes to leading magnates. In effect, Marie bought four years of domestic peace, but to many Frenchmen at court it was clear that there was great unrest with the policies of the regent. Moreover, the leading members of the nobility of the robe, such as Sillery, Villeroy and Jeannin, were incapable of keeping the upper nobility in check.

Court revolt In February 1614, the magnates displayed their hostility by leaving court and retiring to the provinces where they began mobilising troops. At the forefront of this opposition was Henry II of Bourbon, Prince of Condé. In a powerful manifesto, Condé severely criticised the regency government and those connected with it. In Condé's eyes only a meeting of the Estates General could rescue France from collapse. The revolt masked a deep-seated resentment of Concini and the proposed Spanish marriage. To avoid open conflict the government came to terms with Condé at St Ménéhould in May 1614. Marie was forced to concede the following points:

KEY EVENT

Estates General, 1614 This was the last meeting of the Estates General before the revolution of 1789. It made a number of demands but achieved very little.

- The Spanish marriage was deferred until the king's majority.
- The **Estates General** was summoned to Sens in 1614.
- Condé and other magnates were paid off with huge monetary gifts.

Louis reaches majority

Despite Marie's concessions, Condé's opposition changed little. In October 1614, Marie declared Louis' majority and a successful royal progress accompanied the proclamation. The palace clique still monopolised power. In November 1615, Louis married Anne of Austria despite the protests of Condé. After a rather feeble attempt to raise arms, Condé found himself in the **Bastille** in 1616 where he remained until 1619. Concini's creatures continued to prosper at court; men such as Claude Mangot (secretary of state for foreign affairs) and Claude Barbin (finance minister). In 1616, Mangot's office of foreign secretary was handed to a young cleric named Armand du Plessis de Richelieu, Bishop of Luçon. Concini himself had little

KEY TERM

Bastille The Bastille was the foremost royal prison in Paris.

political ambition and appeared interested only in amassing great wealth. Between 1610 and 1616, he accumulated vast amounts of property, land and titles in Picardy. In 1617, Concini turned his attentions towards Normandy and the former lands of Condé.

By 1617, even the 16-year-old Louis was beginning to resent Concini's actions. Louis had learned much from his short rule. In particular, he had become accustomed with faction and power struggles at court. Royal coups appeared commonplace and Louis recognised that Concini's position ultimately rested with his favour. Louis increasingly relied upon his confidant, the 20-year-old Provençal in charge of falconry, Charles d'Albert de Luynes. After Condé's arrest, the dukes of Mayenne and Nevers expressed the shared resentment of the nobility with a show of force in Berry, Champagne and the Île de France. As royal troops were deployed and despatched to Soissons, Concini became more and more a figure of hatred.

Concini's death On Monday 24 April 1617, as Concini made his way to the Louvre, he was separated from his escort and then shot by the king's bodyguard, the Marquis de Vitry. Justified by a royal death warrant and decree, **Concini's assassination** had exactly the opposite effect of the murder of the Guises in 1588. The siege at Soissons was lifted peacefully while Leonora was tried by the *parlements* for treason and witchcraft before being executed in July 1617. Concini's body was later dug up by the mob and further mutilated before being hung up on the Pont Neuf. Following Concini's death:

- An assembly of notables met in 1617 to decide how best to put into effect the principal demands of the Estates General of 1614.
- The *paulette* was abolished forthwith while venality was condemned as an abuse that deprived the king of control over his subjects but was not outlawed. Marie de Medici was effectively under house arrest in Blois and the dominant figure at court was the Duke of Luynes.
- In May 1618, the Duke of Epernon retired from court in disgust at the refusal of a cardinal's hat for one of his sons. When the queen mother was not even invited to

the wedding of her youngest daughter, Christine, to Prince Victor Amadeus of Savoy, it became clear that the two malcontents might unite.

- In April 1619, Louis was forced to deploy 20,000 men in order to show force against the joint forces of his mother and Epernon. In summer 1620, a second war between mother and son resulted in the massacre of hundreds of rebels at the Château of Pont de Cé. A peace treaty was drawn up that allowed Marie de Medici to return to the capital where she installed herself in the Palais du Luxembourg. When Luynes died of a fever in December 1621, Marie was readmitted to the royal council.

Several issues are worth noting from this rather fractious and fragmented period:

- Power and position at court was dependent upon the favour and trust of the king. Both Concini and Luynes found to their detriment that royal favour could soon turn to disapproval.
- Ministerial power tended to be fragile and brief. Loss of office was usually accompanied by a charge of fraud and presumption of political crime.
- Public opinion transmitted through broadsheets and pamphlets was becoming increasingly important and political ambition necessarily required manipulation of these mediums.
- The brevity of successive ministerial reigns was greatly to the advantage of Richelieu.

SUMMARY QUESTIONS

1. How did Henry IV set about restoring peace?

2. How far was the Edict of Nantes based upon the principle of religious unity?

3. To what extent was the depression in the second half of the sixteenth century caused by the Wars of Religion?

4. Why did court faction once more emerge after the assassination of Henry IV?

CHAPTER 8

Richelieu, 1622–42

RICHELIEU'S RISE TO POWER, 1624

Cardinal Richelieu

Armand du Plessis de Richelieu was born in 1585 of a second rank noble family in Poitou, his father François having been part of the entourage of Henry III. Armand entered the church after the early death of his father in order to keep the bishopric of Luçon in the family and in 1607 he was consecrated as bishop. He set about God's will with zest and energy:

- reforming the diocese in accordance with the decrees of the Council of Trent
- giving sermons, making visitations and holding synods to restore the material and spiritual health of Luçon.

At once his devout Catholicism shone through and he was soon championed by the devout faction at court. In 1614, Richelieu was elected to the Estates General as a spokesman for the clergy. His talents were noted by Marie and Concini, and there seems little doubt that Richelieu used his speech at the Estates General as an opportunity to impress them. Recruited to the king's council, Richelieu was given responsibility for foreign affairs. Nevertheless the fall of Concini thrust Richelieu into the political wilderness, although he did accompany the queen mother into exile and negotiate the truces of 1619 and 1620 that reconciled mother and son.

Political qualities

Above all else the **intellectual ability of Richelieu** was clear. The death of Luynes in 1621 cleared the way for Louis to back Richelieu's claim for a cardinal's hat, an honour bestowed upon him in 1622. Such an honour brought with it not only prestige and privilege but also political status that elevated Richelieu above many of the princes of the blood. In April 1624, Marie de Medici campaigned for Richelieu's return to the royal council. Louis, although suspicious of the cardinal, was increasingly frustrated by the failure of his present ministers, Sillery and Puysieux, to assert French diplomatic rights over the **Valtelline**. Richelieu's ambition and abilities were viewed in a positive light by the French king, who was eager to promote his prestige and dignity on the European stage. By August 1624, Richelieu had secured the disgrace of his last remaining rival, the *surintendant* (chief minister) La Vieuville, and his rise to power was complete. Richelieu could now begin to install his own supporters and dependants in key positions. Quick-witted, brilliant and politically astute Richelieu had a perfect understanding of courtly intrigue. Already we can see the makings of a political leader in Richelieu's rise to power:

KEY PLACE

The Valtelline The Valtelline was an important strategic area for the French to the north of Italy, giving vital access to the Alpine passes. Similarly, the Valtelline was highly valued by the Spanish as free access allowed them to transport men and supplies along the Spanish Road into Flanders.

- patronage of Marie de Medici and the Estates General of 1614
- experience at court as foreign secretary under Concini
- peace brokering between mother and son 1619–20
- appointment as cardinal in 1622
- destruction of La Vieuville.

Richelieu was an effective political operator and he was more than ready for office.

Richelieu's aims and objectives

Richelieu was concerned about how his actions and policies would be viewed by his contemporaries and also how he would be remembered in history. His *Political Testament* describes the values of absolute monarchy and good government. Doubt remains as to just when the *Testament* was written, although it is accepted to be near the end of the cardinal's life. The *Testament* revolves around five key objectives:

- ruin the Huguenots
- humble the pride of great men
- bring subjects to their duty
- raise the name of the king abroad
- extend the authority of government.

The aims appear rather negative, as the first three are concerned with destruction rather than reform. While Richelieu's aim was clear, there was no grand plan for the extension of royal authority. Richelieu was an opportunist introducing reforms when required. Furthermore, Richelieu recognised the weaknesses of royal power and used tried ideologies and methods to prompt a revival of monarchical strength. In this context Richelieu's period of ministerial dominance ought to be seen as part of a process; a brilliant ministry but one that was evolutionary not revolutionary.

Consolidation of power

Above all else Richelieu recognised that the trust and affection of his king were crucial in the maintenance of power. The cardinal was careful to consult the king over important policy decisions and he played the king far more effectively than his ministerial predecessors in terms of judging when to consult him and how to sound him out over potentially contentious issues. The issue over which Richelieu was able to consolidate his power was that of royal succession. Thus far the marriage between Louis and Anne had provided no heirs and with the king's health prone to bouts of fragility, courtiers began to speculate as to what might happen in the event of his death. According to Salic law the crown would revert to Gaston, the younger brother of Louis. In 1624, the marriage of Gaston became one of great political significance.

- Louis and Richelieu supported a marriage between Gaston and Marie de Bourbon Montpensier, a princess of the blood.
- Gaston himself along with his tutor Jean Baptiste d'Ornano favoured a foreign princess allowing him greater freedom and prestige.
- Anne of Austria and the Duchess of Cheuvreuse (Luynes' widow) meanwhile wanted no marriage, jealous as they were of Gaston's ability and ambition.

Cheuvreuse used her beauty and charms to unite a powerful faction including Condé behind their cause. Gaston and d'Ornano were forced to look for protection from provincial governors sympathetic to their cause and in May 1626 Louis took Gaston's actions as dangerous and potentially treasonable. D'Ornano was arrested and Gaston was married off to Marie de Montpensier. These were examples of **Louis' paranoia** about the security of his crown. Richelieu used this turmoil to his advantage in that he:

- rid the court of any surviving pro-Luynes nobles
- consolidated his position as the protector of the king
- replaced d'Aligré with Michel de Marillac, a loyal follower, and also introduced the Marquis of Effiat, another trusted adviser
- had executed the **Count of Chalais** for conspiring with Gaston against the king. The Duchess of Chevreuse was driven into exile in Lorraine.

The queen mother

Between 1624 and 1630, France was ruled by the king, his mother and the cardinal. In November 1630, Louis was forced, against his will, to drop one of the trio. Tension had been growing for some time between the *dévots* group represented by Marie de Medici and the keeper of the seals, Michel de Marillac. One-time allies of Richelieu, the *dévots* now began to drift away from their former champion. The principal reasons for this were:

- After the successful siege of La Rochelle (see p. 113), Richelieu was less respectful to Marie de Medici and less eager to seek her advice.
- Marillac opposed Richelieu's policy of armed intervention in Italy believing that the cardinal should root out heresy at home rather than fight Catholic Spain. Richelieu did not share their Counter-Reformation politics. The cardinal was a nationalist Catholic, who put the crown of France above all else.
- Marillac blamed Richelieu for the financial ruin of the crown, as every year since 1620 had seen a royal army raised and costly foreign adventures were reflected in increased taxations and loans.

By November 1630, matters had come to a head as Marie demanded Richelieu's dismissal. She argued that Richelieu's policies were unholy: he attacked fellow

Louis' paranoia The king's paranoia can be seen by the arrest of his two half-brothers in June 1626 as well as the removal of the chancellor Etienne d'Aligre who was seen to be disapproving of the king's actions.

Count of Chalais A noble by birth, Chalais was the grandson of the sixteenth-century marshal of France, Monluc. Chalais was also young and he was pursued ruthlessly to his death by Richelieu in August 1626.

Dévots A political faction led by Marie de Medici that regarded heresy as the chief enemy, and promoted an alliance with Spain if it meant upholding Catholic values.

Catholics abroad but in the process weakened France. The Treaty of Regensburg (October 1630) between Emperor Ferdinand II and Louis promised potential peace and hinted that Marillac was gaining the upper hand over Richelieu.

Day of the Dupes

On 10 November 1630, a dramatic and furious showdown occurred between Louis and his mother at the Luxembourg Palace, resulting from Marie's persistent calls for Richelieu's removal. Richelieu sneaked into the room via a secret passageway only to be met with a tirade of abuse from Marie de Medici. Louis made his own departure to his hunting lodge at Versailles, ignoring Richelieu as he departed. All at court believed **Marillac and Marie** to have triumphed. Marillac prepared for a triumphant entry into the Luxembourg Palace while Richelieu prepared to leave for Le Havre where he was governor. Yet Louis valued his cardinal too highly to allow him to become the victim of faction. The king invited Richelieu to his lodge at Versailles and reassured him of his confidence in his abilities. Louis believed that Richelieu's advice was more important than his mother's and that Marillac was to blame for the problems that France was encountering. Richelieu's fall never came, instead 10 November became known as the Day of the Dupes in recognition of the way in which the king fooled all into believing that he was willing to sacrifice his leading light. Richelieu was triumphant and the Day of the Dupes marks a significant turning point in the administration of the cardinal and the development of royal absolutism. All of the leading magnates were now under no illusions as to who was in control of policy at court. Richelieu could embark upon a period of ministerial absolutism in the name of the king and with his full backing.

RELIGIOUS POLICY

In 1621, France was once more on the verge of civil conflict. The Edict of Nantes had given legal recognition to the religious, political and military organisation of the

---

KEY THEME

Marie and Marillac Marie was put under house arrest in her château at Compiegne. In July 1631, she escaped to the Spanish Netherlands, never to return to France. Marillac was imprisoned while his half-brother was arrested and executed, having been charged with treason.

Huguenot communities but still many Protestants feared for the future of their faith:

- The edict left many royal offices open only to Catholics, while popular Catholic resentment of Huguenot rights of worship manifested itself in violence.
- Moreover, the Catholic Church was enjoying a revival in the seventeenth century. Louis XIII's friendship with Spain further convinced many Huguenots that their days were numbered.

Huguenot nobles such as Rohan, Turenne and Bouillon were eager to increase their strength, and with over 200 strongholds and 20,000 men this was a distinct possibility. In 1617, the king decided to impose the edict of Nantes in the region of **Béarn**. This action provoked the Huguenots. A national assembly of Reformed churches met at La Rochelle in 1620. In response, royalist forces under Louis and Luynes set out southwards in 1621 with the aim of striking at specific Protestant strongholds and bringing the Huguenot nobility to the negotiating table.

Military action

Huguenot military strength under Rohan and Soubise was great and, despite a successful siege of St Jean d'Angély in June 1621, the following assault by royal armies on Montauban was called off in November after heavy casualties and a typhus epidemic. In 1622, the conflict resumed in the Huguenot heartland towards the west of France. In April 1622, the royalists inflicted a significant defeat on the Huguenots at Rie, a victory that was followed by the occupation of Guyenne and a siege of Montpellier. The **Peace of Montpellier** that followed saw a dilution of Huguenot rights from the Edict of Nantes. Two key issues need to be highlighted here in the context of Richelieu's forthcoming religious policies:

- Protestant rebels were not questioning the authority of the crown as they had been in the late sixteenth century, but merely the crown's interpretation of the edict of Nantes
- The strength of La Rochelle as a Huguenot stronghold was clear for all to see. Rich in commerce and tied

KEY ISSUE

Béarn Louis decided to transform the sovereign court of Béarn into a *parlements* in which only Catholic magistrates would sit, thus ensuring the enforcement of the Edict of Nantes.

KEY EVENT

Peace of Montpellier, 1622 The Huguenots gave up the right to 80 of 200 safe havens granted in 1598, and the policy of independence adopted by the Huguenots in 1620 was severely undermined.

closely with the Dutch Calvinists, La Rochelle was the headquarters of Huguenot operations.

Richelieu and the Huguenots

Richelieu was a zealous Catholic but he believed first and foremost in the power of the French crown and he was interested only in the good of the monarchy. With regard to the Huguenots, Richelieu believed that he should, as he put it in his *Political Testament*, 'ruin the Huguenot party'.

In January 1625, Soubise, a leading Huguenot nobleman, seized the islands of Rie and Oléron which offered important access routes into La Rochelle. Richelieu collected a major fleet and sent a royal army to expel Soubise from his refuge. A truce was agreed, brokered by the English (Louis' sister Henrietta Maria had married Charles, Prince of Wales), but suspicion remained high on both sides. Yet English goodwill did not last long and the **Duke of Buckingham** saw an opportunity to assist the Protestants of La Rochelle.

Officially Richelieu's rebuilding of the French navy was the reason for the breakdown in Anglo-French relations and renewed English piracy in the Channel did little to help. France responded by impounding over 200 English vessels in the port of Bordeaux in 1627. In July 1627, over 80 English ships arrived in La Rochelle under Buckingham to lead an open revolt against Louis XIII. La Rochelle was besieged under the supervision of Richelieu and Louis. In November, the English fleet retreated having suffered serious losses in a skirmish off the island of Rie. Buckingham promised another fleet in the new year but a hastily constructed embankment over 1.5 km long blockaded the way and the English fleet was warded off. The subsequent assassination of Buckingham by a fanatic put paid to any further hopes of English assistance and La Rochelle was left to fend for itself. Famine and disease ripped through the city and on 29 October 1628 the gates were opened to the royal troops. Amnesty was granted to the rebels by a triumphant Louis who entered the city on 1 November 1628. Credit for the triumph went to Richelieu who had remained in personal control of the siege. The enterprise had been expensive and risky, yet

---

KEY PERSON

The Duke of Buckingham
Buckingham wished to intervene in order to undermine Louis' rule. Such action would prove popular in Protestant England where Louis was viewed as an oppressive Catholic despot.

the outcome greatly benefited the cardinal's political standing.

The Edict of Grace, 1629

In June 1629, the king issued the Grace of Alais (the Edict of Grace). The 1598 edict was renewed in religious and judicial terms but the military and political terms were suppressed. The Huguenot military organisation was to be dismantled, fortresses and strongholds demolished and Catholic worship revived wherever it had formerly existed. No more state finance was to be used for maintaining Protestant garrisons or educating Protestant clergy. The Edict of Grace was important:

- Henry IV had always meant for the concessions to the Huguenots in the royal brevets to be temporary, and now through force they had come to an end.
- The Huguenot state within a state was finished although Protestant worship had not been outlawed.
- The Huguenots remained a separate order in France, retaining their churches and synods, but all of their political and military influence had been shattered.

The campaign against the Huguenots, culminating in the Edict of Grace, should be viewed in the overall context of Richelieu's centralisation of government. The Atlantic coast was now once more under strict royal control. The cycle of religious war ended in 1629 and the restructured Edict of Nantes kept the peace for the next 30 years.

ROYAL ABSOLUTISM

Richelieu's reforms

The administration of Cardinal Richelieu was of crucial importance in the development of royal absolutism in France. Yet centralising, administrative reforms were not part of a grand design, rather they were introduced when required. **Richelieu's reforms** were not particularly innovative, but they were more wide reaching and systematic than those of his predecessors:

- Richelieu recognised the weakness of royal power and

used tried and tested means of centralisation to revive the authority of the crown.

- Richelieu effectively practised ministerial absolutism in the name of the king.
- Louis was fully aware of what Richelieu was attempting to achieve and the king gave his minister authority to carry out reform in his name.
- The achievements of Richelieu can be seen by 1661 after Mazarin had overcome the Fronde and Louis XIV felt sufficiently confident to take over full control of his kingdom. Louis XIV owed his security and power to the work carried out by Richelieu.

KEY TERMS

Conseil d'en haut The inner council where important policy decisions were made.

Conseil des dépêches A sovereign court established to enforce the king's will in the provinces.

Intendants Agents of the crown in the provinces, responsible for the effective enforcement of royal edicts. *Intendants* also watched over the work of royal officials in the localities, controlled troops and provided the king with valuable information on public opinion in the provinces. While the office of *intendant* was not new, the responsibility of those in that office was greatly enhanced. According to Robin Briggs (1997), 'The presence of an *intendant* became the normal rule where it had been sporadic before and without any clear intention the crown was establishing a parallel system of non venal administrators, with tremendous potential as a tool for centralization.'

From 1630, Richelieu strengthened the power of the crown by clarifying the job of the bureaucracy. The trend after this date was towards a more streamlined conciliar system, with more emphasis being laid upon the role of key ministers in the *conseil d'en haut*. Contact with the provinces was maintained by the *conseil des dépêches*, and later increased through the role of *intendants*. Richelieu maintained the trend of reducing the size of crucial decision-making bodies.

Richelieu and the *intendants*

Richelieu not only diluted the power of the provincial governors but threatened them with dismissal if they resisted royal absolutism. By the end of Richelieu's administration, twelve out of sixteen governors had been replaced. The powers that had traditionally rested with the governors gradually passed over to the *intendants*.

The key to understanding *intendants* like much else in Richelieu's administration is the way in which their role became more defined and more important:

- By 1637, these officials, regarded still as temporary in order to enhance royal authority, had been established throughout the kingdom.
- *Intendants* controlled provincial subdivisions known as *généralités*, and their responsibilities were further increased by Richelieu's successor Mazarin who gave them authority in the realm of tax assessment. The rise of the *intendants* combined with the control of the army

(Richelieu had raised the strength of the French army to 100,000 by 1634, a figure which doubled by 1640) were the twin instruments by which royal authority was bolstered under Richelieu.

Richelieu's network of clients and friends was enormous and all the more significant because it extended beyond the court. Richelieu amassed governorships of towns and provinces for himself and his family. He also purchased large amounts of land and established a very strong political foothold as a consequence throughout Brittany, Anjou, Poitou and Saintonge. Throughout western France, Richelieu became hugely influential through his direct personal authority and patronage.

Financial policy, 1620s

Having chosen Richelieu over Marie de Medici and Marillac, Louis was committed to a policy of war and glory. The consequences were increased taxation and financial crisis. On top of this Richelieu's financial policies in peacetime were far from successful:

- During a period of domestic peace in 1626, he proposed the abolition of venality and a reduction in the *taille*.
- Richelieu put forward the concept of a standing army, numbering over 18,000 men to be paid for and maintained by all the provinces of France. He also persuaded the assembly of notables to support an increase in the size of the navy and the creation of trading companies.
- Richelieu's vision of a centralised French state centred on a thriving mercantile class consisting of nobles who were willing to invest heavily in trade and commerce. A scheme to repurchase ex-crown lands from the nobility over a six-year period failed to come to fruition as the assembly of notables extended the period to sixteen years and in doing so made it redundant. The plan to make all provinces responsible for the provision and upkeep of an army similarly met resistance, and in the end it was the treasury that paid over two-thirds of the bill.

Resistance to financial policies, 1630s

In the 1630s, the focus of Richelieu's fiscal programme changed as the pressures of war served to double expenditure. Although the sale of offices declined in this period it was due to a fall in demand rather than a specific policy. The *taille* in 1643 was two and a half times what it had been during the reign of Henry IV. There was resistance to the policies:

- Resistance to taxation emerged from the estates of Normandy in 1638, as the crown sought to abolish local privileges and exemptions concerning the *taille*.
- Special levies and forced loans were necessary but equally unpopular. In the spring of 1636, there was a popular uprising by peasants calling themselves *croquants* in Angoulême that rapidly spread throughout south-west France. Troops had to be withdrawn from the front to meet the challenge and it was clear that, as the government attempted to increase revenue, disorder was always close at hand.
- In 1639, an insurrection consisting of 20,000 peasants took place in Normandy. The revolt of the Nu-Pieds

Richelieu's financial policies

It is difficult to view Richelieu's financial policies as a success given the misery that they caused the population of France. However, such hardships were not entirely the fault of Richelieu: harvests were poor and there was a shortage of bullion. There are three major points to make about Richelieu's fiscal policies:

- The demands of war after 1630 provoked intensive fiscalism that extended taxation and made Richelieu along with his financial ministers (the Marquis of Effiat and Claude Bullion) look for new means of raising money.
- Popular disorder and peasant insurrection were common in the 1630s as a consequence of fiscal demands.
- Reform was limited and generally unsuccessful, particularly with regard to trade and commerce. Social values and local privileges impeded Richelieu's vision of a French state.

(the barefooted) was in reaction to Richelieu's attempt to extend the *gabelle* to a previously exempt region. Local gentry and clergy joined the revolt and once again the royal army had to fight long and hard to bring the area under the control of the crown. The royal order was revoked in the face of such hostility, although the rebels were punished harshly. Normandy was put under martial law and the population terrorised by royal troops. Summary judgements and mass executions highlighted Richelieu's harsh and repressive sense of justice.

- Also in 1639 Richelieu had abolished the *taille* in the towns, replacing it with a 5 per cent sales tax. Again fierce resistance made it entirely unworkable, and soon after Richelieu's death the tax was abolished, although in practice it had died long before the cardinal.

CONSPIRACIES OF THE NOBILITY

While Richelieu maintained the trust of the king, he was unchallenged in his position as supreme statesman of the kingdom. Yet, danger existed from those who felt excluded from court, and from those who resented the patronage and power of the cardinal himself. Money from Madrid and Brussels was always forthcoming to fund rebellions against the French king. While Richelieu's clientele network was great and vast, those who did not benefit from the cardinal's patronage turned to violence. Until 1638, Richelieu's opponents looked to **Gaston, heir to the throne**, and the younger brother of the king:

- The Day of the Dupes confirmed Richelieu's rise to power, and the fall of Marillac. Marie survived in exile and Gaston too left court in 1631 to begin a series of conspiracies and rebellions.
- In 1632, Henry de Montmorency raised an army in reaction to the extension of taxation in Languedoc, a *pays d'états* province. Partly a rebellion against centralisation and partly one of noble discontent, it ultimately failed. Gaston was implicated again as he sought to unite the nobility against Richelieu. Captured

Gaston, heir to the throne
The king's younger brother was Gaston d'Orleans who until 1638 was heir to the throne. Gaston, along with the queen and the duchess of Chevreuse, was at the centre of the Chalais conspiracy of 1626. That attempt to assassinate Richelieu and perhaps usurp Louis had failed, and Chalais was killed. Gaston soon found himself excluded at court and naturally blamed Richelieu for his position. In 1632, Gaston found support from the duke of Montmorency and raised arms in Languedoc. Failure resulted in the execution of Montmorency.

KEY EVENT

Execution of Montmorency
The fact that the princes of France failed to rise in defence of Montmorency demonstrates how disunited noble opposition was to Richelieu. Montmorency's rising had centred on Languedoc; those nobles from elsewhere felt little loyalty to Montmorency's cause. Injured by royal forces at Castelnaudary, Montmorency was treated by royal doctors and his wounds cared for so that he could stand trial and face execution in October 1632. The execution of one of the foremost noblemen in France sent a stern signal to the rest of the kingdom.

KEY PERSON

Cinq Mars The historian J. H. Elliott wrote in *Richelieu and Olivares*, (1989): 'In the Cinq Mars conspiracy all the elements conducive to the overthrow of the cardinal looked as if they were about to coalesce at last – aristocratic opposition, subversion by Spain, war weariness, and palace intrigue.'

Montmorency

at Castelnaudary, **Montmorency was executed** in Toulouse.

- Gaston once more survived and after a brief reconciliation he found another noble ally in the count of Soissons, another prince of the blood. Like Montmorency, Soissons was an independent noble of the sword who fronted a plot to overthrow the government. The Soissons conspiracy reached its peak in 1641 and was perhaps the most serious threat to Louis' throne. Only the death of Soissons on the battlefield of La Marfée as his troops closed in on victory, thwarted his plans.
- As Spanish power in Europe began to dwindle in 1639–40, Philip IV and his statesman Olivares increasingly viewed noble malcontents in France as a way of weakening the French crown. Already in 1637 Anne of Austria had been discovered carrying out secret correspondence with her Spanish relatives, and her reputation was only partly restored by the birth of Louis, the Dauphin, in 1638.

Cinq Mars The last great anti-Richelieu conspiracy occurred in 1642, and was partly of his own making. In a bid to counter the king's obsession with Mlle de La Fayette, Richelieu introduced to court a favourite of his own, the Marquis of Cinq Mars. Louis and Cinq Mars soon became friends as Richelieu had hoped; the idea being that the cardinal could keep a close watch on the king, maintain his trust and good relations with Louis through the 17-year-old marquis. However, Richelieu made a major miscalculation in the character of Cinq Mars in that he soon became uncontrollable and keen to further his own political ambitions. Richelieu became a rival to Cinq Mars, and by 1642 Cinq Mars became the centre of a conspiracy to assassinate the cardinal:

- In March 1642, the conspirators made a secret treaty with Spain in a plot to persuade Louis to switch to a pro-Spanish *dévots* policy through an invasion fronted by Gaston. Richelieu would be assassinated and France would abandon its Protestant allies.
- Richelieu discovered the plot and personally interrogated François Auguste de Thou, a friend of Cinq Mars.

- The type of correspondence that Cinq Mars had been involved in with Olivares was wholly inappropriate and treasonable. Cinq Mars was arrested and in September 1642 he was executed.
- By threatening resignation Richelieu forced the king to remove all remaining associates of the young marquis and obtained a royal assurance not to take advice from anyone not on the royal council.

Richelieu and the nobility

We can make five conclusions about the seriousness of noble conspiracies against Richelieu:

- Serious conspiracies were concentrated in the periods 1626–32 and 1641–2. Outside these periods fear of the government (note here the treatment of Chalais, Montmorency and Cinq Mars) and Richelieu's clientele network kept explicit noble discontent to a minimum.

- The most serious threat to Richelieu's power probably came from the count of Soissons whose victory at La Marfée in eastern France may have succeeded in toppling the cardinal had the former not died on the battlefield.

- Opponents of the regime were treated harshly, no matter their status or previous service to the crown. Such practice acted as a deterrent to other malcontents. The lack of reaction to such repression demonstrates the disunity of opposition. Territorial magnates were independent in their power base and in their opposition.

- Richelieu maintained the trust and respect of the king throughout this period, and in many ways noble opposition was inevitable. The defeat of men such as Montmorency strengthened the cardinal's position at court further. Richelieu worked hard to maintain his privileged position at court and recognised that his power ultimately rested with Louis.

- Spain consistently funded attempts to overthrow Richelieu in an attempt to undermine Louis and latterly attain a favourable peace settlement. Richelieu's foreign policy was consistently anti-Spanish after 1630, and this created resentment among the *dévots* and unpopularity on the ground because of increased taxation.

However, in November 1642 Richelieu fell ill, and on 4 December he died. In his will Richelieu left a vast fortune, totalling 22.5 million livres and to the king he bequeathed the Palais Cardinal along with his **epitaph** addressed to his majesty.

SUMMARY QUESTIONS

1. How serious was noble opposition to Richelieu?

2. How far was Richelieu able to strengthen the majority of the French crown?

3. To what extent did Richelieu fulfil the aims of his Political Testament?

CHAPTER 9

Mazarin as Chief Minister, 1643–61

In May 1643, Louis XIII died leaving Anne of Austria as regent, with Gaston d'Orléans as lieutenant-general. The new king, Louis XIV, was only 4 years old, and already his council appeared divided:

- Louis XIII had attempted to ensure from his deathbed that Richelieu's policies would be maintained by demanding the inclusion of secretaries of state and Jules Mazarin in the decision-making process.
- After her husband's death, Anne held a *lit de justice* in *parlement* that freed her from any restraints. As regent the power of appointment and dismissal lay with her.

Richelieu's heir-apparent as Chief Minister was **Jules Mazarin**, formerly Giulio Mazarini. Nevertheless, despite the power granted to Anne by the *parlements* in 1643 to rule as regent, a faction still existed at court (the *cabale des importants*) that looked to undermine and topple Mazarin just as they had tried to do with Richelieu.

Continuation of Richelieu's policies

The decision to accept Mazarin as Chief Minister ensured an element of continuity in foreign and fiscal policies:

- The Westphalia treaties of 1648 would leave France in a very strong position on the European stage, yet the price of war was being paid in the provinces of France itself.
- Despite continuing fiscal problems (accumulated as a consequence of war with Spain) and the return of Richelieu's political enemies from exile, actual resistance was minimal in the early years of Mazarin's ministry.
- The need for order and stability was recognised by the great men of the realm, many of whom had actually benefited from war through office and position. Yet the continuing search for funds between 1643 and 1648 created friction between the *parlements* and the regency

KEY THEME

Parlement The *parlement* was not comprised of radicals, in fact the opposite is true. Men such as the president Mole and the advocate-general Omer Talon were conservative royalists, both of whom recognised that their authority derived from the crown.

KEY PERSON

Jules Mazarin (1602–61)
Neapolitan by birth, Mazarin entered the French court as a papal nuncio, and soon he attracted the attention of Richelieu. Entering the service of Louis XIII in 1630, Mazarin became a naturalised Frenchman in 1639. Soon after this Mazarin became a cardinal and the lover of the queen. Rumours abounded of a secret marriage between Mazarin and Anne. Whether this was true or false, the intimate bond between cardinal and regent at least ensured an element of stability and cooperation at the centre of government.

Jules Mazarin

government. However, the *parlement* always took on a more influential role during a time of minority rule in terms of checking unlawful royal practice. Certainly the extension of taxation and supplementary levies kept it busy.

Financial problems

In the period 1643–8, *parlement* also clashed with the finance minister Particelli d'Emery. D'Emery's unscrupulous policies allowed royal expenditure to rise in the short term, but created long-term discontent:

- D'Emery raised loans from the *traitants*, financiers who had bought/been given approval by the crown to sell offices and levy taxation. D'Emery's borrowing allowed the war to continue, on the back of *traitants'* credit and such loans were negotiated with high levels of interest.
- The *toise* was an edict of January 1644 that imposed a tax on the houses built outside the ramparts of Paris. It created uproar in the capital.
- An edict of 1646 increasing the tariffs on goods imported into Paris was only registered by *parlement* after a delay of nine years.
- By 1647, the crown was nearing the end of its resources, symbolised by an increase in the *paulette* and a *lit de justice* in 1648 to register a new set of financial measures with the *parlement*.

In short, the same old problems existed as taxation caused unrest in the countryside, new demands for taxation caused mistrust in the *parlement* and unpaid officials became disillusioned at court. With Spain wilting, Mazarin was reluctant to bring peace at any price; he was going to continue Richelieu's policy of breaking Habsburg power. Yet this goal rather obscured Mazarin's sight of internal discontent. Even the diplomatic successes of Westphalia failed to ease the pressure on Mazarin as war with Spain dragged on. The image of Mazarin as an Italian adventurer in the Concini mould, out to enrich only himself at the expense of his adopted country, soon took hold.

OPPOSITION TO THE REGENCY GOVERNMENT, 1643–8

Mazarin had already experienced noble intrigue and dissatisfaction at the hands of the cabal known as the *Importants* led by the duke of Beaufort (grandson of Henry IV) and organised by the Duchess of Chevreuse (previously exiled in Touraine). Insurrection took place in 1643 with the following aims:

- obtaining Brittany for Beaufort
- restoration of those privileges of the nobility that Richelieu had destroyed.

The *Importants* represented the remnants of the anti-Richelieu faction that now opposed Mazarin, aiming to reverse foreign policy and further their own ambitions. In the end the plot failed, and Beaufort was arrested. The others retreated into the provinces. Popular rebellion had also erupted in 1643 as hopes of immediate peace and a reduction in taxation were dashed by Mazarin's continuation of Richelieu's foreign policy. Over two-thirds of France was in rebellion in 1643, centred on the *croquants* of Rouergue. However, those rebellions were crushed, and the war with Spain was going well in the period 1644–7. Rebellious nobles accepted positions in the army, and *intendants* set about increasing tax collection in the localities. But by 1648 the build-up of fiscal pressures and the failure to conclude peace with Spain combined to produce the most serious revolt against Mazarin's ministry.

The Fronde, 1648

The Fronde of 1648 had a number of **distinct causes** that would seem to unite groups that were normally rivals:

- unpopularity of Mazarin as a self-seeking, low-born Italian
- discontent with Mazarin's continuation of war with Spain, heightened in 1648 with peace elsewhere in Europe. Mazarin was seen as Richelieu's creature as the satirical poem of 1643 'Richelieu Reincarnate' highlights:

Importants The conspirators were called *Importants* because they adopted an air of consequence and some important provincial nobles such as the brothers Condé and Conti were on the fringes of the rebellion.

The Fronde The name Fronde comes from the slings used by the street children of Paris to throw stones at the rich as they passed by in carriages. This implied that the rebels were like schoolchildren throwing criticism but running to hide when the archers appeared. Historians have interpreted the Fronde in many different ways. Some view the insurrection as a remake of the English Civil War, initiated by a *parlement* eager to defend constitutional liberties and the freedom of its people. Others regard the Fronde as a blip or farcical interlude (Pennington) in the rise of absolutism in France. Still others of a more Marxist persuasion see the Fronde as a continuation of the peasant revolts of the 1630s and 1640s – a form of class war against crown and aristocracy.

Causes of the Fronde One thing seems certain – while the revolts of 1639–43 in the countryside demonstrated the suffering of the people, the Fronde itself began in Paris and was directed by leading nobles.

He is not dead, he's merely changed his age
This cardinal, the object of men's rage.

- fiscal pressure exacted by d'Emery and Mazarin which reached new heights in 1648. Taxation in the countryside and new demands to the *parlement* made this a grievance shared by rich and poor alike
- the ministerial network of clients revolving around Mazarin
- centralisation of royal authority to the detriment of local privileges exacerbated during wartime
- the use of *lits de justice* by Anne of Austria to push through policies and demands that were fundamentally opposed by the *parlement.*

The Fronde was aimed at the perceived abuse of power by Richelieu and Mazarin. While the popularity of strong monarchy was beyond doubt, the minority government was desperately unpopular in 1648.

Financial requests

In the spring of 1648, Anne of Austria presented a new package of fiscal demands to the *parlement* at a **lit de justice.** The government demanded a forced loan or a gift from office holders equivalent to four years' salary in return for a renewal of the *paulette.* The king's advocate-general Omer Talon presented the decrees and challenged the constitutional right of the government to use such a procedure. Members of the *parlement*, most of whom were

The Paris Fronde

of course major office holders, joined in opposition to the royal demands with representatives of other sovereign courts in Paris. The amalgamation of the *cour des aides*, *chambre des comptes*, *grand conseil* and the *parlement* itself produced an *arrêt d'union* authorising joint meetings of the four courts. They met in the one of the chambers of the Palais de Justice called the Chambre de St Louis, in utter defiance of the regent. Indeed, Anne formally opposed these proceedings by letters signed with the royal seal.

Assembly at the Chambre de St Louis

In principle, the assembly was revolutionary; in reality it was peaceful and constitutional. Indeed, the *parlementaires* regarded themselves as fathers of the country, protectors of civil liberties and guardians of the state:

- The main objections were to the *lits de justices* held in 1645 and 1648, which in the eyes of many present in the Chambre de St Louis were an abuse of the crown's power.
- At the end of June, Mazarin and Orleans persuaded the regent to compromise and the Chambre de St Louis was given authorisation to meet and duly produced a charter of 27 articles around which the state was to be reformed. The reforms would demolish much of the centralisation established under Richelieu, eliminate financial abuses and give the *parlement* control over taxation. In short, a new form of consultative government was being proposed in which the monarch lost his absolute power. The government had little option but to concede and consent to such proposals.
- The *surintendant* d'Emery was dismissed, *intendants* were recalled, tax farmers disappeared and tax collection was temporarily stopped.

The Chambre appeared to have won because the whole administrative machinery established since 1635 was overthrown. With the fiscal machinery of the crown in chaos, bankruptcy appeared inevitable. Perhaps more than any factor it was the accumulating fiscal pressures exacted by the crown to fund war against Spain that led to the disobedience of 1648. Even after the concessions granted to the Chambre de St Louis, Mazarin continued to borrow from financiers who gambled on the crown returning to power and thus making a vast fortune.

War against Spain and revolt in Paris

To Mazarin the concessions were temporary, as he set about the final defeat of Spain. The foreign war simply continued, and in late August news filtered through of Condé's long-awaited victory at Lens. Encouraged by this success, Mazarin persuaded Anne to order the arrest of three leading *parlementaires*. Among those targeted for arrest was the ageing **Pierre Broussel**.

This action led to open revolt in Paris and the barricades were manned by, among others, **Paul Gondi**, a cleric whose ambitions could only be realised at the expense of Mazarin. The Parisian display of defiance provoked a climbdown by the government and the leaders of the *parlement* were released. The Declaration of St Germain in October 1648 reinforced concessions to the frondeurs. Although the peace of Münster (also October 1648) did not bring peace with Spain, it did allow some French troops to return to Paris. Mazarin was aware that the next stage in the frondeurs' plan, especially in the minds of Gondi, Châteauneuf and Molé, was to remove him from power. Therefore, Mazarin sought the help of Condé's army, in a bid to subdue Paris by force. The young king was removed from the capital so that he might not be taken hostage while Paris was to be starved into submission. The *parlement* which had set out upon a peaceful constitutional revolution was now faced with violence and, with the queen unwilling to negotiate, the frondeurs prepared for civil conflict. Mazarin was named by the frondeurs as the sole cause of the problems; they demanded that he should be exiled. *Parlementaire* strength was bolstered by the support of Condé's brother, the prince of Conti, and his brother-in-law, the Duke of Longueville. Aristocratic influence appeared to be coming to the fore, something that the *parlementaires* had never intended. A compromise peace was negotiated in March 1649; the peace of Rueil confirmed the existing reforms of the Chambre de St Louis.

KEY PEOPLE

Pierre Broussel A leading radical who was very popular with the Paris mob. His wit at the expense of the government had endeared him to most Parisians.

Paul Gondi One of the leading frondeurs who was aiming to displace Mazarin.

The first phase of the crisis was over. It was known by many as the Fronde *parlementaire*.

By March 1649, several issues had become apparent:

- What had begun as a peaceful constitutional revolution in the *parlements* had become submerged and overwhelmed with grievances of other malcontented parties, most notably the aristocracy.
- The alliance of *parlementaires* and rebellious nobles was unlikely to last given that the status and position of the *parlements* ultimately rested with a centralised state.
- Mazarin united opposition, both noble and *parlementaire*. He made several misjudgements in 1648–9, most notably the proposed arrest of Broussel, the use of force against Paris and his obsession with defeating Spain.
- Royal authority and fiscal solvency were deteriorating rapidly throughout the crisis.

The Fronde of the nobles

The frondeur nobles who had taken to the barricades in 1648 continued to press for the dismissal of Mazarin while Condé's relationship with the cardinal rapidly deteriorated. Condé expected monetary rewards and promotion for his loyalty and he probably also began to view himself as a successor to Mazarin. The victor of Rocroi and Lens was now a threat rather than an ally to Mazarin. As a consequence the cardinal ordered his arrest in January 1650, along with Condé's brother Conti and Longueville. The idea was to secure his own grip on power and rally the support of Paris. Yet, while there may have been celebrations among Gondi's frondeurs, provincial nobles were gathering arms in preparation for war:

- Despite an armed royal progress through the provinces in spring 1650 it became clear that the Midi and south-west in particular were hotbeds of anarchy. Opposition to and hatred of Mazarin united those in revolt.
- Gaston d'Orleans, now playing a leading role at court, feared that if Mazarin remained at court there would be more unrest.

- Gondi and Gaston obtained the release of the political prisoners from the *parlements*. Mazarin was aware of the potential consequences, and in a final gamble he travelled to Le Havre in February 1651 in order to oversee the release of the princes personally and attempt to win their support.
- The princes inevitably ignored his offers and instead travelled to Paris where they made a triumphant entry into the capital.
- Mazarin now opted for voluntary exile in Bruhl.
- Louis and Anne remained in Paris where Gaston continued to dominate affairs. Therefore, as Gaston sought to summon an Estates General, Mazarin appeared beaten. Condemned by *parlement* and royal proclamation his prospects looked bleak.
- Yet ultimately the cardinal just needed to bide his time as the fragile unity of the frondeurs quickly dissolved. The power struggle developed between Anne and her supporters, most notably Lionne and Servien, drawn up against Condé, Orleans and the moderate wing of the Fronde, represented by President Molé.

Indeed, one of the best things that Mazarin could have done was to seek temporary exile, as he then removed the one unifying factor that bound frondeurs together, himself.

KEY THEME

Condé's vulnerability

Condé and his allies were little loved in the capital and Mazarin could even call upon the support of Gondi in their arrest. When he returned to Paris in 1652, his reception in the capital was lukewarm to say the least, although there were enough malcontents spurred on by Mazarin's return to give Condé hope of a revival. The historian Robin Briggs writes that 'the coalition of his (Mazarin's) enemies promptly fell apart amid a tangle of conflicting personal fears and ambitions'.

Louis XIV reaches majority

In autumn 1651, the battle lines became more clearly defined as Condé became the figurehead of an armed revolt in the south, allied to the invading Spanish forces. Orleans similarly announced his support for the rebels. On 7 September, Louis XIV reached his age of majority (13); this left **Condé and the rebels in a vulnerable position**. The rebels were now in open revolt against the crown, rather than just venting their anger against the regency government.

- By the end of 1651, Condé was gathering considerable support in Bordeaux, but little elsewhere. Guyenne proved infertile ground for Condé, and he suffered a number of military reverses.
- Mazarin had returned from exile in December 1651 with over 6000 German mercenaries behind him.

- In January 1652, Mazarin once more linked up with Anne of Austria at Poitiers.
- Military exchanges were not going Condé's way and in a last gamble he travelled to Paris in April 1652 where he linked up with Orleans. Already Gondi had abandoned Condé and had joined forces with Anne in return for a cardinal's hat.
- In July 1652, as deputies assembled in the Hôtel de Ville in Paris, Condé's army decided to take Paris by force. Condé's army ran riot, the Hôtel de Ville was burned to the ground, and many members of the sovereign courts were murdered.
- Condé established his own government in Paris with Broussel at its head. Yet this new government had been discredited by its violent actions and the *parlementaires* turned their back on the radicalism of Condé. Condé's supporters disappeared and he was forced into exile in the south-west, and then subsequently the Netherlands.
- The one remaining obstacle to a resumption of royal authority appeared to be Mazarin, still hated by the *parlement*. Therefore, in August 1652 the cardinal chose once more to go into self-imposed exile allowing Louis to make a triumphant re-entry into Paris in October 1652.
- Louis immediately held a *lit de justice* in which Condé was condemned as a traitor and his land passed to the crown. Several leading *parlementaires* were banished or, in Gondi's case, imprisoned and a royal declaration forbade the institution to meddle in matters of state in the future. Mazarin was summoned back to the council in February 1653. It was only in **Bordeaux** that resistance continued.

THE FOREIGN POLICIES OF RICHELIEU AND MAZARIN

Richelieu and the Habsburgs

The victory over the Huguenots at La Rochelle not only convinced Richelieu that the Spanish could not be trusted but also strengthened his relationship with Louis and opened up the possibility of military intervention in Italy.

Bordeaux Here, the Ormée (union of the people against the ruling oligarchy) had successfully seized power. However, having wrenched control from the provincial *parlements*, the Ormée was unable to carry out any constructive reforms and, while alliances with Spain and latterly Oliver Cromwell prolonged the revolt, it was only a matter of time before the royal army regained control. The leader of the Ormée, Duretete, was killed and by August 1653 the kingdom was pacified.

Richelieu's alliances
Richelieu was active in foreign policy before his appointment as principal minister in 1630. In 1624, he negotiated the Treaty of Compiegne with the Dutch and successfully drew up a marriage alliance with England that saw Henrietta Maria marry Charles I of England. Both consolidated French ties with important maritime powers.

What does the Fronde reveal about opposition in France?

A major breakdown in royal authority was inevitable in 1648–9, given the financial demands made by the crown through the continued war with Spain.

- Nevertheless, the inability/unwillingness of the frondeurs to seize power highlights their weaknesses. The *parlement* was basically always royalist at heart and wanted only peaceful constitutional change, while Condé although willing to raise arms was erratic and short-tempered in character and unable to unite rebel factions. The fact that he ended up in the Netherlands commanding a Spanish army demonstrates how selfish his own intentions and ambitions really were.

- In the regions of France local considerations fuelled the disturbances in the provinces between 1649 and 1652. The frondeurs lacked direction throughout the period. The small royal army was vulnerable in the summer of 1652 but effective cooperation from the rebels was not forthcoming.

- Only disapproval of Mazarin united the opposition but once he had gone into temporary exile in 1651 and 1652 the diverse objectives of the various frondeurs were highlighted.

- The violence and destruction that increased after 1651 discredited opposition to the crown and convinced many of the need for strong monarchical rule. Parallels with the Catholic League of the 1580s might be drawn here. The revolt began in the Chambre de St Louis as a peaceful constitutional revolt to impinge royal authority. It ended by making Louis XIV aware of the need for strong, absolutist rule.

- Louis XIV never forgot his exclusion from Paris or the disruption of the years 1648–53 and his harsh policies towards the *parlement* later on reflect the mark it made.

KEY THEME

Marillac and the Habsburgs Marillac was very much in favour of a non-interventionist foreign policy in order to preserve internal stability and bolster the economy.

Under the influence of Marie de Medici and **Marillac**, there was a brief shift from the traditional anti-Habsburg outlook towards a more conciliatory policy with the House of Austria and Spain as was shown by the peace of Monzon, March 1626.

- The *dévots* faction at court fronted by Medici and Marillac believed that a Protestant offensive in Europe led by the Dutch and the Swedes was undermining Catholic power and status. Any anti-Habsburg alliance would therefore further promote Protestantism.
- **Richelieu**, on the other hand, was concerned about Habsburg expansion in Europe and considered a Habsburg alliance unrealistic and unworkable. In the early years of his ministry, Richelieu had to pursue a difficult middle line between the pro-Spanish policies of the *dévots* group, from which he was becoming increasingly detached, and the threat that he perceived from Spain to French security both at home and abroad.
- Richelieu saw the advantages of *dévots* policy in that domestic considerations could be prioritised and internal reform undertaken. Yet, he was also deeply suspicious of Spanish intentions, a mistrust that was exacerbated by the Spanish failure to send a fleet on time to help the French fight the English at La Rochelle in 1628.
- Despite clashes of interest and personality at court, Richelieu attempted to prevent Spain becoming too powerful even before 1630. Evidence of this came in 1625 when he encouraged Ernst Mansfeld to divert the focus of his operations from the Palatinate to the Netherlands in order to curb Spanish advances there. French security would once more be threatened by significant Spanish reconquest in the United Provinces and Mansfeld's intervention came at a critical time.

By 1629, the Habsburg offensive in the Netherlands and in Germany was beginning to wane and Spanish finances in particular were at breaking-point.

Mantua

Louis XIII's choice of Richelieu over Marie de Medici in the Day of Dupes was partly a result of his desire to go to war against Spain. In the short term, Richelieu would be content with undermining the Habsburg position in Europe through clever diplomacy rather than outright war. One example of this was the resolution of the succession crisis in Mantua, whereby the Duke of Nevers was installed as ruler of Mantua by the Treaty of Cherasco (June 1631). Richelieu had to show great determination and resolve to

Richelieu and the Habsburgs Richelieu probably overestimated Habsburg strength in 1630, as by this time the tide had turned in Europe in favour of the Protestant forces, and French intervention did little more than tip the balance even further away from the House of Austria and Spain. It was not until 1635 that Richelieu finally decided to commit France to the Thirty Years' War.

continue the struggle in favour of Nevers as he came under increasing pressure at home from his one-time allies in the *dévots* group. Yet Richelieu recognised that French interests were better served by occupying Savoy and eroding Spanish influence abroad than by pursuing the concept of a grand Catholic alliance. Spanish finances and resources were further stretched by the **Mantua Crisis**, and the Treaty of Cherasco was an outright success for Richelieu. Yet with Spanish forces seemingly still on the offensive in Italy, the empire and the Netherlands the Mantua crisis looked certain to signal full-scale conflict between France and Spain. However, the costs of intervention in Mantua had been heavy for both sides.

Cold War

France did not formally declare war on Spain until May 1635, four years after the peace of Cherasco. The intervening years were those of **Cold War**, as Richelieu sought alliances with the enemies of Spain. Inevitably such enemies were Protestant, moves that further compromised Richelieu's position as principal minister in France and his master's position as defender of Christendom. Nevertheless, war and the erosion of Spanish power were, in a foreign-policy context, viewed as more important than religious conscience:

- In 1630, the Dutch alliance was renewed.
- In 1631, the **Treaty of Bärwalde** was concluded with the Swedes.

Such alliances were nothing new, as in 1624 Richelieu had intervened in the Valtelline on behalf of the Protestant Grisons. Richelieu firmly believed that what he was doing was right; there was a genuine conviction about his actions. In his eyes the real aggressor in Europe was Spain.

Richelieu's policy appeared to be successful, as a powerful coalition now stood against Spain and Austria. Yet the policy had to be carefully managed as the last thing that Richelieu wanted was a complete overhaul of the balance of power to favour the Protestants. The Swedish offensive of 1632, led by Gustavus Adolphus, was initially a great success and the emperor feared that the Catholic states of

Germany might be overrun. It was probably with some relief that Richelieu heard of the death of Gustavus Adolphus at the Battle of Lützen in 1632. This Swedish catastrophe allowed Richelieu to resume his policy of maintaining checks and balances. The policy could no longer be maintained after the Swedish defeat at **Nördlingen** in 1635. Richelieu, recognising war to be imminent, set about rebuilding alliances with Sweden and the Dutch while also courting Bernard of Saxe-Weimar to fight in the Rhineland. Spain was determined to continue operations in the Netherlands and thus a secure land route up the Rhine was critical. The Rhine became a central focus of Richelieu's war against Spain.

War between France and Spain

War broke out between France and Spain in 1635; Richelieu believed France to be capable of winning a rapid victory. Given the dispersed nature of Spanish forces and the previous years of warfare it appeared that French intervention would be the decisive factor in finally destroying Habsburg power in Europe. Yet Richelieu was too optimistic:

- French alliances with Sweden and the Dutch were ineffectual as both nations were too concerned with their own interests to drive forward Richelieu's ambitions.
- Richelieu was perhaps overly ambitious in mobilising large armies that could not be kept in the field for long periods of time.
- The nature of the conflict against Spain was one of attrition dominated by sieges and defence rather than swift offensives.
- While Spanish financial resources were stretched the crown could still pull together massive resources for war.

In 1636, the combined forces of Spain and the empire won a series of victories over untried and outdated French forces, resulting in an invasion of Picardy. Richelieu's decision to declare total war on Spain appeared to have backfired. However, by the end of 1636, Imperial troops had been forced off French soil and, as long as the new Emperor Ferdinand III (his father Ferdinand II died in 1636) refused to cede Pomerania to the Swedish, Richelieu could continue to count on Swedish aid. In 1638, the strategically important fortress of Breisach fell to the French marshal Turenne. As Spanish strength slipped in the Netherlands and in Germany, Richelieu made significant if not startling gains. Artois in the southern Netherlands and Rousillon in the Pyrenees were occupied by French forces. Revolts in Catalonia and Portugal in 1640 underlined Spanish weaknesses. Richelieu was determined to fight Spain to the finish, but he died in December 1642 followed shortly by Louis himself in May 1643. Both sides now sought an advantageous settlement; France buoyed by considerable reserves and Spain by the prospect of a long royal minority in France.

Continuity with Mazarin and Louis XIV

Mazarin followed Richelieu's lead in foreign policy, pursuing the ultimate defeat of Spain and the House of Austria and the strengthening of the French frontier:

- Within a week of Louis XIV's accession, a French army under the Duke of Enghien had destroyed the Spanish army of Flanders at Rocroi. This is widely regarded as the battle that sealed Spain's military demise, and put paid to any hopes of Spanish success in the Netherlands.
- In August 1645, the French were victorious in a second battle at Nördlingen although they were shortly forced to retreat to Alsace.
- In July 1646, Turenne invaded Bavaria, a conquest that persuaded Maximilian to agree to a truce which was later broken in 1647 and led to a second French invasion in 1648.
- Peace negotiations had been ongoing since 1644 and on 20 August Enghien hastened proceedings with a crushing victory over Ferdinand's brother, Archduke Leopold, at the Battle of Lens. Enghien (now with the title Prince of Condé) and Turenne had proved themselves to be peerless in this French overturning of Habsburg supremacy.

Treaties of Westphalia and Pyrenees

The results of Mazarin's foreign policy can be seen in the **Treaty of Westphalia** (1648) and the Treaty of the Pyrenees (1659). Westphalia concluded the wars in the

KEY EVENT

Treaty of Westphalia, 1648 Westphalia may be an impressive memorial to Mazarin's capabilities, but contemporary French opinion slated him for failing to make peace with Spain, and shortly Mazarin had to use all of his political skill to survive the Fronde. Mazarin could not settle with Spain while France continued to support the Catalan rebels, and the continuation of war undermined Mazarin's position at home.

Netherlands and Germany, but the direct conflict between France and Spain continued for another eleven years until the Treaty of the Pyrenees. Nevertheless, Westphalia very much vindicated the policies of Richelieu and Mazarin:

- The status of the Habsburgs was greatly reduced.
- France acquired Metz, Toul, Verdun, southern Alsace, Breisach, Philippsburg and authority over ten Imperial cities.
- French borders were secured, and influence in the empire increased, while Austria left the peace talks empty-handed.

The Treaty of the Pyrenees (1659) concluded France's conflict with Spain. Brought about by a Franco-English alliance of 1657 which made inroads into the Netherlands and continuing problems in Portugal for Philip IV, the peace of the Pyrenees represented another major success for Mazarin. France received Artois and Roussillon from the Spanish Netherlands, along with fortresses in Hainault, Flanders and Luxembourg. Spanish dominance in Europe had come to an end, and now France was emerging as the major player on the European stage. Yet at what cost? The suffering of the French people through oppressive taxation and loss of life were terrible by-products of the foreign policies of both Richelieu and Mazarin.

SUMMARY QUESTIONS

1. How serious was noble opposition to Mazarin?

2. Why did the Fronde fail?

3. To what extent did Richelieu and Mazarin fulfil their aims and objectives in foreign policy?

4. How far did Richelieu and Mazarin strengthen the power of the monarchy?

CHAPTER 10

Louis XIV's France, 1661–1715

Louis XIV

Louis XIV believed in his God-given task to rule over France and, in contrast to his father, he did so personally. He was devoted to affairs of state, diligent and conscientious in his duties. Louis appointed no successor to Mazarin, preferring instead to shoulder the responsibility of power himself. Ministers were his servants; secretaries of state to be consulted on policy rather than formulate it. Louis was master and the arrest and subsequent imprisonment of Fouquet in 1661 (see pp. 140–1) demonstrated that there would be no royal favourites.

CONTINUITY

Nevertheless, a conciliar system of government remained, and few major alterations were made to the system that had been in place since the fifteenth century:

- The royal councils, namely the *conseil d'état*, the *conseil d'en haut*, the *conseil des finances*, the *conseil des dépêches* and the *conseil privé* remained a labyrinth of bureaucracy. Louis had no more direct control over these councils than his predecessors. In many respects, Louis still relied upon these councils for information and acted upon the news that they fed him.
- However, Louis did select his secretaries of state carefully, and membership of the *conseil d'en haut*, where important decisions were made, was closely monitored.
- Personal control of such a vast and complex system was just not feasible, and to replace entirely the structure of government was equally impractical.

Despite these limitations, Louis identified himself with the state more than any of his predecessors. He ignored the Estates General and *parlements*, ruling instead with the idea *L'état c'est moi*.

VERSAILLES

At the centre of Louis' court and the building most identified with his reign and rule was the great palace of **Versailles**. Between 1631 and 1634, Louis XIII transformed the lodge by extending the main building, reconstructing the wings and flanking the angles with four jutting pavilions. During the early years of his reign, Louis XIV rarely visited Versailles, but once married he took the queen and court there. From 1661, work commenced to rapidly transform the retreat into a royal palace beyond comparison anywhere in Europe.

- On the first floor two symmetrical apartments were created for the king and queen, linked by a central reception room.
- The gardens were landscaped by Le Nôtre while Le Vau built the orangery.
- The castle became a place for entertainment and in May 1664 a pantomime entitled 'Pleasures of the Enchanted Island' was performed. In July 1668, the Grand Royal Entertainment took place marking out Versailles as a centre of culture, extravagance and fashion.

The king wanted to enlarge the castle further and Louis Le Vau was entrusted to draw up plans. Louis could not decide whether to pull down the old castle and replace it with a palace in the Italianate style or just add a new wing in stone at each end. Ultimately, he compromised and adopted a combination of both, preserving the old castle and surrounding it on three sides by a taller stone building with a flat roof. Louis may have had the intention of destroying the old brick building later but the wars of the second half of his reign left the project unfinished. Versailles is therefore formed of two castles and only the façade overlooking the gardens represents a true expression of Louis XIV's wishes. Louis XIV's decision to transfer the seat of the court and the government to Versailles was a crucial one: from May 1682 onwards the court ceased to travel around. Versailles became the centre of royal government and at the same time a way of life for the nobility.

KEY PLACE

Versailles Originally a mere hunting lodge, used extensively by Henry IV and his eldest son, Louis XIII. Under Louis XIV it developed into the grandest palace in Europe.

Louis XIII's palace of Versailles

FINANCE

Royal finances

In order to fight wars and pay for the grand court he had assembled, Louis looked to reform the royal finances. In 1662, **Colbert** assumed authority for financial administration and in 1665 he was appointed controller-general. Colbert's influence in the financial sphere was reinforced by his appointment as *surintendant des maisons* (building projects) and *surintendant du commerce* (trade) in 1665 and then secretary of state for the navy in 1669. Colbert had two main priorities:

- liquidating past debts left by war
- bringing order and efficiency to the financial system.

To this end a *chambre de justice* was established. Colbert persuaded Louis that those financiers and speculators who loaned money to the crown at very high rates of interest and creamed off the profits of taxation had to be brought to account:

KEY PERSON

Colbert Not particularly innovative in the realm of finance, but he was immensely diligent and purposeful. Jean-Baptiste Colbert was even known as the 'north wind' because of his cold and calculating demeanour.

KEY TERM

Chambre de justice A special court established to investigate cases of malpractice and corruption among financiers and entrepreneurs who lent money to the crown at high rates of interest.

- The previous finance minister, Fouquet, had been reluctant to alienate leading nobles on whom he believed the financial security of the crown depended.
- Colbert, on the other hand, saw it necessary to demonstrate the power of royal justice, and Fouquet himself served as a useful scapegoat.

From now on the crown received the equivalent of one year's income from those speculators brought before the chamber of justice. Colbert was rewarded for his judgement with a place on the inner council in 1665, but he still had much to do in terms of increasing royal revenue. Much of the money from the chamber of justice was used to buy back offices and *rentes*, in order to free up cash that had already been committed elsewhere. With the royal debt standing at over 400 million livres Colbert had to improve royal credit gradually while also seeking to increase existing areas of revenue.

Taxation

Colbert managed to increase the yield from taxation while lightening the burden of the *taille* on the third estate:

- The net yield of the *taille* was reduced from 42 million livres per annum to 35 million. Nevertheless, **tax exemptions** were reduced much to the annoyance of the nobles. Just as speculators had been taken to task in 1665 so others were made aware that royal justice would seek out those who profited at the expense of the crown.
- The age-old problem of tax farming was addressed by Colbert with some vigour, and the annual cost of collecting the revenue was reduced from 52 million livres to 24 million livres. Colbert did not seek to outlaw tax farming nor get rid of the *rentes*. He worked within the system and made existing practices work in favour of the crown. Louis did not want to take the risk of fundamentally reforming the financial system, and therefore the yield from indirect taxation increased from 36 million to 62 million livres per annum.
- The tax on salt known as the *gabelle*, resented for its unequal distribution across the kingdom, was collected on a more efficient basis taking in 4 million livres more than it had done under Fouquet.

Colbert

- As the crown's credit rating improved Colbert borrowed at a more favourable rate of interest while royal lands were recovered.
- Diligent book-keeping, vigilance towards corrupt practice, hard negotiating with speculators and tax farmers and the use of *intendants de finance* to ensure more effective collection of taxation all contributed towards a successful financial recovery.

Still malpractice existed, still parochial trade barriers obstructed a national economy and still Louis believed that any foreign adventure would be easily bankrolled, but the financial yield quadrupled between 1661 and 1672 and for this alone Colbert must receive credit.

Stimulating industry

Colbert's promotion of a state-sponsored economy was based around the twin principles of stimulating economic growth and strengthening the state by trade.

Colbert recognised that speculators would be reluctant to invest in industry as there was no quick or visible profit to be made. He firmly believed that more money would increase the power, the greatness and the affluence of the state. He therefore set about devising a programme of state investment and intervention designed to bring industry under the close supervision and control of the crown:

- Large-scale enterprises such as that of Van Robais at Abbeville were subsidised by the state to produce textiles at competitive rates. By 1700, the woollen factory at Abbeville was the largest industry in France, employing over 2000 people.
- On a lesser scale the same principles of state subsidies and supervision were applied to the lacemakers of Auxerre and the silk factories in Lyons.
- Small groups of craftsmen were established, such as the hosiers of Troyes or the tapestry manufactory of Gobelins and in the process they were given the status of *manufactures royales*.

Now such manufacturers had the promise of royal support and protection. Workers in these industries were exempt

COLBERT VISITANT LA MANUFACTURE DES GOBELINS

from the *taille* while foreign craftworkers were encouraged to settle. At the same time, protective tariffs were introduced to bolster such royal patronage and place French industries at an advantage against their powerful Dutch, English and Swedish competitors.

Lesser trades were regulated by guilds, and an edict of 1673 required inspectors to be sent out into the provinces to ensure that appropriate measures were being taken. Unquestionably, workers were made to work harder and festival days and holidays were reduced, perhaps in an attempt to replicate the Protestant work ethic of the maritime powers. Overall, output increased, French goods became synonymous with quality and workers' wages were high. Colbert had recognised the challenge being laid down by the maritime powers of England and the Netherlands, meeting it head on with a policy of state intervention. In the process, national identity and inland communications were improved, the most notable example being the showpiece Languedoc Canal. However, manufacturers felt stifled by the overmighty state, and private entrepreneurs were still out to make profit rather than adhere to Colbert's quality regulations and standards. Furthermore, the industrial priorities laid down by Colbert and the emphasis on luxury goods were perhaps not the best foundation on which to base the French economy.

KEY THEME

Favourable economic climate Colbert was perhaps fortunate to be operating in a conducive economic environment in which food prices were low and the world market was expanding.

Foreign trade

Perhaps Colbert's most progressive ideas came in the realm of foreign trade and, as with domestic reforms, he was lucky to be operating in a **favourable economic climate**. In 1664, he founded the East India and West India companies, and later the Levant (1670) and Northern (1669) companies. Again royal capital subsidised such ventures, and new trade routes were built up. Most notably the West Indies proved to be a valuable source of sugar and by the 1680s more than 200 French ships were operating on this route:

- West coast ports such as Bordeaux and La Rochelle began to prosper and private enterprise became a more attractive proposition for entrepreneurs.
- The number of individual merchants trading overseas doubled between 1664 and 1704. Overall, however, such trading ventures were a failure and most of the companies failed to outlive Colbert.

Nevertheless, Colbert had once again given the stimulus for progression and offered the lead in the form of state subsidy. Future companies such as that formed in 1698 for trade with China proved more successful and some credit has to be given to Colbert for these future developments. Nevertheless, in comparison with well-established Dutch and English rivals, French overseas companies had fallen short of the mark. Indeed, it became increasingly clear that French commerce could only expand at the expense of the Dutch.

The French navy

Colbert quickly recognised that the promotion of overseas trade depended upon an increase in the size of the navy. New forests were planted and the Ordinance des Eaux et Forêts of 1609 ensured that future resources would be conserved. Toulon and Brest were developed as dockyards and naval arsenals were established in these ports. Consequently, demands for iron stimulated a growth in related industries. Maritime conscription combined with foreign sailors provided Colbert with a large naval personnel that could compete with the major Protestant maritime powers. Indeed, by 1677, the French navy was the largest in the Mediterranean. The rationale behind naval expansion was practical and aggressive: if France was to challenge the Netherlands and England in foreign trade and establish new markets, a powerful navy was essential.

Mercantilism

The term **mercantilism** is one often used to describe Colbert's economic policies. With the circulation of money limited, the basis of Colbert's mercantilist outlook was bullion reserves. His vision depended upon the increase in bullion and exports to the benefit of the state. This mercantilist outlook certainly stimulated French industry and promoted trade but simultaneously undermined his domestic rehabilitation of French finances. The primary reason for this was that Colbert's priority increasingly became the defeat of the Dutch. Tariff wars began in 1664 and in 1667 duties on textiles were doubled. Ultimately, mercantilism led to a French declaration of war on the Netherlands in 1672, a war that did little to harm Dutch superiority but much to increase state expenditure in France.

RELIGION

Protestantism

One of the main charges brought against Louis XIV was his decision to destroy French Protestantism by **revoking the Edict of Nantes** (1598). Louis was determined to invoke the principle enshrined at the Religious Peace of Augsburg in 1555, namely *cuius regio eius religio*. One can see why Louis wanted the Huguenots to conform; as the Most Christian King it was his duty to stamp out heresy and promote the glory of his rule through Catholicism. Yet the Huguenots had proved extremely loyal to the crown, even during the Fronde, and they were an important part of the industrial growth that France was experiencing. The timing of Louis' persecution of the Huguenots lay in the personal life of the king and France's standing within Europe.

KEY TERM

Mercantilism Mercantilism entailed an economic system in which trade was promoted as a means of acquiring gold bullion. The promotion of trade necessarily entailed defeating one's enemies and establishing trade routes and markets. State intervention also played a crucial role in promoting domestic industry and protecting production.

KEY THEME

Impact of the Edict of Nantes, 1598 The edict was born out of the French Wars of Religion and, while its long-term aim had been unity, the edict had served to create a committed but loyal Huguenot minority in the Midi. The edict essentially protected this Protestant minority as it recognised their right to worship and offered basic civil rights.

KEY CONCEPT

'Cuius regio eius religio' 'The religion of a country is that of its prince'. It was therefore the responsibility of the prince to decide upon the faith of his subjects. This principle was established at the Religious Peace of Augsburg in 1555. Louis was determined to stand by his coronation oath and rule over a kingdom united in faith and loyal to its ruler.

Were Colbert's policies a success or failure?

- Colbert's great achievement was in reforming a financial system that had ceased to benefit the crown in terms of revenue. Obstructions and privileges remained, but on the whole speculators were made aware of their loyalties to the crown and royal authority over tax collection was greatly enhanced. Colbert was pragmatic, recognising where accumulated old debts just had to be written off and levying the *taille* at an affordable rate.

- Colbert's economic expansion had mixed results in terms of trade and industry. He failed to break the Dutch stranglehold on trade and overseas enterprise. Tariff wars did more harm to the French than the Dutch, while Dutch overseas colonies were well established and able to undercut French goods and corner the specific market. The Dutch War (1672–8) did much to destroy the financial recovery initiated by Colbert, and plunged the economy into debt once again.

- State intervention proved unpopular at a provincial level, and many local merchants failed to share in Colbert's national vision. Local tariff barriers remained and guilds protected their own privileges. Regulations were often ignored as merchants looked to make increased profits for themselves rather than the crown. Local taxpayers resented paying for Colbert's construction projects such as the Canal des Deux Mers linking Bordeaux to the Mediterranean. While Colbert's outlook was national, the merchants' was often local.

- Colbert was also dealing with a merchant and noble class stuck in their ways. The French nobility, unlike the Dutch, took a snobbish view of mercantile activity, and were reluctant to invest in Colbert's schemes. The reservations and self-interest of a nobility under pressure from Colbert is understandable. Age-old issues of status, hierarchy and class would not disappear, and this put France at a disadvantage against the Dutch.

- Finally, Colbert invested heavily in luxury industries and trading companies to the detriment of agriculture. The lowered *taille* gave no excuse for evasion, and the ordinary peasant benefited little from Colbert's reforms. The Dutch War put extra fiscal pressures on the peasantry and the serious Breton revolt of 1675 was testament to the crippling effect of that conflict on local economies.

- By 1680, Louis was increasingly manipulated by the devout and pious **Madame de Maintenon** who was eager to persuade him of the error of his ways in allowing a Huguenot minority to exist.
- Following the end of the Dutch War with the Peace of Nijmegen (1678–9), Louis was in a position to turn his attentions to his own kingdom and demonstrate his own orthodoxy to Innocent XI.

The terms of the Edict of Nantes upholding Catholic values were enforced with growing strictness. Huguenot schools were closed down, professional jobs were closed to non-Catholics and financial incentives were even offered to Protestants to convert to Catholicism. Pressure was increased on Huguenot populations. Royal troops drawn from the dregs of French society were billeted on Huguenot households in Poitou. The aim was clear: the soldiers were to enforce conversion using any means at their disposal. Toleration of Huguenots within the edict was regularly flouted. The rate of conversions rose and Louis was further encouraged by the accession of the Catholic James II to the English throne.

Finally Louis was eager to make an explicit demonstration of his orthodoxy to Pope Innocent XI. **Louis' relations with the papacy** had been distinctly strained since 1675 when Louis sought to extend his traditional right of *regale* which allowed the king to administer vacant bishoprics and take the revenue from them. In 1682, with Franco-papal relations worsening, Louis published the Gallican Articles which stated in law the privileges and rights of the French king over the church as outlined in the Concordat of Bologna (1516). In 1683, Louis refused to join a crusade against the Ottoman Turks and consequently it was left to Emperor Leopold I to relieve Vienna from the threat of the Infidel. Louis was therefore keen to demonstrate French orthodoxy to the rest of Europe and, spurred on by Madame de Maintenon, the **Edict of Fontainebleau** was signed in October 1685.

KEY PERSON

Madame de Maintenon (1635–1719) The king's mistress and later secret wife (1684) wrote in 1679 that 'Louis confesses his weaknesses and recognises his faults.' More worryingly for the Huguenots, she added, 'We must now wait for the spirit of grace to reveal itself.'

KEY THEME

Louis's relations with the papacy Papal authority over appointments to bishoprics had for a long time been little more than theoretical, and now Louis reminded Innocent in no uncertain terms of the independent traditions of the Gallican church over which he presided.

KEY EVENT

The Edict of Fontainebleau, 1685 Annulled and replaced that of Nantes, proscribing the practice of the Protestant religion. Huguenot ministers were to convert or go into exile while all remaining Huguenot schools and churches were to close. The death penalty awaited anyone that defied the edict. A century of Huguenot culture and history was wiped out.

Destruction of Protestantism

Successive French kings in the second half of the sixteenth century had looked for ways of exterminating heresy from the realm. Over three decades of religious wars had not resolved the issue. Yet Protestantism was an entirely different prospect in the 1680s to the aggressive and arrogant movement of the 1560s buoyed by noble and foreign support. Louis achieved his aim. **Huguenot emigration** totalled about 200,000 people: approximately 10 per cent of the Huguenot population left the country in the decades following 1685. Many fled to the United Provinces, England or Brandenburg where they could worship freely. It can be argued that Louis' persecution of the Huguenots weakened the economy in the late seventeenth century. Entrepreneurs, industrialists and craftsmen took their skills elsewhere. Moreover Louis did not entirely succeed in wiping out Protestant worship in France:

- Many Huguenots continued to worship in secret and in the outlying provinces open worship took place.
- In 1702, a Protestant rebellion broke out in the mountains of the Cévennes in south-eastern France. It was known as the revolt of the Camisards, and it proved to be an embarrassment for Louis XIV. The king was forced to send a royal army under one of his leading generals, Marshal Villars, to suppress the rising, and even then the rebels held out until 1710.

Jansenism

The Catholic doctrine of **Jansenism** came from Cornelius Jansen, bishop of Ypres. Bishop Jansen was greatly influenced by the writings of St Augustine and put great emphasis upon the omnipotence of God. He viewed Jesuit doctrine as weak and asserted that man could only achieve salvation through the acquisition of divine grace. Such grace was bestowed only on a few and the rest were destined for damnation. Followers included the nuns of the Cistercian convent of Port Royal in Paris, and its sister house of Port Royal des Champs near Versailles adopted Jansen's ideas. Under the influence of the Arnauld family, Port Royal emerged as the headquarters of Jansenism.

KEY EVENT

Huguenot emigration Just how damaging the loss of Huguenot labour and technical expertise was is debatable. France was bound to suffer economic stagnation and depression anyway given the pressures of war, although the loss of this workforce did not help matters.

KEY CONCEPT

Jansenism Jansen's doctrine resembled that of Luther and indeed Calvin in places, although Jansenism was portrayed as a Catholic teaching. Jansenism was taken up by a committed minority attracted by its austere and rather pessimistic outlook.

Louis XIV came to detest Jansenism for a number of reasons:

- Jansenists were nonconformists. Unity in religion underpinned the French monarchy, so Jansenism undermined the principles upon which Louis' monarchy rested.
- Jansenism had political overtones of disloyalty as the Cardinal of Retz, the Prince of Conti and the Duchess of Longueville were all implicated in the Fronde while at the same time were sympathetic towards Jansenism.
- Jansenists explicitly rejected the hierarchy and wealth of Louis' court and scorned the magnificence of Versailles.

Those at Port Royal laid an emphasis upon the influence of ordinary priests in church government and a democratic spirit that was the opposite of the order that Louis was looking to impose upon his kingdom. On a spiritual and secular level, the Jansenists undermined Louis' kingship.

Louis XIV and Jansenism

Throughout the 1650s, papal bulls had condemned aspects of Jansenist doctrine as heretical. Antoine Arnauld had been expelled from the Sorbonne while a series of devotional texts had been outlawed. Worryingly also for Louis was the fact that Port Royal attracted important intellectuals such as **Blaise Pascal** and Jean Racine:

- Schools attached to the convent at Port Royal were closed down but an all-out attack was put off in 1661 as a number of French bishops doubted the authority of papal condemnation of Jansenist doctrine in the context of Gallican liberties.
- A truce was eventually agreed brokered by Pope Clement IX in 1668, known as the Peace of the Church. Little had changed, however; Louis remained hostile to the existence of the Jansenists and the king's cause was not helped by the election of **Innocent XI** in 1676.
- In 1679, after the Peace of Nijmegen Louis forbade confessors and novices from residing at Port Royal and in 1681 called a general assembly of the French church.

KEY PEOPLE

Blaise Pascal (1623–62) A brilliant mathematician, physicist and theologian. He is credited with the invention of a calculating machine and later the barometer. Pascal's sister was a member of Port Royal and he even wrote a defence of Jansenism entitled *Lettres Provinciales* (1656–7) which was promptly denounced by the government.

Innocent XI, 1676–89 Innocent admired the morality of the Port Royal Jansenists and as the argument with Louis over the *regale* (royal prerogative to take income from vacant bishoprics) intensified so the Jansenist controversy once more came to the surface.

The result was the Gallican Articles, designed to strengthen the liberties of the Gallican church. While the struggle with Rome went on Jansenism was put to one side.

- The death of Innocent XI in 1689 and election of Innocent XII paved the way for more amicable relations between the French crown and the papacy. Louis withdrew the Gallican Articles and was in a position to attain papal approval for an attack on Jansenism.

- The attack came in 1692 when a text called *Moral Reflections on the New Testament* appeared, written by Pasquier Quesnel, a Jansenist priest. In 1705, Clement issued the bull *Vineam Domini* condemning aspects of Jansenist doctrine relating to Augustine.

- The nuns at Port Royal insisted on reservations refusing to accept the bull without qualification. Eventually Louis was moved to expel the nuns of Port Royal by a council decree of 1709 and followed this up with the complete destruction of Port Royal des Champs in order to prevent it becoming a place of pilgrimage.

- In 1713, the bull *Unigenitus* condemned Jansenist teachings and Louis insisted that this papal declaration be adhered to and observed.

KEY THEME

Unigenitus The archbishop of Paris was joined by other Gallican militants in denouncing the bull as another example of papal imperialism. Louis banished them to their sees and ordered that the bull stand. In doing so, Louis shifted from being one of the staunchest defenders of Gallicanism to a staunch defender of the papacy. Louis's determination to overcome Jansenism had made him dependent upon the very power that he had sought for so long to exclude from French affairs.

SUMMARY QUESTIONS

1. How successful was Colbert in stimulating industry and promoting trade?

2. What purpose did Versailles serve for Louis XIV?

3. How successful was Louis XIV in his religious policy?

4. How far was Louis' power based on image and patronage?

CHAPTER 11

Louis XIV and foreign policy, 1661–1715

National security; **La gloire**; the Spanish succession; domination of Europe; commercial interests; peace; religion – all could be put forward as the motivating factors behind Louis' foreign policy. Indeed, over such a long period of rule, 1661–1715, priorities were bound to shift and Louis had to adapt to new circumstances. Also many of the factors became interlinked as Louis aimed to maintain security and pursue a glorious inheritance for his successors:

- Initially, French diplomacy operated on similar lines to those laid down by Richelieu and Mazarin. The War of Devolution against Spain (1667–8) demonstrated that Louis continued to view Spain as the major threat in Europe.

La gloire Louis's pursuit of *La gloire* is seen by the historian François Bluche as the primary justification for French foreign policy. French reputation, prowess, status and integrity could only be bolstered by promoting French power abroad. The lure of the Spanish succession lay behind many of Louis's foreign-policy initiatives.

The destruction of Port Royal des Champs

- By 1670, there was a shift in French foreign policy as the power of Spain declined. The Protestant maritime powers of England and the Netherlands now became the major enemies of France.
- Hostilities with the Dutch became inevitable for a number of reasons. Louis XIV perceived the Dutch to be ungrateful for French support against the Spanish during their long struggle for independence. The Dutch had even joined the Triple Alliance against France during the War of Devolution in 1668. Moreover, the Dutch were a major obstacle to French commercial interests, and even Colbert seemed to recognise that only by defeating the Netherlands in war would France open up new trade routes. Finally, the Stadholder of the Netherlands, William of Orange, became king of England in 1688 thus altering the balance of power once again.

Louis' chief occupation was foreign policy and his primary goal was to maintain the security of his state. Inevitably, he had to be reactive and opportunistic to adjust to the changing European environment and circumstances. Louis was concerned with defending French frontiers to the north-west and east, thus consolidating gains made at Westphalia (1648) and the Pyrenees (1659), as well as expanding into the southern Netherlands and towards the Rhine.

The War of Devolution, 1667–8

The balance of power was shifted in France's favour with the death of Philip IV of Spain in September 1665. He was succeeded by his 5-year-old son, Charles II. The **Spanish Empire** was still vast despite its declining fortunes in the 1640s and 1650s. The boy king was weak and there was a distinct possibility that he might die leaving no heirs. Still surrounded by Habsburg territories Louis began to prepare his own claim to the Spanish succession:

- Louis and his team of legal advisers paved the way with careful manipulation of the domestic law of the Spanish Netherlands that stated the children of a first marriage took precedence over those of a second. Charles II was a product of Philip IV's second marriage while Louis' own claim rested on his descent from Philip II and his

---

KEY THEME

Spanish Empire Milan, Naples and Sicily were all ruled by Spain; to the east of France, Franche-Comté was a Spanish possession; to the north-east lay the Spanish Netherlands.

marriage to Philip IV's daughter. It was on Maria Theresa, the elder half-sister of Charles, that Louis rested his hopes of **devolution**. The prize was potentially the entire Spanish Netherlands.

- Le Tellier and his son Louvois were ordered to amass a large army, and in 1669 an invasion of the Spanish Netherlands was launched. French military superiority soon began to tell and a number of gains were made. Indeed, it was well within the capabilities of the French to seize all of the Spanish Netherlands but mediation from the Triple Alliance persuaded Louis to back off and focus his attentions on Franche-Comté.
- The Treaty of Aix-la-Chapelle (1668) saw France acquire the fortresses of Tournai and Charleroi, both of which were in the Spanish Netherlands.
- Yet even more importantly for Louis was the secret partition treaty that he signed with the Holy Roman Emperor Leopold I in January 1668. In the event of Charles II dying without heirs France was to attain the Spanish Netherlands, Franche-Comté and Spanish Navarre as well as Naples and Sicily. This represented a remarkable concession by Leopold, as it explicitly recognised the legitimacy of the Bourbon claim to the succession. Louis had given up Franche-Comté despite its occupation by Condé in return for strengthening French presence in the north-east and with a guarantee of future spoils if Charles II died young.

The Dutch War, 1672–9

The newly acquired French territories in Flanders made the Dutch increasingly suspicious of French interests in the Netherlands, and the formation of the Triple Alliance illustrated how wary the Dutch were of Louis XIV. From Louis' perspective the Dutch had replaced the Spanish as the number one enemy of the French.

- Louis hated the commercialism of the United Provinces which together with Dutch republicanism and Calvinism stood in stark contrast to Louis' France.
- Louis believed the Dutch were ungrateful for his support of their struggle against the Spanish, and his declaration of war on England in 1665. The Treaty of Aix-la-Chapelle had been rather forced on Louis by the **Triple Alliance**,

and Louis disliked the idea of anyone dictating terms to him with an implicit threat of force in the background.

- Above all else, Louis coveted the Spanish Netherlands in order to bolster the north-eastern frontier once and for all. National security was the overriding motivation behind Louis' declaration of war on the Dutch, as he knew that his designs on the southern Netherlands would not be met favourably by the United Provinces.
- Even Colbert agreed with war in 1672 because he recognised that future economic growth depended on annihilating the Dutch. Tariff wars had already severely disrupted trade between the two countries.

In 1672, French armies crossed the Rhine via Liège and entered the Dutch republic. Louis had already secured English neutrality thus isolating the Dutch diplomatically. A French army of 100,000 men, led by Louis himself, quickly carried all before them. Arnhem was captured, followed by Utrecht and the way seemed open to Amsterdam. The Dutch States General sued for Peace, offering generous terms including the secession of Maastrict. Such terms would have allowed the French to attack the southern Netherlands from north and south, but Louis refused, intent on an unconditional surrender that might bring further lands in the United Provinces.

Nevertheless, the French had moved quickly, and outpaced their supply lines. Also their situation was not helped by the fact that the Dutch had flooded the countryside in order to defend Holland. The newly installed stadholder of Holland was William of Orange, who immediately called upon European assistance against the French threat.

- In 1672, the Emperor and the Elector of Brandenburg joined the Dutch, and were followed by Spain and Lorraine the following year; all of their interests were affected by French supremacy in Europe. Still French victories under the brilliant Turenne were forthcoming against the combined forces of the anti-French coalition.
- In 1674, Charles II abandoned the secret Treaty of Dover (1670) and withdrew from the war, leaving France to fight it alone. Valenciennes, Cambrai and Saint Omer were all captured in Flanders but at great

cost both in terms of lives and livres. Franche-Comté was annexed from Spain in 1674, but stretched resources and Dutch resistance forced Louis to the negotiating table in 1676.

Two more years of fighting ensued before the **Peace of Nijmegen** was signed in 1678. Despite territorial gains the original objective of the war had not been achieved. The Dutch were undefeated and France even had to return Maastricht as well as rescind Colbert's harsh tariff law of 1667. Louis realised that the Netherlands could not be forced to give up large amounts of territory and that his ambitions in the Spanish Netherlands and to the east were always likely to unite the powers of Europe against him. Nevertheless, Louis had taken advantage of an exhausted Spain at Nijmegen and made substantial gains in the process.

The Nine Years' War, 1689–97

Thus far Louis was concerned with national security, aiming to block off potential routes of invasion into the kingdom. The fortresses in the north-east acquired at Nijmegen and the purchase of Dunkirk in 1662 from Charles II of England are two good examples of this defensive strategy. After 1679, Louis turned his attention towards the eastern frontier, already bolstered by the acquisition of Franche-Comté. *Chambres de réunions* were established in order to return favourable decisions on Louis' right to annex important frontier territories in the east. All of these territories were insecure frontier regions that had nominally come under French jurisdiction at one time or another since Westphalia. The reunions gave Louis the legitimacy he wanted to occupy and govern these territories:

- Alsace had been rather ambiguously ceded to France at Westphalia in 1648, but after the reunion it came under effective royal control.
- Strasbourg had always been kept out of French hands, so a reunion would do little to advance Louis' claims here. Instead French troops occupied the city in 1681, much to the horror of Leopold I.

KEY EVENT

Peace of Nijmegen, 1678–9 The French gains made at Aix-la-Chapelle were recognised, and the key fortresses of Condé, Valenciennes, Ypres and Saint Omer were acquired from Spain. All were strategically situated along the frontier between France and the Spanish Netherlands. Moreover, Spain also ceded Franche-Comté in the east.

KEY TERM

Chambres de réunions These special courts gave a quasi-legal backing to Louis's actions and allowed him to reunite Metz, Toul and Verdun to his heritage in December 1679. Further reunions were set up at Breisach (Alsace), Tournai (Flanders) and Besançon (Franche-Comté).

KEY EVENT

The Truce of Ratisbon
Intended to last for twenty years, during which time French control over Lorraine, Strasbourg, Luxembourg and the reunion territories was to be observed.

KEY THEME

Louis' rivals Charles II of England was reluctant to intervene in foreign affairs, William of Orange could not persuade the United Provinces to go to war against France while the emperor had only just managed to resist a Turkish attack on Vienna.

Further military expeditions into the Spanish Netherlands eventually provoked Spain into a declaration of war in 1682 but without Imperial support it lost Luxembourg to Vauban's army. The policy of reunions backed by military force where necessary had proved very successful. Louis had consolidated territories, acquired new ones and had not incurred the major expenses of a long conflict in the process. In 1684, both Spain and the Emperor agreed to the **Truce of Ratisbon.** The defensive strategy appeared to have reached its conclusion with the eastern and north-eastern borders secure from invasion. Ratisbon marked a high point in Louis' foreign policy and, while he had shown some diplomatic skill and no little military presence in securing the favourable peace, we must also look at the weak state of **Louis' rivals**.

Opposition grows

Although Louis' concerns may primarily have been defensive, his outlook appeared aggressive to the rest of Europe. A city such as Strasbourg may well have been an important eastern frontier territory and a buffer against invasion but it was also a gateway to the Danube and Vienna. Therefore, what could be portrayed as defensive strategy on the one hand could also be viewed as aggressive on the other. The Emperor, Spain and the Netherlands would look to redress the balance. The revocation of the Edict of Nantes (1685) united Protestant opposition to Louis and the prospect of a grand anti-French coalition drew closer:

- In 1686, the rulers of Saxony and the Palatinate joined with Spain and the emperor in the League of Augsburg, established to warn Louis from further territorial acquisitions on the eastern frontier.
- Leopold was buoyed by recent victories over the Turks, and Imperial armies were growing in experience and strength. Louis paid the League little attention, however, sure of French military superiority, and knowing that if this alliance was a real threat then he would have to strengthen the eastern frontier even further.
- It was to this end that Louis turned his attentions towards the Electorate of Cologne and the fortress of Phillipsburg, both of which were situated in the

Rhineland. Cologne was of critical strategic importance both as a defensive bulwark against attack from northern Germany and as an offensive base from which to strike the Dutch republic.

Cologne

The opportunity to press French claims in Cologne came in 1688 when the Archbishop-Elector died. The deceased archbishop had allowed Louis to use Liege as a French base in the previous Dutch War.

- Even before the archbishop's death, Louis had organised his successor, namely Cardinal Fürstenberg, bishop of Strasbourg and of course loyal to Louis XIV.
- Yet Pope Innocent XI had other ideas. Franco-Papal relations were at a real low over Louis' attempts to further royal power over the church in France at the expense of Rome. The Pope refused to allow Fürstenberg to become archbishop of Cologne, instead conferring the post on a brother of the elector of Bavaria who was loyal to William of Orange and the emperor.
- Consequently, Louis ordered a French army to march into Cologne and then across the Palatinate to Phillipsburg.
- As in the War of Devolution, Louis possessed a claim to the Palatinate through his sister-in-law the duchess of Orleans who was sister to the late elector. The claim was relatively weak, however, and Louis' main aim was to take the fortress and protect Alsace in the process. Phillipsburg fell to the French in October 1688, although it became increasingly clear that the German princes were not going to allow Louis to pick off frontier territories one by one.

The Nine Years' War had begun with the fall of Phillipsburg and with William of Orange lately installed as king of England, the prospects for Louis became increasingly gloomy. England and the Dutch Republic naturally joined the League of Augsburg in an alliance that grew more threatening by the day. Louis, recognising the Netherlands to be the major threat, ordered a retreat from the Palatinate. The order included a **scorched earth policy** to deprive enemy armies of resources and at the same time offer a show of destructive force to the German princes.

French victories in the Nine Years' War were more numerous than those of the allies, although crucially the **Grand Alliance of Vienna** had gained control of the sea after a decisive victory off The Hague:

- The ensuing blockade of France brought famine to some parts of the kingdom.
- Modest French victories at Fleurus (1690), Beachy Head (1690), Steenkirk (1692) and Marseilles (1693) did little to ease a domestic situation exacerbated by bad harvests.

In 1695, William recaptured Namur, a town captured by the French in the early throes of the conflict. With the French economy near breaking point and with no outright victory in sight, Louis came to terms with the allies at the Peace of Ryswick (1697). At the heart of Louis' willingness to compromise, however, lay the Spanish succession. Charles II had somehow lived into the 1690s but it became clear that he was going to die shortly and certainly childless.

The issue of the Spanish succession

Louis XIV was willing to negotiate another partition treaty regarding the Spanish inheritance in 1698, probably in a bid to avert another war. The **First Partition Treaty** drawn up by England, France and the emperor was an attempt peacefully to split up the Spanish inheritance among the various claimants. News of the treaty was soon leaked to Spain, who had not been consulted over the division of its lands. Charles II was furious and decided that all his possessions would go to the young Prince Joseph. However, in 1699, the prince of Bavaria died, aged only 7 years old, negating both the First Partition Treaty and the desires of Charles II. A **Second Partition Treaty** was signed in 1700. William III accepted the proposals, but Leopold did not, preferring to advance his own claims to the Spanish succession. Relations between the Austrian and Spanish branch of the Habsburg family had steadily declined over the course of the late seventeenth century, and Charles II left in his will the entire Spanish

KEY EVENTS

Grand Alliance of Vienna
This anti-French alliance was made up of the Dutch, the empire, Brandenburg, Spain, England and Bavaria. The numerical odds were stacked against France, although unity and effective leadership would compensate for this.

First Partition Treaty, 1698
Gave Spain, the Spanish Netherlands, Sardinia and America to the electoral prince of Bavaria, Joseph Ferdinand. He was grandson of the emperor and his Spanish wife. Leopold's second son, the Archduke Charles was to receive Milan, while Louis XIV's heir, the dauphin, would take Naples and Sicily as well as Guipuzcoa in the Basque country.

Second Partition Treaty, 1700 The Archduke Charles would acquire Spain, America and the Netherlands while the dauphin would get Naples, Sicily and Lorraine. The duke of Lorraine, as compensation for the loss of his duchy, would take Milan. Such an exchange demonstrated Louis's wishes to fortify the eastern frontier at the expense of lands in Italy.

succession to Louis XIV's second grandson Philippe, Duke of Anjou.

The succession On 1 November 1700, Charles II died and Louis now had to decide whether to accept the validity of the will or not:

- There was no guarantee that, once installed, Philippe would rule in the interests of France while the partition treaty gave quick territorial gains to France that might be more beneficial in the short term.
- In reality, Louis had little option but to accept the validity of the will as the immediate alternative to Philippe as stated in the testament was the Archduke Charles. In light of Leopold's rejection of the Second Partition Treaty, Louis was well aware of Habsburg ambitions in Spain. Louis had always believed in his **family's claim to the Spanish succession** and now was the time to collect.

Louis' acceptance of the will was always likely to provoke hostilities with Leopold at some stage, yet the French king's next action was to revive the Grand Alliance. England and the United Provinces had already recognised Philippe as Philip V of Spain when Louis passed a decree through the *parlements* of Paris stating the hereditary order of succession to the crown. In doing so, Louis proclaimed his grandson's right to the French succession as well as that of Spain. To his rivals it seemed as if Louis was paving the way for French domination in Europe. Added to this rather unnecessary antagonism was the fact that Louis also ordered French troops to take over the Dutch barrier fortresses in the southern Netherlands. Louis claimed to be acting as his son's regent for the southern Netherlands but such actions were always likely to rile the Dutch who had long feared a French presence on their southern frontier. As a result of Louis' actions, Europe once more mobilised for a war of Spanish succession in 1701.

The war The combined forces of France and Spain were formidable, but resources were stretched over four fronts:

KEY THEME

Louis and the succession
Louis probably never envisaged that the crowns of France and Spain would be united under one ruler, instead believing that the Orleans branch of the family would acquire Spain if Philippe should inherit the French crown.

Castilians and Catalans
Castilians come from the central region of Spain known as Castile. Catalans come from Catalonia.

Marlborough Marlborough was a great military leader who coordinated activities well both with Prince Eugene of Savoy and Anton Heinsius, leader of the United Provinces after the death of William III in 1702.

- In Italy, French forces were put on the defensive by the Imperial army commanded by Prince Eugene, suffering a major defeat outside Turin in 1706.
- In Spain, things went much better for Louis. To the **Castilians**, Philip V was the rightful monarch and they rallied to his cause. The fact that the Archduke Charles was supported by Protestants and the **Catalans** made the choice much easier.
- In the Low Countries, Louis' armies came up against the commander of the Anglo-Dutch forces John Churchill, **Duke of Marlborough**, whose greatest contribution came not in the Netherlands but in Bavaria. In 1704, a combined Franco-Bavarian army under Tallard was destroyed at the Battle of Blenheim (on the Danube). Tallard was captured and the elector left Bavaria for the Netherlands. France had lost not only a significant battle, but also its only German ally.
- Marlborough turned his attentions back to the Netherlands and in 1705 he broke through French defences to take Brabant and, despite the procrastination of the Estates General, Marlborough inflicted another serious defeat on the French at Ramillies in 1706.
- By 1706, Brabant, Flanders, Louvain, Brussels, Ghent and Antwerp all fell to the allies. The Archduke Charles was recognised as sovereign by the Estates of Brabant and Flanders, both of which were relieved to get rid of French rule that had already eroded local privileges and tax exemptions. To many of the Flemish nobility the Anglo-Dutch alliance was preferable to the French on political grounds alone. Marlborough had essentially succeeded in uniting the Netherlands although a permanent reunification was unlikely given the political and economic differences between the two states of north and south.
- In May 1708, Louis' armies suffered their final humiliation in the Netherlands, a crushing defeat at Oudenarde at the hands of Marlborough and Eugene. Marlborough wanted to push on and invade north-western France, yet the Dutch remained obsessed with their own security and in particular the fortress barrier on the southern frontier that they did not want to leave unguarded. The allies instead laid siege to Lille, the fortifications of which had been designed by Vauban.

Consequently the town held out for over six months in 1608, and when it finally capitulated in December the opportunity for an invasion of France had gone.

- In the spring of 1709, the campaigning season got under way again, and the allies were soon on the offensive capturing Tournai and laying siege to Mons. The decisive battle came at Malplaquet, north of Mauberge. The threat of a major allied invasion stirred French patriotism and, under the command of the recently recalled Villars, the French troops inflicted massive casualties on the coalition forces. The French withdrew and gave up Mons, but once more any plans to invade Paris had to be shelved.

Despite such heroics Louis recognised that peace had to be made sooner rather than later in order to preserve national security and relieve the enormous strain on his people.

Peace

Peace was realistically the only long-term solution for Louis, and in the preliminary negotiations of 1709 Louis showed himself willing to give up Ypres, Menin, Furnes, Condé and Lille in the Netherlands as well as Strasbourg in Alsace. Moreover, Louis agreed that he would remove French troops from Spain. The allies did not trust Louis to give up his conquests, and insisted upon the removal of Philip V from Spain. The aims and objectives of Louis' foreign policy lay in the balance. The concept of Bourbon control over the Spanish Empire and secure eastern frontiers would have been destroyed in 1709 were it not for Castilian support for Philip V. The preliminary agreement required Louis to take up arms against his grandson if Philip resisted the terms of agreement and refused to abdicate. A settlement in Spain in favour of the Archduke Charles was a central part of the peace process. With many of the frontier fortresses already lost, Louis' position looked weak, yet he could not surrender unconditionally to the allies:

- In December 1710, a small French force with Castilian backing defeated the troops of the self-proclaimed Charles III at Viciosa, leaving Philip V as ruler of Spain once again. In the context of Bourbon-led Spanish

KEY THEMES

Continuation of war Louis wrote to his provincial governors in 1710, urging them to support his continued war against the allies, emphasising that their demands of unconditional surrender would endanger French national security. The war may be one that Louis had little chance of winning, and was certainly one that would cause further hardships for his people, but it was one that had to be fought.

Peace negotiations The key sticking point was again the status of Philip in Spain and France. Ultimately, Philip agreed to renounce all claims to the French throne in return for remaining king of Spain.

revival, Louis had little option but **the continuation of war**.

- The allies had missed their chance to impose a peace settlement on Louis as their demands were too extreme and unreasonable. Indeed, the Dutch had been willing to accept Louis' concessions in 1709, but it was the English that insisted upon Charles III being installed in Spain.
- On the death of Emperor Joseph I in 1711, Charles was elected to take his place and after this date it appeared that the allies were fighting for a return to Habsburg domination of Europe.
- Therefore despite Marlborough's continuing military successes in 1711 that threatened Paris, the new Tory government in England shifted policy towards one of achieving peace. Marlborough was withdrawn and the French army under Villars won a crucial victory at Denain (1712). **Peace negotiations** got under way.

Utrecht, 1713

At the Peace of Utrecht, France was allowed to keep Alsace, including Strasbourg, as well as the ring of fortresses on the Netherlands frontier namely Mauberge, Condé and Lille. The emperor acquired the Spanish Netherlands, Naples and Sardinia. The duke of Savoy took Sicily while the Dutch lost out. The barrier on the southern frontier which had guided their foreign policy over the past decade was maintained but the fortresses given to France severely weakened it. Considering that they ended up on the winning side, the Dutch gained little. Although they could hardly keep fighting on their own, the Dutch resented the concessions given to France at Utrecht and felt betrayed by their ally England which made commercial gains out of the treaty at the expense of the Dutch.

Louis had lost the southern Netherlands and much of Italy to the Austrian Habsburgs, although he had maintained the fortress defences. His grandson was also undisputedly king of Spain and the Indies. When one considers what terms may have been imposed on Louis in 1709 and what he himself was willing to concede, he appears to have salvaged a great deal from Utrecht.

The consequence of war for the third estate

The glory of Louis XIV's foreign policy came at the cost of his people, particularly the peasantry who suffered enormously under the continual pressure of heavy taxation and scarcity of resources. Poor harvests combined with defeat abroad and war weariness led to a number of revolts:

- The controller-general in 1709 wrote that troops had been needed in nearly every province to keep them under control.
- Certainly Louis was not to blame for the natural disasters that occurred in these years such as the great winter of 1708–9 or the bovine epidemic of 1714, but there is little doubt that his foreign policy exacerbated the situation. Louis viewed insurgents as traitors who were holding back his dynastic ambitions. A militia was formed in 1688 to guard grain convoys and enforce hated taxation such as the *gabelle*.
- In May 1675 the peasant community of Brittany revolted against high taxation and overmighty landlords. The Dutch War had severely damaged Brittany's trade and the conflict had increased taxation demands. The government was forced to recall troops from the front in order to crush the revolt. Thousands were executed and 10,000 troops were billeted on the population as a result of the uprising.
- That same year, a smaller yet still significant rising took place in Bordeaux against the *papier timbre* and *marque d'etain*. As a consequence of the riots the town lost its tax privileges altogether and had troops billeted on it throughout the winter. It was clear that Louis would not stand for such behaviour, although he could not prevent future risings such as the revolt of the Camisards (1702–5) further afield.
- In 1707, the Tard Avises of Quercy rose in opposition to proposed taxation on births. The revolt was easily crushed by the royal dragoons, and such shows of force generally appear to have subdued the rebels into submission.

Nevertheless, Louis left France heavily in debt, with trade and agriculture in decline, and a fiscal system that was entirely unfair. Throughout Louis' reign it was the **third** estate that shouldered the burden of Louis' building projects and foreign policy both in terms of lives lost and money. Hundreds died in the construction of Versailles and despite the introduction of the capitation and the *dixieme* towards the end of Louis' reign it was still the peasantry that funded Louis' foreign conflicts.

Was Louis XIV's foreign policy a success or failure?

- The Truce of Ratisbon (1684) marked a high point for Louis's foreign policy, as eastern and north-eastern frontiers were secured.
- After Ratisbon, Louis's foreign policy became less aggressive as he sought to hold on to what he had acquired through aggression, reunions and diplomacy.
- French expansion into the empire and towards the southern Netherlands inevitably united opposition as shown by the League of Augsburg and the Grand Alliance. The opposition was united in its mistrust of Louis XIV. Maritime propaganda also focused on his persecution of Protestants after 1685, portraying Louis as an ideological threat. The imposition of Catholicism on Strasbourg was further evidence of this increasingly *dévots* line.
- Louis was capable of shrewd and skilful diplomacy. He used legal precedents and backing to pave the way for the War of Devolution, justifying his aggression in the process. The reunions were a triumph, exploiting as they did the ambiguities of Westphalia and securing German frontier land.
- Louis was also able to extract favourable terms from less than favourable circumstances. Stalemate over the Netherlands moved Louis to exploit Spanish weaknesses at Nijmegen in 1679 to acquire towns in the Spanish Netherlands. Again at Utrecht in 1713, Louis was able to follow up a welcome victory at Denain with terms that hardly reflected the weak state of France.
- Louis was also capable of making disastrous decisions such as his reluctance to agree peace terms with the Dutch in 1672, instead committing France to a further six years of warfare. The reunions antagonised German princes and the devastation of the Palatinate in 1688

stirred German patriotism and stiffened the resolve of the League of Augsburg to defeat Louis. Finally, in 1701 Louis' decision to take on the role as regent of the Spanish Netherlands and expel Dutch troops from frontier fortresses hastened the road to war and portrayed him as the aggressor once again.

- The issue of Spanish succession was unavoidable and the extreme nature of the allies' terms in 1709 meant that Louis had to fight on in order to preserve the security of the state. Dynastic considerations were still crucial to Louis; he would not wage war on his grandson as the allies had requested and he was concerned with the legacy and glory of his kingship. Nevertheless, reason of state was also becoming more of a consideration as illustrated by Louis's appeal to his provincial governors in 1710 to ensure the state's security come what may.

THE ACHIEVEMENTS OF LOUIS XIV

France was in many ways weaker in 1715 than it had been in 1661. The economy that had been so rigorously transformed by Colbert lay in tatters. War had imposed major suffering on the people of France and Louis' own reputation had suffered both at home and abroad. Yet, on the other hand, Louis had established the outline of modern France with the acquisition of Metz, Toul and Verdun along with Alsace, Strasbourg and Franche-Comté. Maubeuge, Condé and Lille were also added to the kingdom in the north-east. Therefore, not only were frontiers secure but the border of modern France had been established. The Spanish succession had been resolved in favour of the Bourbons, even if Philip was precluded from succeeding to the French throne. Louis had perhaps been too ambitious for his own good and, while dominating the European scene for large parts of his reign, the wars that he committed France to steadily increased in terms of size, longevity and scale. Accordingly, opposition became more unified and concerted. Utrecht marked for France what Westphalia had marked for the Habsburgs:

- The strategy, might and effectiveness of the French army waned throughout the period of Louis' rule. The reforms of Le Tellier and his son had produced a fighting force that was the envy of all European rulers in the 1670s and 1680s. However, by the War of Spanish Succession the Anglo-Dutch forces had caught up, and this was aptly illustrated at Blenheim in 1704 and again at Ramillies in 1706.
- Foreign policy and war took priority over domestic reform and therefore centralising initiatives at home were left incomplete.
- Louis was not the sole warmonger in Europe, and Leopold and Charles II along with William III should be held equally responsible for the period that the European powers spent at war in the seventeenth and early eighteenth centuries. Indeed, we could argue that it was the Grand Alliance that imposed the later wars upon France, and that Louis was only out to defend his acquisitions from previous campaigns. Of course it was precisely the acquisitions Aix-la-Chapelle and Nijmegen along with Ratisbon that provoked such an anti-French coalition in the first place. Nevertheless, Louis fought for an achievable and necessary goal in the 1670s, primarily that of national security. Perhaps it was the failure of his statesmanship to portray these goals as non-threatening that was his real downfall.

KEY THEME

Louis's testament On his deathbed in 1715, Louis was reported to have told his infant son 'not to imitate my love of building nor my liking for war, but try, on the contrary to live at peace with your neighbours'. Saint-Simon is a notoriously unreliable source, and Louis may never have uttered these words. However, dynastic concerns on the battlefield and the pursuit of *la gloire* continue to cloud the reputation of Louis.

- In contrast to Richelieu and Mazarin, Louis' foreign policy appeared short-sighted and poorly planned. Of course there had to be flexibility about foreign policy, and an element of opportunism but Louis appeared set on provocation and antagonism at times when it was not in the interests of France to be so. The reunions and the reaction to Charles II's will are two examples. At crucial times Louis found himself without allies, most notably the lack of papal support for the French candidate for the bishopric of Cologne. Similarly, the two cardinal ministers proved more adept at ignoring religious loyalties when striking the most favourable alliance for France. Sweden and German princes were courted by both Richelieu and Mazarin in a bid to promote French interests. Louis XIV, under the influence of Madame de Maintenon, persecuted Huguenots, ostracised Protestant support abroad, and bound maritime opposition together. Moreover, Louis continued to recognise the right of the exiled James II and subsequently James' son the Old Pretender to rule England, reinforcing his outright belief in divine right but provoking opposition within England and the Netherlands.

SUMMARY QUESTIONS

1. What does the way in which Louis XIV dealt with Huguenots and Jansenists reveal about his character?

2. Why does Ratisbon (1684) mark a turning point in the foreign policy of Louis XIV?

3. How far was the foreign policy of Louis XIV an extension of that under Richelieu and Mazarin?

4. To what extent can Louis XIV's foreign policy be seen as a success for France?

AS ASSESSMENT: FRANCE: 1500–1715

SOURCE-BASED QUESTIONS IN THE STYLE OF OCR AND EDEXCEL

Source A
Loménie de Brienne (Secretary of State) describes Louis XIV's announcement that he would rule personally in 1661

> *The king arranged for the meeting in the room of the Queen Mother, where Council meetings had previously been held, of all those whose services he had been in the habit of employing – the princes, the dukes and the ministers of state. He wished to make it clear to them in his own words that he had decided to govern the state himself, relying only on his own efforts.*

Source B
Louis XIV reflects in his memoirs of 1671 on his choice of ministers in 1661

> *I could have chosen persons of higher social standing as my ministers but none with better qualifications. To be perfectly honest with you, it was not in my interest to select individuals of greater eminence. It was above all necessary to establish my own reputation and to make the public realise, by the very rank of the ministers whom I selected, that it was not my intention to share my authority with them.*

Source C
Louis XIV instructs Turenne about the use of force against French subjects in 1662

> *We find ourselves obliged for the conservation of the state as much for its glory and reputation, to maintain in peace as well as in war a great number of troops, both infantry and cavalry, which will always be in good condition to act to keep our people in the obedience and respect they owe, to insure the peace and tranquillity that we have won.*

Source D
Colbert writes to La Barre in 1662

> *The king has received a number of complaints that, during the weeks of the harvest, troops have been used to aid the collection of taxes in your generality, thus causing widespread disorder and bringing great hardship to the people, who have already*

suffered a bad year. I have firmly assured His Majesty that in your capacity as intendant of Riom, you will quickly remedy this situation, and that, in the months of July and August, you will not allow anyone to exert pressure of any kind on the parishes.

(a) Study Source D. From this source and your own knowledge explain the reference to *intendant*. (20)

(b) Study Sources A and B. Compare these sources as evidence for Louis XIV's treatment of the nobility. (40)

(c) Study all the sources. Using all the sources and your own knowledge, assess the view that Louis XIV was an absolutist monarch. (60)

How to answer these questions

(a) Look to spend ten minutes on this question. The focus here is on explaining a particular issue, in this case the significance and role of the *intendant*. Answer the question directly and sharply. There is no need for an introduction, just get straight to the point. Explanations need to be clear and convincing with some linkage to the source. Some of the key points are listed below.

- *Intendants* were royal representatives in the localities working alongside provincial officials in order to uphold the authority and policies of the crown.
- Source D demonstrates how useful and important *intendants* were to Colbert in maintaining control, law and order and the royal prerogative.
- Colbert gradually increased the responsibility of the *intendants* and they became a particular feature of Louis XIV's system of government. Uniform tax collection was one area in which they were heavily involved, and Source D outlines some of the difficulties in this area.
- Although important as a centralising agent of the crown, there were only thirty-one *intendants* and their effectiveness should not be overestimated.

(b) Allow twenty minutes for this question. The key here is to offer a genuine comparison between the sources and to interact confidently with the material in front of you. Contrast areas of agreement and disagreement but also comment on usefulness and typicality. Below are some ideas.

- The two sources largely agree on how Louis was going to govern the realm although Source B is more explicit about the king's motives.
- In Source B Louis has the freedom to express his attitude towards the nobility more freely as he is established on the throne and writing from a position of strength.
- Whilst similar in content, the two sources differ in tone.

- Source B outlines the king's reluctance to promote great nobles to important political positions, something we know to be correct although those of higher social standing were still encouraged to reside at court.

(c) Spend 30 minutes on this question and make sure that you plan your answer carefully. There must be a balance between analysis and evaluation of the source material as well as own knowledge. Own knowledge means material not found in the sources. It does not need to be lengthy but rather sharp and relevant. Sources and own knowledge should be integrated into your argument. You might consider the following key points.

- Both sources A and B outline how Louis ruled without a chief minister and reduced the nobility to what seems like subservience. This is clearly a major point regarding Louis' absolutism, and one that needs careful examination. The old nobility were not mere puppets of the king and were still crucial to strong government. Noble privileges and status remained intact although traditional opinion would lead us to believe that the appointment of men of lesser social standing and the use of Versailles as a means of controlling the old nobility served to avoid the faction fighting that had marked Louis XIII's reign.
- Source C demonstrates how Louis was prepared to use force against his own subjects although in reality the government often showed mercy rather than vengeance. A standing army and the effective use of force to set an example are two hallmarks of an absolutist monarch but again the reality in Louis' case was necessarily different. Examples such as the Breton revolt of 1675 demonstrate how compromise was often sought and how the government was keen to avoid provoking influential nobles.
- Source D reveals the usage of *intendants* as a tool of centralising government, although in reality Louis' absolutism in the provinces remained obstructed by traditional obstacles.
- Specific own knowledge may draw upon the privileges inherent within French society and the obstacles that barred the way to complete absolutism. Candidates might take the line that Louis increased the power of the crown and centralised government but such achievements were limited. The discrepancy between image and reality may be outlined, and problems with enforcing laws or continued corruption in tax collection could also be utilised.
- Try to make some kind of balanced judgement on the question.

For Module 3 you will be asked to complete a course essay. The main focus of the question is on explanation. Below are examples of the types of questions you might be asked:

- Explain why…
- With what success…?
- Examine the factors…

The course essay title will be sent to your school or college two weeks before you are to write your response under timed conditions. This will give two weeks to prepare your notes and plan effectively.

Question 1

> How significant was noble support for Calvinism as a factor in explaining the outbreak of the French Wars of Religion?

How to answer this question
- The key to a successful course essay is a detailed plan.
- Your main points of argument need to be clearly thought through.
- You need to link the main factors together in your plan and throughout your essay.

General points on structure
It is important that you think about how you will structure your answer before you try to tackle the question. You will be able to plan before you write your timed essay. To answer these types of essay questions you need to do the following.

- **Read the question** carefully and identify what the question is asking you.
- **Provide a direct and to the point response** to the question.
- **Before you start to write**, plan your answer carefully.
- **In your plan include** a list of points that will form the basis of your argument/judgement. Then briefly map out what you plan to put in each paragraph.
- **Start your answer with a brief introduction.**
- **Keep your paragraphs to the point.**
- **Choose evidence that is relevant** and that substantiates the points you have made.
- **Conclude** in such a way that you clearly state the judgment you have made in response to the question.

Plan
Plan your essay around analytical themes rather than events. Avoid a purely descriptive approach and instead look to use your evidence to reinforce specific points.

Content
Ensure that this is focused and relevant. In this case the focus is on noble support for Calvinism but other factors will also need consideration. Make reference to the following in your essay:

- The rise of Calvinism in France throughout the 1550s and the influence of Calvin himself.
- The power vacuum created by the deaths of Henry II and Francis II.
- The moderating policies of Catherine de Medici.
- The growth of faction at court.

Style
In your answer you need to be direct and to the point. Your introduction will contain your main points of argument. Here is an example of a direct introduction made in response to the question above:

The protection and legitimacy offered to Calvinism by nobles such as Coligny and Condé was crucial to the movement's survival and development during the 1550s. Yet as the Huguenots became more confident and powerful, tension grew in the towns, as Catholics vented their anger at having to live side by side with heretics. Furthermore, illegal church building, synods and the singing of psalms on the left bank of the Seine built up a Calvinist identity that further provoked Catholic hatred. In the long term noble support for Calvinism would be especially important but in the years leading up to 1562 it was the misgovernment and naivety of Catherine de Medici that inevitably led to violence.

Question 2

Why had Henry III lost the confidence of his Catholic subjects by 1588?

How to answer this question
The main point of the question is to test how well you understand the importance of the role of the individual.

Plan
In your plan you need to identify the main points of argument. Below are some examples:

- Primarily, Henry was unable to defeat the Huguenots on the battlefield and eradicate heresy.

- Catholicism underpinned the authority and status of the monarchy. In failing to defeat the Huguenots Henry had failed to uphold his coronation oath.
- Henry was financially bankrupted by the prolonged nature of the wars and unable to fight effective campaigns. The financial strain on the third estate led to peasant unrest.
- The Day of the Barricades and Henry's subsequently rash decision to have the Guise brothers murdered was the final nail in the coffin of his legitimacy and standing as monarch.

Style

You need to be direct in your response throughout. It is important that your course essay gets off to a good start with a direct introduction that answers the question. Here is an example:

In many ways Henry was unable to detach himself from the vicious circle of events that had blighted Catherine de Medici's regency. Inadequate peace treaties that offered toleration, an inability to defeat the Huguenots on the battlefield and a subsequent peace edict ensured that his Catholic subjects rapidly lost confidence in Henry's ability to uphold Gallican principles. The final humiliation came in 1588 when the Sixteen in Paris put their faith in the more militant Guises rather than their monarch.

Further questions

Here are some examples of the types of questions asked on this subject. Try to write plans and introductions to each one of these:

Examine the importance of Catherine de Medici in the origins of the French Wars of Religion.

To what extent did religion provoke and sustain violence in France, 1562–98?

Why did the French Wars of Religion last so long (1562–98)?

A2 SECTION

Introduction: Historiography Analysis and Interpretation

RENAISSANCE MONARCHY

Historians tend to characterise Louis XII, Francis I and Henry II as Renaissance monarchs. **Glenn Richardson** (*History Review*, September 1998) argues that the transition between medieval king and Renaissance prince can be seen with Louis XII (1462–1515). On the one hand, Louis XII might be regarded as a Renaissance monarch in the way that he began centralising government, codifying the legal system and controlling the power of the nobility; but on the other, he might be seen as a medieval prince in the sense that few of his reforms could really be labelled innovative. Richardson cites the example of the Ordinance of Blois (1499) as a piece of legislation that came out of meetings with the Estates General and assembly of notables – not a tool to curb noble power but a royal directive to improve the judicial system that was acknowledged by the nobility in return for recognition of their status by the crown.

CHANGING CHARACTER OF THE NOBILITY

In *A History of France, 1460–1560* (Macmillan, 1995), **David Potter** picks up on a central theme that runs throughout this period: the rise of the nobility of the robe. Traditionally, the rise of this new administrative class of nobility has been viewed as being at the expense of the old nobility of the sword. In short, the crown deliberately sold offices and created the new nobility in order to weaken the old magnates who continually posed a threat to the monarchy. Potter, **Mack Holt** (*Society and Institutions in Early Modern France*, University of Georgia, 1991) and **Philip Hoffman** have done much to add caution to this argument. Certainly a new noble class did emerge in the sixteenth century and venality was a constant means of increasing the royal income. Yet, although major noble families such as Guise and Montmorency were not so powerfully independent of the crown as they had been in the fifteenth century, nor were they excluded from power. Holt and Potter emphasise that the old nobility retained their social prominence throughout the sixteenth century, and during the Italian Wars played a critical role in raising and leading armies for the king. Moreover, while the new nobility undoubtedly attained greater political influence, not all received offices that led to an increase in power or got them closer to the king. In *The Nobility of the Election of Bayeaux, 1463–1666* (Princeton, 1980), **J. B. Wood** has demonstrated in his study of Bayeaux that the nobility of the sword and the nobility of the robe were almost indistinguishable rather than being two separate groups. Some old nobility held offices just like the new, while some new nobility lived nobly as we would expect the old to. The key to understanding the fate of the nobility in sixteenth-century France, according to Wood, was not old or new nobility but rich or poor nobility and the general trend in Bayeaux was towards a richer noble class.

NOBILITY IN CRISIS?

The traditional line fostered by historians writing in the first half of the twentieth century was that of a nobility in crisis. The economic decline of the nobility went hand in hand with their political and social fall from power at the expense of the crown. **Lucien Romier** (1922), **Gaston Roupnel** (1955) and **Paul Raveau** (1926) undertook local case-studies that shaped our view of the nobility in France during this period. The trends appeared to be the same, that of an economic boom in the first half of the sixteenth century that gave way to depression and consequently noble decline. Noble landowners made good in the 1520s and 1530s when labour was cheap, harvests good and land plentiful; and suffered ruin in the 1570s and 1580s when inflation was high, rents fixed, harvests poor and civil war rampant. Yet Wood, Holt and **J.-M. Constant** ('*Nobles et paysans beaucerons aux XVIe at XVIIe siècles*', thesis, Lille, 1981) have shown such a portrayal to be false. Both Constant and Holt have demonstrated that many of the very wealthy nobility made a profit out of the Wars of Religion and, far from selling land, many nobles actually bought it during the Wars of Religion. While some lesser nobles went under, and perhaps those who had begun to live nobly at the start of the sixteenth century slipped back into the third estate, the main core of the nobility survived and thrived. As **R. J. Knecht** writes in *The Rise and Fall of Renaissance France 1483–1610*, Blackwell, 2001.

> *the traditional view of aristocratic decline rested on three assumptions: first, that siegneural rents were fixed and paid in money; secondly that war helped to ruin the nobility; and thirdly that extravagant living and a lack of business sense contributed to that ruin. All three are questionable.*

The king continued to rely upon the old nobility in the provinces and court did not attract the number of nobles that was once thought. As Richardson writes,

> *the two groups (old and new nobility) formed an expanded oligarchy which was prepared to deal with the monarchy in order to secure for itself the lucrative pensions, positions in the royal household and the myriad of offices in the localities.*

Therefore, there has been a significant reappraisal of the role of the nobility within French society over the past two decades. The picture of a nobility in crisis has given way to one in which the old aristocracy actually suffered little change and in many senses benefited from the chaos and turmoil of the sixteenth century.

ABSOLUTE MONARCHY?

Another major point of debate among historians is the extent to which the authority of the crown increased during this period, reaching its zenith under Louis XIV. The nature of Renaissance kingship under Francis I and Henry II, and in particular the extent of the limitations on their authority, remain contentious points. Were the Valois monarchs paving the way for Bourbon absolutism? **George Pagès** believes that Francis and Henry were absolutist, with few obstacles to their outright authority. Yet other historians, such as **Henri Prentout** and **J. Russell Major** (*Representative Institutions in Renaissance France, 1421–1559*, Madison, 1960) are cautious about such an outright endorsement of absolutism, drawing attention to the rights and privileges of the *pays d'états* alongside the decentralised political structure within France that naturally curbed royal authority. Russell Major sees the reign of Francis I as popular and consultative rather than absolutist. He points to dealings with the *parlements* and the way in which Francis consulted his subjects over foreign policy as evidence of a monarch prepared to seek advice and consent before embarking upon important policy decisions. Yet Knecht takes issue with Russell Major, demonstrating that in many ways Francis's reign had the hallmarks of an absolutist monarchy: for example, the way in which the Concordat of Bologna was forced through *parlements* despite impinging upon clerical Gallicanism, or the way in which Francis treated the provincial *parlements*, most notably that in Rouen. Moreover, neither Francis nor Henry ever called a meeting of the Estates General and an assembly of notables was called in 1527 only to raise a large subsidy to pay the ransom of Henry's two sons held captive in Madrid. Knecht points out that even when provincial estates were asked to ratify a treaty the decision had already been taken by the king's council: the deputies were simply rubber-stamping the decree. The way in which the king pardoned the salt tax rebels of 1542 at La Rochelle has also been put forward as an example of how Francis treated his subjects with compassion and magnanimity. Yet, as Knecht points out, the *gabelle* was not scrapped and in the midst of a war with the emperor troops could not be freed to deal with the 10,000 armed rebels. Francis had no option but to be conciliatory.

Therefore, historians debate the extent to which Renaissance monarchy was absolute, that is without subordination to any other human authority or institution; or contractual, that is answerable to institutions and expected to consult with them on major issues of state. The reality probably lay somewhere in between. Provincial liberties and *parlements* continued to prove an obstacle to royal authority. Less so in the long and stable reign of Francis I admittedly, but they became more politically prominent in the second half of the sixteenth century. Law and order in the localities was erratic even in the reign of Francis and political power so decentralised that to use the term absolutist would be false. Yet, on the other hand, the image of a benevolent, caring and contractual monarch has to be treated with caution. Francis rode roughshod over provincial liberties whenever he could, pandering to them only when he needed money. No consultative institution had the chance even to meet during the reigns of Francis or Henry! Therefore, in the context of the sixteenth century the reigns of the Renaissance monarchs were closer to Knecht's authoritarianism than Russell Major's consultation.

IMPORTANCE OF RELIGION IN THE WARS OF RELIGION

Numerous recent local studies have increased our awareness of the centrality of religion in sixteenth-century France. In *The French Wars of Religion 1562–1629* (Cambridge, 1995), Mack Holt even talks about 'putting religion back into the wars of religion', after decades of political and economic analysis of the causes and progression of the French Wars of Religion. Certainly recent work on individual localities, such as that of **Philip Benedict**, *Rouen during the Wars of Religion* (Cambridge, 1981), **Barbara B. Diefendorf**, *Beneath the Cross: Catholics and Huguenots in Sixteenth-Century Paris* (Oxford, 1991) and **Penny Roberts**, *A City in Conflict: Troyes during the French Wars of Religion* (Manchester, 1996), has enriched our understanding of the impact of civil war on the local populace. While the importance of the nobility and economic pressures should not be forgotten in any discussion of the wars, it is the role of religion that recent scholars have emphasised as being critical in fuelling the violence and preventing compromise. Holt emphasises the influence of religion in a social rather than a doctrinal context: it was not necessarily the intricate doctrinal details of the eucharist or predestination that mattered but more the centrality of belief and faith within the community. Clearly, this becomes important when we consider how the Catholics viewed Huguenots as seditious, dangerous rebels. The popular, mob violence that erupted in 1572 had, according to Diefendorf, been simmering near the surface for some time within the capital. The executions of Philippe and Richard Gastines in 1569 and the mob violence that accompanied them were prime examples of how Protestant and Catholic could not live side by side. The inadequate peace treaties that followed each of the Wars of Religion are used by Holt to demonstrate the centrality of religion in a social context. None of the clauses discussed transubstantiation or the route to salvation, but rather where and when Huguenot worship could take place. Philip Benedict notes that compromise between Catholic and Protestant had proved unworkable at Poissy in 1561 and that Poissy had given way to toleration in 1562 with the Edict of January. Benedict writes that

> *when Catherine de Medici granted Protestantism legal toleration in 1562 she broke dramatically with the prior traditions of the French monarchy.*

This is a point picked up by recent academics such as Holt and Knecht, and it clearly recognised by contemporaries: the existence of heresy severely undermined the crown. After 1572 there was less mob violence because confessional allegiance was organised more along geographical lines with a Protestant hardcore in the Midi. However, while **Stuart Carroll** in *Noble Power during the French Wars of Religion* (Cambridge, 1998) outlines the strength of the Guise clientele network as a political force during the turbulent 1580s, Holt notes that religion continued to provide the unifying force behind the Catholic League. When Henry of Navarre abjured in 1593 he at once removed the issue that held the League together, the Catholicity of the crown.

Therefore, recent emphasis has very much been upon the role of religion in the Wars of Religion rather than political or economic concerns. Certainly Alençon looked to further his own cause in 1576; many nobles adopted Calvinism for material gain; and peasants revolted in the 1580s because of grievances against oppressive landlords. Yet local studies have shown that the advent of Protestantism severely shook communities of believers throughout France and undermined the Gallican principles upon which stability rested.

HENRY IV'S REIGN: A TURNING POINT?

The reign of Henry IV has traditionally been viewed as one of inevitable recovery after the chaos of civil conflict. The political and financial recovery overseen by Henry IV was, in the eyes of Edmund Burke writing in the 1790s, an almost automatic process as France moved seamlessly towards Bourbon absolutism in the seventeenth century. More recent scholarship by **Jean Pierre Babelon** (1982) and **Mark Greengrass** in *France in the Age of Henri IV* (Longman, 1987) has demonstrated that Henry IV had to 'consciously create the stability of his rule after the wars' (Greengrass). The assassination of Henry IV in 1610 clouded the judgement of successive commentators and historians, argues Greengrass, who portrayed the reign of Henry as a golden age in which royal authority was enhanced and the nobility put back in their place. Henry became something to everyone in the seventeenth and eighteenth centuries: to Catholics he was the pious king who restored unity, to monarchists he was the ideal of good kingship, and to Parisians he was the king who was interested in social welfare and enlightened toleration. Yet Greengrass has endeavoured to portray a more realistic assessment of Henry IV that shows the extent to which the lines of authority were indeed redrawn in this period. Mack Holt reinforces the line taken by Greengrass that Henry IV consciously worked at the restoration of royal authority. His pragmatic policies of appeasement of leaguer nobles and ultimate aim of unity in religion are highlighted by Holt as evidence of this proactive approach. Similarly, while Greengrass acknowledges that in some senses Henry IV was fortunate to be ruling over a France tired of war and in a period of general economic recovery, the policies of Henry and Sully were nonetheless shrewd and carefully planned. However, much research has also been carried out by **Janine Garrison** (*Royaume, Renaissance et Reforme, 1483–1559*, Paris, 1991), **Jean Pierre Babelon** (*La Renaissance*, 1976) and **Emmanuel Le Roy Ladurie** (*L'état royal de Louis XI et á Henri IV*, Paris, 1987) to demonstrate that problems still existed with regard to unification and centralisation by the time of Henry's assassination in 1610. A Huguenot minority still existed and fiscal pressures remained harsh on the third estate. Henry IV did not carry out an expansionist foreign policy necessarily through compassion for the plight of his subjects. Indeed, as Greengrass points out, the fact that he mobilised three times between 1600 and 1610 suggests that given more time Henry would have committed France to a costly and probably disastrous foreign war against Spain. The Saluzzo question that was left over from Vervins caused future conflict and the Huguenot question left over from Nantes caused future conflict. Thus, recent work has done much to penetrate the myth of Henry IV as the outright saviour of France and the ruler who laid the foundations for absolutism. The reign was not without problems and strife but, viewed in comparison to what preceded it and viewed in the context of what succeeded it, it becomes convenient to see Henry IV's reign as the turning point in monarchical fortunes.

LOUIS XIV AND LIMITED ABSOLUTISM

Modern scholarship on Louis XIV has tended to focus on the obstacles to reform and innovation, and therefore stresses the limited nature of absolutism. Nineteenth- and early twentieth-century French historians such as **Ernest Lavisse** and **P. A. Chéruel** viewed Louis XIV's power and subjugation of the nobility as almost effortless and inevitable. In short, to these historians the state steadily increased its power at the expense of traditionally autonomous institutions such as the church and the nobility. Alternatively, **A. Lossky**, in The absolutism of Louis XIV: reality or myth? (*Canadian Journal of History*, 11, 1984), examines the discrepancy between the image of Louis' kingship and the reality on the ground. **S. Kettering**, in *Patrons, Brokers and Clients in Seventeenth-Century France* (New York, 1986), maintains this theme by outlining the importance of noble clientele networks in the provinces to maintain law and order as opposed to the lure and attraction of Versailles. Such research builds upon that of **Roland Mousnier** who also emphasises the importance of venality in upholding loyalty and order in the localities. **William Beik**, in *Absolutism and Society in Seventeenth-Century France* (Cambridge, 1988) uses a detailed study of Languedoc to present the idea that absolutism in the localities was based upon a new feudal society which maintained privilege and inequality. The authority of the king was still very much dependent upon personal loyalties and the idea of clientele networks in the provinces was crucial. Yet, image was clearly a crucial element in projecting the kingship and power of Louis XIV: **Peter Burke**, in *The Fabrication of Louis XIV* (1992), has successfully demonstrated how the arts and architecture were used to glorify France, with Colbert at the forefront of this cultural manipulation. Even **François Bluche**'s sympathetic biography of Louis XIV (1990) comments that the practical limits to the exercise of absolute power were considerable. He makes the point

> that it was understood in France in the seventeenth century that *monarchia absoluta* (absolute monarchy) signified a monarchy without shackles, and not one without limits.

Therefore, modern opinion is one that sees through the image of Louis XIV's absolutism and stresses the limitations to his power that remained. Moreover, recent local studies have attempted to show just how Louis did maintain control in the provinces: the emphasis here appears to be on continuity and reinvention rather than change and innovation.

SECTION 1

France in the sixteenth century: the making of a nation-state, 1498–1610

THE KING

One of the central themes in any study of sixteenth- and seventeenth-century France is the rise of monarchical authority: it reached a low point during the Wars of Religion (1562–98); then recovered once more along the lines laid out by Renaissance monarchs to reach its zenith of absolutism under Louis XIV. In hindsight, the process looks straightforward and simple: in reality there was no grand plan for absolutism and the development of France into the most powerful state in Europe in the seventeenth century was more complex than it seems. Monarchical attempts to extend royal power and centralise government predictably met with some opposition, and the development of a nation-state highlighted the limitations of royal authority as well as the strengths. Nevertheless, at the heart of the kingdom in 1500 was the king, and it was through him that policies and developments relating to language, culture, religion and war were driven: during periods of weak monarchy, such as the minority rule of Charles IX, control over such means of development was limited. Imagery and ritual were all-important in developing the concept that French kings were appointed and ordained by God to rule over the kingdom, and selling this idea to their subjects was a major part of royal propaganda.

French kings were not only ordained by God but were themselves thought of as gods. Myths developed reflecting their sacred powers; for example, one touch from the French king after his coronation would allegedly cure the horrible skin disease scrofula. Such ritual was an important part of the relationship between king and subject, as it reinforced the idea that royal authority was sacred. Moreover, each new French king was anointed with the holy oil of the sacred ampulla which linked that king to all his predecessors. Thus the ancient and sacred nature of French kingship was visible in the ceremony. After consecration the king was presented with his crown, sceptre and regal vestments. The king's duties were outlined in his coronation oath, namely to promote peace, protect his subjects, dispense justice fairly and expel heretics from his kingdom. The king also received the eucharist in both kinds, that is both the bread and the wine, a measure only received by the clergy. Again, the purpose here was to boost the king's secular and sacerdotal status. The royal propaganda of the sixteenth century portrayed the king as a divine ruler and the one man capable of unifying the diverse elements that made up the French kingdom.

Yet sixteenth-century France was largely feudal and the king, for all his power and prestige, still had to respect the rights of his subjects. Provinces, towns, guilds, nobles, the church and corporations all enjoyed a measure of independence. Often Frenchmen owed greater allegiance to province than to realm, as the former was so remote from the centre of power. Particularism, then, was a major problem for French kings in the early modern period, and, despite patronage and careful management, attaining the unstinting loyalty and submission of their subjects was often impossible. Throughout the period 1498–1715 notions of royal absolutism evolved which envisaged a French monarchy free of external restraints such as councils or *parlements*, and with all power vested in one man. According to this doctrine, the king was appointed by God as his vicegerent on earth: it was the king's right to make laws, dispense justice and create offices. Any institution which curbed or eroded royal authority could be abolished under the royal prerogative and local traditions and privileges could only remain with the king's consent. Lawyers and humanists throughout the sixteenth century, such as Guillaume Bude and Jean Bodin, articulated this theory and successive French kings sought to fulfil the role of absolute monarch. There were opponents to this theory, such as Claude de Seyssel who put forward three restraints on royal power, namely religion, justice and established ordinances. Seysell was still advocating royal authority, but in a different context. In practice, however, the king of France remained bound by certain obligations and rights with regard to his subjects and administrative machinery was necessary to oversee the effective rule of the kingdom. Certainly, the French crown and government were more centralised by the end of Louis XIV's reign, with increased control over the outlying provinces, yet checks on the power of the crown remained and absolutism was an unrealised political theory. Nevertheless, one of Louis XIV's successes was the ability of his propaganda team to sell the image of an absolute monarch, ordained by God, and answerable only to Him for his actions. Thus, Louis encountered few obstacles to his policies despite the fact that his wars caused unprecedented suffering for the people of France. Louis also attempted to unify the kingdom religiously, depriving Protestants of any protection and ordering them to abjure. As we have already seen from the king's coronation oath, in which he swore to protect the canonical privilege, due law and justice, the bond between king and church was very strong and both legitimacy and order emanated from this relationship.

THE CHURCH

The symbolism of the coronation ceremony emphasised the unique relationship between the French monarchy and the Catholic Church. The French king had the papal endorsement of *rex christianissimus*, the Most Christian King. Moreover, the French church operated virtually independent of Rome after the passing of the Pragmatic Sanction of Bourges in 1438 which increased Gallican liberties and curbed papal intervention. The sanction allowed cathedral chapters to elect both bishops and abbots independent of royal and papal control. Gradually, however, this clerical Gallicanism was impinged upon by the crown, a process accelerated by Louis XI who was essentially controlling clerical appointments himself by 1471. Such practice was officialised in 1515 by the Concordat of Bologna which gave Francis I the right to nominate candidates directly for vacant bishoprics and archbishoprics thus increasing the power of the crown over the church, and giving rise to what one may describe as royal Gallicanism. With such power of appointment and as recognised guardian of the church it was to the king rather than the pope that Frenchmen looked to for spiritual protection. Yet royal Gallicanism also allowed for corruption in terms of clerical appointments and, as in other parts of western Europe, the church witnessed lowering standards of education and practice. Few of the bishops appointed by either Francis I (1515–47) or Henry II (1547–59) had any theological training, with only three out of 80 appointments made by the latter monarch having a degree in theology. On the other hand, control of clerical appointments gave French kings great power and allowed them to distribute their patronage among the nobility and reward Italian allies of the French who opposed the Habsburgs.

Calls for reform emanated from learned humanists such as Jacques Lefèvre d'Étaples who rejected scholasticism and instead focused on improving the Christian life through education, a return to the original scriptures and moral reform. Lefèvre d'Étaples soon joined with a like-minded humanist named Guillaume Briconnet, bishop of Meaux, and the humanist Circle of Meaux was born. The scriptures were read to parishioners in the mother tongue while Lefèvre d'Étaples translated the New Testament into French in 1523. Although all participants in the circle were orthodox Catholics and loyal to their king, the group came under suspicion in the 1520s because of the actions of Luther in Germany: despite the patronage of Francis I's sister Marguerite, it was suppressed in 1525. Whether we regard the Circle of Meaux as a forerunner to reform or not, the issue of reform and heresy became a more pressing one for successive French kings after Francis I. As reformist views became more radical, persecution was stepped up and, although the German Luther made little impact in France, the native John Calvin had much greater success operating from his base in Geneva. French

Protestantism emerged as a strong minority in the 1550s and divided the kingdom and weakened the monarchy until the conclusion of the French Wars of Religion in 1598. Ultimately, to the vast majority of Frenchmen, Catholicism was the one true faith, and heresy was intolerable. The failure of French monarchs in the second half of the sixteenth century to defeat the Huguenots on the battlefield and stamp out Protestantism led to a decline in the fortunes of the crown both at a political and popular level.

Catholicism tied the king to his subjects and bound the nation together as a community of believers. The church legitimised the king's authority, and tied him to his subjects. The eucharist and the mass lay at the centre of people's lives as much in a social sense as doctrinally. Therefore, the threat of Protestantism was to the perceived hierarchy within French society and to the community as a whole.

THE NOBILITY

The nobility held a privileged and powerful position within French society. As French nobles did service to their king on the battlefield they were exempt from direct taxation. Therefore, those who could afford to pay most actually paid least. They had seigneurial rights over the peasantry which meant that they acted as landlords towards the peasantry and as independent judges. The leading nobility in France were known as the *noblesse d'épée* (or the nobility of the sword) because of their military obligations to the crown, and membership of this exclusive club relied upon the ability to trace family lineage back for at least two centuries. Indeed, the crown became increasingly eager to pass legislation prohibiting people from just claiming noble status without actually holding a title. The rather fluid nature of social mobility at the beginning of the sixteenth century had meant that many rural landlords had merely assumed noble status, and begun living nobly, exempting themselves from taxation and therefore depriving the crown of income. It was not until the personal rule of Louis XIV (1661–1715) that the crown got hold of this problem and began to exploit the wealth of those that claimed noble status without being able to prove it. At the head of the nobility of the sword were the royal princes of the blood and beneath them dukes, peers, cardinals and marshals all with varying degrees of wealth and prestige. In 1469, Louis XI created the order of St Michael the Archangel, a chivalric order that grouped together the most important nobles in the realm. A hierarchy was beginning to develop within the nobility itself, shaped by the crown. The result was that the leading noble families were showered with distinctions and royal patronage, consequently increasing their power and status. The lesser nobility found it increasingly difficult to survive, and during periods of hardship many went under. Indeed, the aristocracy as a whole was coming under threat and no little criticism at the beginning of the sixteenth century for a number of reasons. Enlightened humanist opinion portrayed them as barbaric, interested only in military adventures and their own worldly ambitions rather than learning and the fate of others.

In the early sixteenth century, the house of Bourbon was the most powerful of all families. Founded in the fourteenth century, the family held large amounts of land in central France and as with other such nobles the territories were very much the demesne of Charles of Bourbon, who effectively ruled over the provinces. In 1515, Charles was made constable of France which made him leader of the French army in peacetime. While this might be viewed as an effective use of the king's patronage, a crisis arose in 1521 on the death of Bourbon's wife, the Duchess Suzanne, who had actually inherited all of the Bourbon lands herself in 1488, and married her cousin Charles in order to unite the two branches of the family. Suzanne's will naturally left all of the Bourbon land to her husband but its validity was challenged by Louise of Savoy, the king's mother, on the grounds that she was Suzanne's nearest blood relative. The claims were put before *parlements*, but in the meantime the king began to dispose of Bourbon lands, selling them for profit. In 1523, Charles turned against his king and allied with France's most bitter enemies, namely Charles V and Henry VIII. While Francis was in Italy, Charles led a rebellion with English and Imperial aid. The plot was uncovered and Charles forced to flee the kingdom in disgrace. Bourbon lands were assigned to the crown, a transfer which became almost permanent on the death of Charles at the sack of Rome in 1527. Power factions were, therefore, a constant source of trouble for French monarchs in the early modern period. Moreover, such factions were exacerbated by the fact that a relatively large number of nobles, including the Bourbons and Châtillons, were attracted to Calvinism in the second half of the sixteenth century. Such support, often based on political or financial profit, gave Calvinism the necessary legitimacy and power it required to survive amid persecution and served to lengthen the Wars of Religion.

The final major development within noble ranks during this period is the emergence of the *noblesse de robe* (or nobility of the robe) in the seventeenth century. The concept of venality, the sale of offices for royal profit, created thousands of new administrative and bureaucratic positions which were eagerly snapped up by ambitious gentry or merchants keen to better themselves. Ennobled through office and service to the king, such individuals challenged the traditional political power of the nobility of the sword and the latter did not dominate the king's council in the seventeenth century in the same way it had in the sixteenth. Although the new nobility could not challenge the social prestige of the old nobility, they were a more attractive prospect to French kings after the Wars of

Religion, a point highlighted by the fact that Louis XIV appointed only two members of the upper nobility to his inner council. The downside to venality was that it created further layers of bureaucracy which hampered royal authority.

Of course, the royal court became an increasingly important source of power and patronage for the French nobility throughout the sixteenth and seventeenth centuries, culminating in the extravagance and splendour of Versailles under Louis XIV, the Sun King. Royal titles, jobs, money, land, tax-farming contracts and contacts became the prizes on offer for those wealthy and important enough to reside at court and receive the king's patronage. Throughout the sixteenth century, it became increasingly important physically to reside at court, and by 1670 not to be known at court could be a form of social death. From a monarchical perspective, it has been argued that court became an important control mechanism for the king, somewhere that nobles were compelled to reside and where they could be closely monitored. Yet, while Louis XIV did move the court permanently to Versailles in 1682, the nobility resided there out of choice rather than compulsion. The frequency of noble revolts against the crown throughout the sixteenth and early seventeenth centuries are testament to the fact that the nobility represented a powerful body of opinion and at times an obstacle to the extension of monarchical power.

GOVERNMENT

During the sixteenth century, there were three main organs of government in France, namely the king's council, the *grand conseil* and the *parlement* of Paris. The king's council, once made up entirely of the princes of the blood, the peers of the realm and other great magnates, was by the sixteenth century changing in its composition as French monarchs sought to guard against noble domination. Trained lawyers and clerics found increasing royal favour and an inner council (*conseil d'affaires*) selected personally by the king also existed. Here in the inner cabinet crucial policy decisions on matters such as foreign affairs were made. Since 1497, the *grand conseil* had also grown in stature with regard to judicial activity, and fixed membership allowed for continuity and stability. The *grand conseil* acted as the king's own portable law court, following him on his travels and adjudicating on appeal cases or complaints against royal officials. The chancery made the council's decisions into law through royal enactments, but as royal legislation increased greater responsibility was handed to officials under the control of the chancellor and attached to the royal council, namely the *maîtres des requêtes*. Trained in the law, these officials served to link departments of administration and the majority were ennobled for their service.

Of the seven *parlement* which existed, the oldest, most powerful and most prestigious was the *parlement* of Paris. It acted as the highest law court and its jurisdiction covered two-thirds of France; although still considered part of the king's council, the *parlement* regarded itself as the guarantor of liberty and acted as a check on royal authority. All royal legislation had to be ratified by the *parlement*, and remonstrances or objections to the king were not uncommon. If *parlement* continued to object, the king might himself attend the court in person and preside over the ratification of the law in question, a measure known as a *lit de justice*. Such actions were rare and were often viewed as the trait of a weak monarch. The six provincial *parlements* were largely a result of France extending its boundaries in the fifteenth century, and the provinces of Toulouse, Bordeaux, Dijon, Grenoble, Aix and Rouen all had institutions based on the Paris model. Each *parlement* held sway in its own province with regard to ratification of legislation.

The only elected national body was the Estates General which was made up of representatives of the clergy, nobility and third estate. With the right to ratify treaties and approve taxation, theoretical power was great. Yet the Estates General tended to meet only in times of crisis and on the king's authority. It was never summoned under Francis I or Henry II, and it met on only five occasions between 1560 and 1615. Therefore, the Estates General was largely inconsequential in reforming French government and its inactivity highlighted the failure of the French nobility to fulfil a crucial political function as a consequence of religious division and faction.

Often the Estates General achieved nothing, as meaningful discussion and debate soon gave way to the traditional selfish bartering. The nobility called for the abolition of the *paulette*, claiming that commoners were acquiring offices in perpetuity that should have been the preserve of the nobility. One demand debated at length that was important to the development of monarchical authority was the article *de la sûreté des rois* which asserted that the king held his crown from God alone and that no power on earth had a right to deprive him of it. Such views resurfaced in 1626 at the assembly of notables and were found in the *Political Testament* of Richelieu. The concept of setting royal power above all other human authority, making it absolute, emerged over the coming decades.

Local or provincial government was based around the provincial estates which, unlike the Estates General, played an influential role in the distribution of finance and the regulation of taxes and customs duties. Provincial governors, drawn from the ranks of the aristocracy, were important figures of authority in the eleven border provinces of France. The powers of the provincial governor were vague, however, and often the post was used as a reward for good service to the crown; furthermore, often the governor spent more time at court than in the province. Ultimately, the king could hire and fire governors at will and French monarchs were wary of appropriating too much power and authority to influential and ambitious individuals far from the centre of royal authority. Beneath provincial governors came the *baillis*, who were in control of the 86 *bailliages*. At a local level, the *bailliage* was an important facet of government and one which was open to corruption from officials who were poorly paid.

A major trend in government administration in the sixteenth and seventeenth centuries was the creation of offices and increase in the level of bureaucracy. Francis I had one office holder to every 3000 inhabitants, a reflection not only of the increase in royal business in institutions such as the chancery (the body which turned council decisions into law), but also of the lucrative nature of venality.

TAXATION

Ordinary revenue from sources such as the king's crown lands together with extraordinary revenue from taxation made up the king's annual fiscal haul. Annual revenue fluctuated and difficulties in the collection of taxation reflected the decentralised nature of the kingdom. The *taille* was the direct tax, levied annually and in two forms. The *taille personnelle* was based upon the individual's ability to pay while the *taille réelle* was a land tax and applied to all social ranks and was unquestionably fairer. Yet the *réelle* was used only in certain areas such as Languedoc and Provence. From the reign of Charles VII, French kings could tax at will, although it must be remembered that the nobility and clergy were exempt from the *taille* as were other groups such as lawyers and royal officials. In fact, the burden of taxation fell upon the peasantry and the sixteenth and seventeenth centuries saw a number of sporadic but nevertheless significant peasant uprisings against taxation. Indirect taxation also existed; one example being the *gabelle*, a tax on salt, a crucial commodity for the preservation of food. The *aides* were similar duties on commodities sold regularly and in large quantity, such as wine or livestock.

Given the decentralised nature of the French kingdom, collection of taxation became a thorny issue for the French crown. Exemptions, both noble and provincial, reduced the number of people who could be taxed, while effective collection in outlying provinces proved difficult. Arrears often accumulated in times of war when levels of taxation were higher. Various measures were introduced throughout the sixteenth and seventeenth centuries in an attempt to increase the efficiency of tax collection in the provinces. Royal agents (or *intendants*) represented the culmination of such efforts and while ministers such as Sully and Colbert did much to enhance the amount of money returned to the royal coffers, the same problems continued to exist, exacerbated in the sixteenth century by civil war and in the seventeenth century by foreign war.

Effective tax assessment and collection was further hampered by provincial traditions and privilege. While in the *pays d'élections* tax was levied by royal administrators on orders from the royal council, in the *pays d'états* taxation was levied by the local estates. Therefore, in provinces such as Brittany, Languedoc and Provence the responsibility for levying taxation fell on local estates rather than the crown, a privilege that was fiercely defended by these territories, and a clear obstacle to uniformity, efficiency and national identity. While the *taille* was assessed and collected by an elected representative, the right to collect indirect tax was auctioned to the highest bidder. The victorious bidder was allowed to collect and keep the tax in question after prior payment of a fixed sum to the crown. Therefore, the opportunity for profit and corruption were vast, although it did ensure a regular return from the provinces for the king with few administrative problems. In general, the *taille* brought in about 2.4 million livres out of a total revenue of 4.9 million; the *aides* contributed 0.8 million livres; the *gabelle* cashed in 6 per cent of the total revenue.

THE THIRD ESTATE

The third estate is a general term to describe all those who did not belong to the noble or clerical classes. At the upper end of the scale were wealthy merchants, royal office holders and lawyers: men of ambition who perhaps had designs on ennoblement. In an urban context there were also artisans and lesser merchants who could count on a comfortable income and standard of living. Yet the vast majority of the third estate were peasants. France was an overwhelmingly rural society with only one person in twenty living in a city of over 10,000 inhabitants. The vast majority of Frenchmen and women lived in small village communities dispersed throughout the kingdom. Communal spirit was created by the intimacy of village life, the parish church, public farmland and general cooperation among villagers. That is not to say that movement from villages was static during the course of the sixteenth century. Indeed, new opportunities to buy land elsewhere or earn higher wages in another village encouraged movement. Consequently, cheap land and favourable tenancy rates saw the rise of a wealthy middle class within the villages throughout the first half of the century. Thereafter, rising taxation, split inheritance, the dislocation caused by civil war and poor harvests changed the dynamic of the village again. In this environment, a very small number of very wealthy farmers prospered on the back of financial reserves and connections. The gap between rich and poor widened between the village elite and the day labourers.

In the lead up to the sixteenth century, the lot of the peasant had improved considerably. Between 1450 and 1560, after the ravages of the Black Death and the Hundred Years' War in the fourteenth century, the French population had almost doubled. Consequently, there was an upsurge in agriculture to meet the growing demand for grain. Land clearance and reclamation provided territory for cultivation while the emancipation of serfs gave incentives for labour. Yet by the mid-sixteenth century grain production failed to keep up with the demographic increase and scarcity soon led to inflation and starvation. Moreover, wages failed to keep up with rising grain prices and there was a surplus of workers on the land. Small peasant holdings were often sold to pay back debts, a trend which was exacerbated in the second half of the sixteenth century by the Wars of Religion. Often such land was bought by the landlords and it was a case of the gap between rich and poor increasing. Unemployment, vagrancy and begging were commonplace in sixteenth-century France and towns witnessed an increase in populations as the poor sought work. With the constant burden of taxation upon their shoulders, life for the peasant was hard, and over 35 years of civil war made it no easier.

Peasant unrest was frequent as a consequence of economic hardships brought about by overmighty landlords looking to make as much profit as possible out of their relatively short land leases, poor harvests, and taxation. Local hardships brought about by economic depression often led to sporadic outbursts of popular protest. Often the revolt was aimed at hated royal tax collectors or agents of the crown in the provinces. Occasionally, as in Brittany in 1675, the rebels targeted local landlords. Yet it tended to be urban officials or royal representatives that were the object of hate, as they were perceived to be encroaching upon the parochial liberties of rural life. The larger peasant revolts often culminated in an attack on the local town, and increasingly peasant revolts appeared to become better organised and focused. In the seventeenth century, lists of grievances were frequently drawn up and presented to *intendants*. Such grievances inevitably pointed out the inequalities of the tax system and asked for arrears to be forgotten. Loyalty was always professed to the monarch and it appears that peasant revolts began to emerge as a legitimate form of political protest. Often concessions were made as royal agents pragmatically realised that collection of the latest tax was more achievable if arrears were reduced or forgotten. At times, force and aggression were used to quell the rebellion and dissuade others from carrying out similar actions. The extent to which French monarchs actually cared about the well-being of their subjects as monarchical power increased is debatable. Despite the various hardships and traumas of the sixteenth and seventeenth centuries, and the increasing fiscal pressures imposed by the crown, the peasantry appeared to get on with life, subdued through fear and a sense of knowing their lot within the social hierarchy into general political ignorance and apathy. Only when their immediate interests came under threat or life became intolerably hard did they make their voice heard, and then their actions could be an unwelcome distraction for the crown and royal troops might be deployed.

CONCLUSIONS

French politics and society witnessed both change and continuity over the course of the sixteenth and seventeenth centuries. Here are some of the major themes:

- Royal authority fluctuated between the Renaissance strength of Francis I and Henry II, and then the civil war weakness under Charles IX and Henry III. Recovery and centralisation marked the reigns of Henry IV and Louis XIII, before the perceived absolutism of Louis XIV.
- Particularism was eroded throughout the period through the codification of law initiated by Louis XII, and the use of royal agents in the provinces, yet local privileges and customs inevitably remained.
- Warfare, both foreign and civil during this period, placed an often untolerable tax burden on the third estate who were already facing pressures of inflation and land shortage.
- The use of venality to fund war and boost the royal coffers increased, thus widening the numbers involved in royal bureaucracy.
- A new noble class, the nobility of the robe, emerged to challenge the traditional political power of the ancient nobility.
- The nobility of the sword remained crucial to the effective rule of the kingdom and their social prestige remained intact.
- The rise of Protestantism in the 1550s threatened the Gallican principles which bound French society together as well as the status of the crown. Only when the civil Wars of Religion finished could the monarchy set about restoring its lost authority.
- French frontiers both at home and abroad extended over the early modern period, reflecting the glory of the French crown, although such gains were offset by the financial costs.
- Noble factions persistently looked to take advantage of the numerous power vacuums which existed in the French crown in order to pursue their own political ambitions.

TO WHAT EXTENT DID FRANCE BECOME A MORE UNIFIED STATE DURING THE PERIOD 1498–1610?

France was hardly developed as a nation in 1498. Nearly one-quarter of the kingdom had been acquired in the previous 50 years; five languages were spoken as well as many regional dialects; the law was uncodified. A nation is built upon a shared culture and common social organisation. In 1500, the state was based much more on the king's sovereignty over his subjects than a defined segment of land. Over the period 1498–1610, the monarchy acted as the central locomotive driving the rise of a nation-state, strengthening the authority of the crown and forging a nation out of diverse beginnings. Through ritual and ceremony, language, law, war and religion a nation was constructed that was more centralised in its government and more unified as a community of Frenchmen. Nevertheless, the process was neither straightforward nor inevitable, nor indeed entirely successful. The chaos of the Wars of Religion in the second half of the sixteenth century highlighted how difficult it was for Frenchmen to imagine a nation: the process of internal unification depended as much on the acceptance of the authority of the king by his subjects as it did on his own will. By 1610, and the untimely death of Henry IV, it is certainly possible to argue that France was more unified and that parochial obstacles had been weakened if not destroyed. The authority of the crown was enhanced, boundaries better defined and centralisation increased. Yet, as we witnessed over the previous hundred years, opposition to such change existed and royal efforts to centralise and unite depended upon political and economic stability.

Territorial boundaries

A unified state requires clearly defined and established territorial boundaries. In 1498, a significant portion of France was new and only recently incorporated. Through marriage, war and inheritance further acquisitions were forthcoming over the next hundred years, forming the geographical outline of what we consider to be modern France. This is an element of change that leaves France as a more definable nation-state by 1610.

The modern hexagon was taking shape but a nation-state also implies shared culture, language, values etc. Did people think of themselves as French or Breton, for example? New *parlements* were established in Provence and Normandy to extend royal authority into newly acquired territories, but centralisation and the development of belief in a nation-state was always likely to be a long and difficult process. Parochial obstacles therefore cast a shadow over territorial unification.

Language/culture

If there is no shared national outlook or identity it becomes difficult to talk of a nation-state. Five principal languages were spoken – French, Occitan, Basque, Breton and Flemish – along with countless dialects: in the north, *langue d'oil* dialect, in the south *langue d'oc*. This was the major split, and while *langue d'oil* spread southwards it was slowly and mainly among the noble, educated classes. The Edict of Villers Cotterêts (1539) decreed the use of French not Latin in legal documents while efforts were made to encourage greater use of French in Metz after 1552 to create a sense of linguistic unity and combat German surroundings. Joachim du Bellay, a poet, wrote the *Defence of the French Language* in 1549.

Yet, while there was a promotion of the French language by the crown, local elites and intelligentsia, regional dialects still existed. At an official and academic level, French triumphed over Latin but it is still difficult to argue that a sense of nationhood was forged through linguistic unity because of the continued use of local dialects.

Law
France was united through 'one king, one faith, one law', yet the one law was the weak link of this chain in 1500. Successive monarchs attempted to unify the diverse legal codes but this process was not completed until the French Revolution. Louis XII commissioned Barme and Baillet to codify and write down the customs of northern France. Many customs were verified and confirmed on paper. Royal commissioners or *baillis* helped this process. The Edict of Villers Cotterêts (1539) ordered the register of births and deaths to be kept by parish priests and French used instead of Latin. The introduction of uniform legal records officialised matters.

However, the Catholic League still used ambiguities in the 1576 Estates General to claim that it was a fundamental law that the French king must be Catholic, and the general chaos of the Wars of Religion hindered progress and a great variety of legal customs and traditions existed all over the kingdom.

Monarchy
The driving force behind centralisation and unification was the monarchy. The process of unification depended upon acceptance of the king's authority by his subjects. Extension of royal authority did not automatically translate into a nation-state.

Royal propaganda and ritual influenced public perception of a nation-state, for example coronation ceremonies and funerals or the king's healing for scrofula.

Louis established a *parlement* in Provence; Francis a *parlement* in Normandy; Henry II a *parlement* in Brittany. The ordinances of Blois

(1499) and Lyons (1510) regulated the role of royal officials. Louis XII introduced the *généraux de finances* (1504) while Francis I utilised *maîtres des requêtes de l'hôtel*. Both Francis I and Henry II increased the power of the crown at the expense of parochial institutions.

Therefore, government was unquestionably more centralised in 1610, although the French Wars of Religion had hindered progress, and obstacles still existed such as tax exemptions. Was the nature of the monarchy consultative or absolutist? Reform and centralisation were possible during periods of economic and political stability. The term nation-state means much more than just centralised government under the crown. Yet foreign adventures such as Milan (1500), Marignano (1515) and the defeat of Spain in 1598 gave some impression of a nation-state. Popular and limited noble opposition represented strength of parochial, local liberties and traditions. France may have been on the road to absolutism by 1610, and to many historians the monarchy was central in defining the nation-state. The heroes here are Louis, Francis and Henry IV but there were factors outside the control of the monarchy that provided problems in the creation of a nation-state.

Religion

In 1498, a clear unifying factor was the Catholic church. The growth of Calvinism in the 1540s and 1550s threatened the Gallican principles which bound a community of believers together. The French Wars of Religion in their scale, length and cost demonstrated how religion became the most disruptive factor in the quest for a nation-state. The recovery and search for unity by a former Protestant, Henry IV, demonstrated the centrality of Catholicism as a factor for stability and unity within France.

Yet, a significant minority of Huguenots still existed in 1610 especially in the Midi. The Edict of Nantes was not revoked until 1685 under Louis XIV. The dissolution of the unity of the church was more than just an intellectual struggle over doctrines and beliefs. Protestantism brought with it the perceived danger of dissolving the nation itself as well as the secular and religious authority on which that sense of nation was based.

TO WHAT EXTENT DID THE STRUCTURE OF SOCIETY AND THE NATURE OF THE ECONOMY CHANGE IN FRANCE 1498–1610?

Nobility

The rise of the nobility of the robe and the role of venality were central to the theme of social change. Venality was constant throughout the period but increased as the financial demands/requirements of the crown increased. Did this constitute social change? There was no real long-term decline of the nobility. Some rural lesser nobles were hit hard by rising prices and fixed rents. However, when they went under it was generally the larger wealthier nobles that bought up their land. Overall the noble class retained its position at the top of the social hierarchy and remained a crucial part of royal government, in terms of maintaining law and order in the provinces.

How were the nobility affected by centralisation and increase in monarchical authority? It is true that during times of monarchical weakness the nobility had greater leeway in the provinces, for example The Day of the Barricades (1588). It can also be argued that strong personal monarchs such as Francis I had greater control over the nobility, for example the execution of Semblancay in 1527. Yet noble opposition continued to exist in strong reigns (Bourbon in 1523) and weak ones (Alençon in 1576).

The monarchy continued to rely upon the nobility to execute the royal will in the provinces and to raise arms. Note how Henry IV bought off the remaining Catholic leaguers in the 1590s. He recognised how crucial noble loyalty was to the recovery of monarchical authority.

Also we must not forget the relatively large number of nobles who committed themselves to Calvinism in the 1550s and 1560s offering the movement much needed protection and credibility. The nobility became polarised during the French Wars of Religion between extreme Catholics such as Guise detached from the crown and extreme Protestants such as Navarre. Ultimately the king found it easier to ally with the latter in 1588.

Peasantry

There were few changes for the peasantry throughout this period. If anything, their position worsened. Peasant unrest demonstrated that even the third estate could take only so much fiscal pressure. In times of war there were heavy fiscal demands made on the third estate and the inequality of society was clear. Any attempts to widen the scope of taxation to include nobles and merchants were unpopular and short-lived.

Social mobility declined in the second half of the sixteenth century and there was a decreasing possibility of wealthier peasants living nobly by the latter half of the sixteenth century.

Economy

Economic change was linked to social change in many respects.

Domestic economy Continuity existed in terms of a fiscal burden on those who could afford to pay least. The French economy initially benefited from the recovery after the ravages of plague and the Hundred

Years' War. Land was plentiful and cheap in the first half of the sixteenth century. Prices were relatively low and rents fixed. In the second half of sixteenth century a different story can be told. Civil war exacerbated what would have been a depression anyway, and made worse the Europe-wide downturn for France. Inflation, rising prices, bad harvests and fixed seigneurial rents would have caused problems but billeting, death and destruction made things much worse. Moreover, the crown was heavily in debt and popular uprisings reflected hard times.

Trade Trade was also underdeveloped in France: communications and small-scale luxury industries mean that France lost out to the major maritime powers such as England or the Netherlands. Parochial tariffs and a lack of national unity did not help matters for French merchants.

Conclusion

That a financial recovery was possible under Henry IV and Sully highlights the importance of peace and stability on the economic fortunes of France. The manner in which Sully liquidated debts and extended royal influence over tax farmers should be applauded, but he was aided by circumstances and a general recovery in the European economy. The French Wars of Religion may not have changed the nature of French society but they did put an enormous burden on the peasantry that was still being felt during Sully's recovery.

TO WHAT EXTENT WAS THE FRENCH MONARCHY SET ON THE ROAD TO ABSOLUTISM 1498–1610?

The traditional view of monarchical power in France highlights the centralising policies of Francis I and Louis XII eroding representative institutions and paving the way for absolutism under Mazarin and Richelieu, culminating in the rule of the Sun King, Louis XIV.

However, the chaos of the Wars of Religion undermined much of the work done by previous monarchs and power swung back to the provinces and local magnates in the second half of the sixteenth century. Abuses by tax farmers and the authority of local estates became more prevalent. It should be argued that the authority and power of the monarchy was undermined by the advent of Protestantism, and the onset of civil war.

Certainly the road towards absolutism was not a straightforward one and it would be wrong to see the increase in monarchical authority as a process. There was no grand plan for absolutism throughout the early modern period. French monarchs recognised the political and economic benefits of a more unified and centralised state, yet we must be cautious in evaluating the extent to which absolutism was achieved. No French monarch was absolutist in the purest sense of the word, in that no king was completely absolved from subordination to any human authority. Not even Louis XIV was absolutist and certainly no sixteenth-century monarch could claim such status. All were limited by the moral conventions of the age, such as the contemporary disapproval of political assassination and of mass murder. Look what happens after Henry III had the Guises assassinated in 1588: resistance theories emerged calling for the assassination of the king himself. The French did not equate absolutism with tyranny as everyone from the king downwards believed that a Christian ruler, however powerful, had duties both to God and his subjects. As the Father of the People he should behave responsibly and remember that although he had no constitutional obligation to keep the law, the law still existed and that it was a Christian king's duty to uphold its authority.

Therefore, the question here is whether Bourbon absolutism was established in some way by Valois rulers and then Henry IV. Obviously we rule out Henry III, although his reign was important in demonstrating the importance of unity through religion and the Catholicity of the crown. The turmoil of his reign showed how necessary strong monarchical rule was in order to avoid such internal disaster. Nevertheless, Mack Holt in *French Wars of Religion 1582–1629* (1996), sees it as a cliché that the disorder of the civil wars led to the absolutism of the seventeenth century. Yet, there is little doubt that the legacy of the French Wars of Religion served as a constant reminder to all later kings of the necessity for a strong monarchy.

Francis and Louis had done much to strengthen the power of the crown at the expense of local, parochial privileges and representative institutions. Both reigns were strongly personal and leant more towards coercion than consultation. *Parlements* still existed and in times of monarchical weakness and political instability they provided a focal point for political opposition. The Estates Generals met rarely but was often an indicator of monarchical weakness, as in 1576 and 1588 (both in Blois). Traditional parochialism too impinged upon monarchical authority in the form of tax exemptions, municipal councils and regional *parlements*. Provinces such as Burgundy, Brittany, Languedoc, Provence, Béarn, Guyenne and Dauphiné were those most recently incorporated into the French realm (since 1453) and they retained many local privileges and liberties as part of their bargain with the crown upon their incorporation. All were *pays d'états* as they retained their provincial estates to assess and collect tax. Regions with provincial estates made up one-third of the taxable population of France yet provided barely one-tenth of the crown's revenue from direct taxation.

Of course, the nobility also could provide an obstacle to absolutism. The king still relied upon the nobility to keep law and order, raise troops and make important decisions. Building up clientele networks through patronage was an important part of royal government. The problem was that major families such as the Guises built up vast clientele networks of their own throughout the realm which could rival or surpass those of the king. The army and military strength are on the absolutism checklist. Yet French military strength declined in the period 1498–1610 from the high point of Marignano to the invasion by German Protestants in 1576 and 1587, and Spain in 1590, 1592 and 1596–7. All these invasions proved impossible to stop and only the last of them was successfully repelled. Fifty thousand was about the limit of the French army at any one time. Funding was unavailable to keep the army in the field for any length of time. This left the king reliant on his great magnates to raise forces: this was satisfactory if they were on his side. The opposition of the Protestant Navarre and the Catholic Guise were visible examples of how precarious noble support could be. Mack Holt believes that absolutism was always more of a prototype of how government was supposed to work rather than how it actually worked in practice. Francis I and Henry IV may not have been the predestined architects of absolutism claimed by traditional historiography but there is no question that their reforms and influence enhanced and centralised the authority of the crown.

SECTION 2

To what extent was Henry IV a modern king?

The reign of Henry IV is often seen as a watershed in the history of early modern France. After almost four decades of civil strife, the first Bourbon king re-established the authority of the crown and brought peace and stability to a kingdom ravaged by war. Henry did much to continue the work carried out by his Valois predecessors Louis XII, Francis I and Henry II in terms of good government and the creation of a nation-state. In particular, Henry is credited with the rebuilding of France after the Wars of Religion through:

- centralisation of government and overriding of provincial powers
- payment of debt and restoration of royal finances
- control of the nobility
- legitimate male heirs
- successful invasion of Savoy.

Yet, we must be aware of limitations to this argument. Financial constraints prevented Henry making a lasting impression on the European stage and, as always, there were obstacles preventing the effective centralisation of government. Moreover, we might consider Henry fortunate in the context of his reign because most of France was war-weary and ready to work towards a lasting peace. For once, confessional antagonism took second place to more pragmatic concerns, and it is worth considering just how many of Henry IV's reforms were innovative.

PEACE, ORDER AND STABILITY, 1583–1610

The year 1598 is a crucially important one in the reign of Henry IV: the Edict of Nantes and the Peace of Vervins were both signed in the spring, bringing France's long period of war to a close. The Edict of Nantes was a compromise peace settlement based loosely on the principle of long-term unity and Gallicanism. Nevertheless, the concessions contained within the royal brevets had the effect of creating a Huguenot state within a state in the Midi region, and to many the Huguenots were a privileged group dependent upon royal favour and finance. Moreover, an edict alone was no guarantee of peace on the ground, as Catherine de Medici had found out. In reality, the Edict of Nantes was little different from the treaties of the previous decades in that Huguenot toleration was still permitted in certain places and surety towns were assured. Henry was fortunate in one respect because, despite the lenient terms of toleration contained within the royal brevets, France was tired of war and ready to embrace peace. This context allowed Henry to take a precarious middle line, appeasing both confessional groups. Yet we must never lose sight of what really sold the treaty to the Catholic majority: the long-term aim of unity. Huguenot privileges were supposed to be temporary. The edict was certainly not innovative in that it laid out and met the same obstacles which previous settlements had encountered. The edict met stiff opposition from the *parlements* resentful of the creation of Huguenot surety towns and *chambres mi parties*. It took two years of forceful persuasion from Henry himself to persuade the *parlements* to register the edict and even then Rouen avoided formal registration until 1609. Furthermore, law and order had largely broken down in the localities, particularly in the south-west where local nobles and office holders had become a law unto themselves raising taxation at will and charging massive interest rates on loans. It took several years to eradicate such brigandage. Finally, Huguenot surety towns and assemblies effectively undermined royal authority and caused general friction. It was no surprise that by 1610 the Huguenots were once more thinking about war. Henry IV should be given great credit for his twin policies of appeasement and unity which combined to produce a lasting peace settlement. Yet to argue that this peace was popular or innovative would be wrong. Henry certainly benefited from the general feeling of exhaustion that most Frenchmen held in 1598.

In 1595, having placated most of the great leaguer nobles, Henry felt strong enough to declare war on Spain. Again, given years of civil war this was a shrewd move because it served to unite the country in a national campaign against Philip II and further undermine an important ally of the League. An immediate victory at Fontaine-Française in June 1595 boosted Henry's status and prestige. The following year, Amiens fell to the French and, when Mercouer, the last leaguer noble holding out in Brittany, turned over to the new king, Philip II was ready to negotiate peace terms. Nearing death and in financial crisis, Philip was ready to make peace on the terms of 1559. The Peace of Vervins was signed on 2 May 1598 and accordingly it stated that all towns captured by either side since Cateau-Cambrésis in 1559 should be returned. The treaty therefore returned Calais, Toul, Metz, Verdun and Amiens to France which importantly maintained France's north-eastern frontier. In return, France agreed to papal arbitration over French claims to Saluzzo (seized by the duke of Savoy in 1588), a responsibility which Clement VIII ignored. In 1600, Henry declared war on Savoy over the Saluzzo question. The resultant peace treaty of 1601 saw Henry give up claims to Saluzzo but receive Bresse, Bugey, Valromey and Gex. Therefore, Vervins as with Nantes sowed seeds of discontent for the future and peace with Spain was always fragile. Again, Henry was limited by financial constraints and for the most part satisfied himself with funding the Dutch rebels in their fight for independence against Spain and encouraging the Turks to attack Calabria and Naples. Spain similarly looked to cause trouble for Henry, supporting discontented French nobles such as Biron and Bouillon. Trade wars were also commonplace and had it not been for financial constraints Henry might have been more aggressive in his relations with Spain, a point reinforced by the fact that the French king mobilised three times between 1600 and 1610. Therefore, the portrayal of a frugal, careful and pragmatic king who did not sap the royal coffers with unnecessary foreign adventures needs some readjustment. Initially, Henry sought peace because he had to, but in the long term there seems little doubt that Henry intended a more bellicose foreign policy.

FINANCIAL REFORM

One of the great achievements of Henry IV was the restoration of royal finances. In 1598, the royal debt stood at 300 million livres while no uniform system of tax collection or assessment existed. By 1608, over half the debt was paid, mortgages on crown property had been redeemed and a large revenue had been accumulated in the treasury. Moreover, central administration had permeated the localities in a more systematic manner than before, and tax farming was better regulated.

Sully

The man who deserves to take much of the credit for Henry's financial recovery is Maximilien de Béthune, Duke of Sully. Sully held the post of *surintendant des finances* (1598–1611), and was unquestionably the most important minister on the royal council. Many on the council such as Bellièvre (chancellor 1599–1607), Villeroy (foreign affairs) and Brulart de Sillery (chancellor after 1607) were noble, conservative and cautious. Many were veterans of Henry III's reign. Sully on the other hand was Huguenot, adventurous, dynamic and more closely aligned with the king.

Sully was diligent, conscientious and energetic as can be seen by the number of areas in which he was involved. Apart from finance, Sully was responsible for royal fortifications, buildings, the navy and artillery and for the general upkeep of highways, bridges and canals. Yet by far his most remarkable achievement was to accumulate a reserve of 15 million livres by 1610.

Debt

The immediate problem facing Sully in 1598 was the royal debt, and the large amounts of money owed to England, the Swiss cantons and individual lenders throughout France. Sully's aim was to reduce the figure bit by bit in order gradually to restore the king's credit rating and secure loans once again from the major bankers. Much of the debt was simply written off or renegotiated as France had declared bankruptcy after the Wars of Religion.

- States such as the Swiss cantons were ready to accept immediate token cash repayments which France could afford, rather than wait for total repayment over a long period of time. In the end, the Swiss cantons received only one-seventh of the 36 million livres owed to them.
- Debts with Tuscany were repaid through Henry IV's marriage to Marie de Medici in 1600, whereby 2 million livres were wiped out as part of her dowry by the grand duke, Ferdinand I.
- France also owed over 4 million livres to England and only when Elizabeth threatened trade restrictions did Henry agree to pay back some of the debts incurred during the Wars of Religion. Even then, Sully persuaded the English queen to allow one-third of France's subsidy to the Dutch rebels to count towards its debt repayments, thus continuing Henry's *cold war* against the Spanish while paying off foreign debts.
- Internal debts and those owed to lesser German princes were often simply ignored and remained unpaid, which provoked resentment and anger but little open hostility.

Sully was not popular during the reign of Henry IV but he was effective in liquidating the past and wiping out the bulk of Henry's debt in quick time. Despite such activity, one-sixteenth of the king's income was still devoted to paying for the Wars of Religion in 1608.

Indirect taxation

One of the principal features of Sully's ministry was a shift towards indirect taxation. The total levy from the *taille* decreased from 18 million livres to an average of 15.8 million livres between 1600 and 1610. Therefore, the burden on the third estate, which had been so heavy during the Wars of Religion, was relieved slightly and Sully instead concentrated on increasing revenue via indirect taxation. In particular, the main indirect tax was the *gabelle*, levied on a variable basis in five out of six areas of France. The problem here was that it was unequal in its distribution and assessment and the areas in which the *gabelle* was high found themselves burdened by increases in the price of salt. The yield from indirect taxes on the whole, however, reflected a strengthened economy after 1600. More efficient collection seemed to be the key although it is worth remembering that, despite the apparent emphasis on indirect taxation, revenue from this source only amounted to around 17 per cent of the total paid into the treasury. Moreover, an innovative indirect tax known as the *pancarte* which constituted a 5 per cent sales tax on all goods for sale at markets in walled towns proved so unpopular that rioting broke out in Poitiers and Angiers in 1601 and again at Limoges the following year. The *pancarte* was abolished in November 1602, thus illustrating the problems in attempting to raise revenue by encroaching upon the privileges of the towns. In reality, while tradition may see Henry IV as a king who genuinely cared about the welfare of his subjects the burden of direct taxation remained heavy and in the *pays d'élections* it contributed an average 49.6 per cent of total revenues (1600–4). Perhaps more importantly Sully was willing to write off unrealistic arrears of tax and at the same time investigate cases of corruption in the local administration of the *taille* and to reapportion the burden around the villages. The breakdown in royal authority during the Wars of Religion had exacerbated the problem of decentralised government and Sully did much to itemise and outlaw abuses in the *taille*.

Tax farming

Sully also tackled the age-old problem of tax farming, described by one contemporary observer as the great destroyer of the kingdom's revenue. Specially constituted commissions of judicial enquiry were established, called *chambres de justice*. Such courts of enquiry did not essentially outlaw or prohibit tax farming, but rather regulated the practice and ensured loyalty and accountability from the officials concerned. Indeed, a properly audited and regulated system of tax farming had its benefits for the crown. Tax farmers were those individuals who collected taxes in the localities. Usually, individual contracts were made with the tax farmers and bids for tax farms went to the highest bidder at auction. The crown would issue the subsequent contract. The problem with the system was that it had been much abused by greedy nobles who took advantage of the semi-anarchy during the Wars of Religion to levy exorbitant rates of taxation and make enormous profits for themselves at the expense of the crown. As well as investigating corruption the *chambres de justice* raised money because many officials preferred offering non-refundable loans to the crown rather than face potential ruin at trial. Increased centralisation led to more effective tax collection, and Sully was aided by a general economic recovery throughout Europe after the recession of the 1580s and 1590s. Nevertheless, uniformity in tax collection remained out of the question given the popularity and power of the provincial estates (or *pays d'états*). The *pay d'états* were those provinces such as Brittany and Languedoc in which taxation was levied by the local estates as opposed to the *pays d'élections* where taxation was levied by officials on orders from the king's council. Henry and Sully attempted to unify the means of tax assessment and collection by eroding the privileges of the *pays d'états* and they partly succeeded in Guyenne where eight elections were established to administer the *taille* on behalf of the crown. However, bitter opposition from the other provincial estates meant the reforms were not applied to the whole kingdom. Provincial estates in Dauphiné, Provence, Languedoc and Burgundy were unwilling to pass tax collection over to royal officials and they were often supported by local nobles in their defence of parochial privilege. Henry risked open revolt by encroaching upon their liberties, but such concessions undermined Henry's authority and both he and Sully regarded the provincial estates as enemies of the crown.

The *paulette*
One lucrative measure which Sully introduced in 1604 was the *paulette*, a device which allowed royal officials to ensure that their heirs would continue to possess their offices, in return for one-sixtieth of the capital value. Knecht likens the *paulette* to an insurance premium payable by office holders to exempt them from the 40-day rule, while Greengrass sees the strength of the heredity tax lying in its equal appeal to all parties. Certainly, to the office holders it made financial sense as the annual rate was a reasonable payment in return for the continued benefit of their investment by their heirs. For the king the *paulette* created a predictable income from royal offices and removed offices from the patronage of leading nobles. Every office holder who paid the annual sum was reminded that he owed loyalty to the king and the long-term political consequences of the *paulette* should not be underestimated. Venality and the sale of royal offices had long been an important source of revenue for the monarchy but such procedures had not always been advantageous to the authority of the crown. Now the *paulette* ensured that venality took place on the crown's terms and the bribery and corruption involved in the process was officialised and directed into the royal coffers rather than the pockets of influential intermediaries.

Assessment of financial reform
- Under Sully the royal budget achieved a surplus by 1610, standing at 15 million livres.
- Foreign debts were effectively liquidated through advantageous renegotiation or, in the case of Tuscany, marriage.
- Sully maintained a tight control on expenditure and kept a strict budget for artillery, roads and bridges. The court was not lavish and Marie de Medici's expenditure was closely monitored.
- Centralisation improved the collection of taxation and, while corruption and privilege were not eradicated, they were turned to the advantage of the crown, for example by the *paulette* and the *chambres de justice*.
- Obstacles to the effective administration of the *taille* were insurmountable and the provincial estates remained virtually autonomous in tax collection.

CENTRALISATION

The provincial estates and the towns jealously guarded their liberties and privileges with regard to tax exemptions and local government. Henry was eager to extend royal influence into the localities, both to strengthen his own position and to increase revenue. Already Louis XII and to a greater extent Francis I had begun this process of centralisation with varying degrees of success. Certainly royal commissioners in the localities (or *maîtres des requêtes de l'hôtel*) were regularly dispatched to ensure that royal proclamations were upheld and adhered to. Such men were drawn from the court and were not the beneficiaries of venality, therefore they owed total loyalty to the crown. Such commissioners were the forerunners to Richelieu's *intendants* who were regular and permanent agents of the crown in the localities. Under Sully provincial problems were dealt with more effectively by royal commissioners but there were not enough of them and their role was as yet ill-defined. As Knecht observes, the *intendants de justice* became the pillar of royal absolutism under Louis XIII and Louis XIV yet under Sully they were used haphazardly and the traditional obstacles to royal authority still existed, namely the *parlements*, provincial estates, the towns and the nobility. After 40 years of near anarchy, Henry and Sully did a remarkable job in restoring royal authority and the prestige of the crown, and the restoration of royal finances is testament to the extent which they were able to penetrate parochial barriers. However, despite the widening powers of the *maîtres des requêtes de l'hôtel* and the planting of royal lieutenants in town governments the centralisation of royal administration still had a long way to go before the king's word immediately became law throughout the kingdom.

HENRY IV AND THE NOBILITY

Until the birth of Louis XIII in 1601 and his brother Gaston in 1608, the Bourbon succession remained uncertain, and therefore aristocratic intrigue continued to remain close to the surface. The legitimacy of Henry IV's divorce and subsequent marriage to Marie de Medici was controversial and the blood relationship between Henry and his Valois predecessor so distant that many princes believed their claim better. This, combined with Habsburg determination to undermine the Bourbon monarch, contributed to sporadic instability and some noble discontent.

Actually, Henry IV did much to repair the damage of 40 years of civil war through generous pensions, careful regulation of provincial governors and limited numbers of new peers. Inevitably there were those who resented the huge pensions handed out to leaguer nobles in order to ensure loyalty, and those omitted from the royal council felt ostracised and isolated. Nevertheless, Henry did much to increase the authority of the crown in the localities through the erosion of duties expected of the provincial governors. The governors were encouraged to reside at court, thus giving them the impression that they were sharing in the decision-making process, while more trustworthy lesser nobles were utilised as provincial lieutenants to ensure that the king's will was carried out in the provinces. Such lieutenants limited the seriousness and extent of noble discontent in the localities although two significant noble revolts occurred around Gascony.

In January 1601, marshal de Biron, who had become an admiral in 1592, marshal in 1594 and provincial governor of Burgundy in 1596 admitted to conspiring with Spanish agents. Despite such treasonable activity, Henry pardoned Biron in the hope that such leniency would be reciprocated with loyalty. Yet Biron was ambitious and very much pro-Spain. After the conflict with Savoy, Biron was once more found to be organising a rebellion to depose Henry IV: in July 1602 he was arrested and then executed in the Bastille. Other nobles in Auvergne and Gascony were implicated and Sully made them beg for forgiveness.

One leading nobleman deeply implicated with Biron and Philip III was the Duke of Bouillon. Like Biron, Bouillon had been close to Henry as a lieutenant-general during the Wars of Religion and he held vast lands in the south-west as well as the principality of Sedan on the German border. Given the fact that Henry IV still owed large amounts of money to German Protestant princes, which had not been forthcoming, Bouillon represented a dangerous focal point for rebellion. Moreover, Bouillon's brother-in-law was Frederick IV of the Palatinate. Bouillon fled to Sedan and attempted to raise support with Spanish money. Few in France or Geneva rallied to his unconvincing Protestant martyr act, and by 1606 Henry IV had become fed up with continued speculation of an aristocratic conspiracy involving former leaguers and Protestant princes. Henry IV travelled in person to Sedan at the head of a large force. Over 1000 nobles came before the king on his travels to profess their loyalty and, as Henry prepared to besiege Sedan, Bouillon surrendered in return for a pardon and confirmation of all of his offices.

Ultimately, both revolts were overly ambitious and never likely to succeed. Henry dealt effectively with them, preferring by and large to show clemency rather than ruthlessness. Loyalty and control were the keys to Henry's relationship with the nobility and he remained rightfully suspicious of leading noble families such as Condé, Soissons and Guise. Henry could not afford to alienate the princes of the blood and exclude them from power although he did not wish to hand such individuals too much authority. Henry looked to organise marriage alliances among the nobility which maintained old rivalries and kept the grandees disunited in the face of increasing royal authority. Moreover, Henry was increasingly able to call upon a new group of nobles, the so called nobility of the robe, who had steadily increased their status and power since 1500. This new administrative noble class had risen through the ranks of office holders and had benefited from the increase in venality. The need for ready cash during the civil wars meant a rapid rise in venality and the number of royal office holders doubled in provinces such as Rouen. The effects were threefold – unsuitable candidates bought positions of power and often profited greatly from them, the associated bureaucracy increased as did the wage bill footed by the crown, and the old nobility of the sword felt threatened by the advance of this new class of noble. On the other hand, the sale of offices provided a lucrative source of income and the introduction of the *paulette* from 1604 ensured that the crown received an annual income from office holders and maintained some control over them. Moreover, few that bought offices held any great power and to argue that the nobility of the robe challenged the social status of the nobility of the sword would be wrong although some families from new and old did intermarry. More and more, the king relied on a trusty inner council to make and break policy – men such as Bellièvre, Villeroy and Sully. The great nobles were not excluded entirely from the decision-making process and certainly they were influential at court. Moreover, it was still the higher nobility that the king relied upon to raise arms and provide loans and Henry dare not antagonise them unnecessarily. Similarly, the nobility depended upon the king for status, power and position and largely it was in their interests to be close to the king. While discontented factions existed within the old nobility, none were united or strong enough to threaten the crown.

FOREIGN POLICY

Given financial restraints, Henry was content to pursue a *cold war* policy against Spain in the period 1598–1609 whereby good relations were maintained with the Dutch republic, England and the German Protestant princes. Subsidies to the Dutch were often poorly disguised as repayments to England but, given the relatively weak position of the Habsburgs and Spain, there was little threat of invasion. Indeed France's enemies reciprocated the more subtle policy of funding and aiding enemies of the king, for example the support offered to Biron and Bouillon. Given the semi-autonomous nature of a number of principalities on France's eastern frontier, such as Lorraine, Franche-Comté and Savoy, tension was inevitable especially with Spain which required safe passage through some of these areas en route to the Netherlands.

Although Henry's main aim appeared to be to keep the Habsburgs weak without resorting to war and sapping the royal coffers, the king was bellicose by nature and, supported by Sully, he mobilised three times between 1600 and 1610. On the first occasion, French force was directed against Charles Emmanuel, duke of Savoy, over the question of Saluzzo.

The fate of Saluzzo had been left to papal arbitration in the Peace of Vervins, but Clement VIII had found such responsibility too onerous and instead a decision was reached by a neutral commission whereby the duke agreed to cede Saluzzo by June 1600 or offer other territories as compensation. Charles Emmanuel had previously sought Spanish aid in seizing Saluzzo in 1588 and followed this with raids on Provence (1589) and Dauphiné (1593). The marquisate itself was strategically important, situated in northern Italy through which Spanish supplies could pass. When Henry received news that the duke was once more enlisting Spanish aid to defend the marquisate he mobilised French forces and a small force of 50,000 men invaded Savoy with great success. All Savoyard territory west of the Alps was captured and, before Spain could intervene on a large scale, Henry made peace in January 1601. France ceded Saluzzo in return for Bresse, Gex and Valromey and 800,000 écus. Given the success of the Savoy invasion Henry appears to have come out badly from the Peace of Lyons. The Spanish had free access across the Alps and through Saluzzo while the principalities France received were much less prosperous. Perhaps Henry was happy to take what he could and replenish his finances in the meantime, but it certainly seems that he was a better soldier than he was a diplomat.

The second cause for mobilisation was the Bouillon conspiracy of 1606 which was dealt with efficiently. However, the twelve-year truce (in which France had acted as mediator) between the Dutch republic and Spain altered the nature of Franco-Spanish relations and made conflict a distinct possibility. In March 1609, the Duke of Cleves, Jülich, Mark and Berg died leaving no heir. His duchy was situated between the northern Netherlands and their German Protestant princes. Should the Habsburgs claim control of the duchy the future of the United Provinces of the Netherlands would be in real danger and the balance of power would unquestionably swing in favour of the Habsburgs. The Emperor Rudolf II ordered his cousin Leopold to occupy the duchy and fend off other claimants, most notably the Dukes of Brandenburg and Neuberg. In July 1609, the emperor proclaimed the sequestration of the duchy and Spanish troops soon occupied Jülich. In October 1609, Henry issued an ultimatum to the emperor to vacate the duchy and, when no reply was forthcoming, Henry prepared France for war. By May 1610, over 50,000 troops had been mobilised with aid coming from England, the Dutch and the German Protestants. Campaigns against Jülich, Cleves and Milan were planned for the summer of 1610 but, before these could be put into operation, Henry was assassinated on 14 May 1610. Some argue that Henry's assassination saved France from a ruinous and disastrous war against Spain while others believe that Henry just planned to give the Habsburgs a sharp lesson in Germany before pursuing his desire to marry his son to the Infanta of Spain. Henry's sudden demise obscures his designs, although his assassination did reveal the dangers of what many construed as an anti-Catholic foreign policy because the assassin, Ravaillac, appears to have acted out of Catholic zeal, certain that Henry was an enemy of the pope and the true faith.

THE ASSASSINATION OF HENRY IV

More than twenty attempts were made on Henry's life over the course of his reign, mainly by Catholic extremists who doubted the sincerity of his conversion from Protestantism to Catholicism. Henry's foreign alliances with the Dutch republic, England and the German princes convinced zealous Catholics that he was merely a lapsed heretic.

On 14 May 1610, the king travelled from the Louvre to the Arsenal by coach. As the coach stopped in traffic on the rue la Ferronnière, Henry was stabbed three times through the open carriage window by Ravaillac. Henry died almost at once while Ravaillac, seemingly acting alone, was brutally tortured and then had his body pulled apart by horses.

WAS HENRY IV A MODERN KING?

Henry IV, the first Bourbon king, takes his place in French history as the monarch who arrested the decline which France had experienced since 1562. In the process he showed great concern for the welfare of his subjects and restored political and social order to the kingdom. Above all else he put the monarchy on a firm footing economically and enhanced the authority of the crown, paving the way for the absolutism of Louis XIII and Louis XIV.

There is little doubt that Henry achieved a great deal in a short period of time, although his reputation was heightened by the fact that he became a royal martyr at the hands of Ravaillac and through the vastly inflated picture of him offered in Sully's memoirs written in 1611 and entitled *Sage et royales économies d'état … de Henri le grand.*

The extent to which Henry cared for the welfare of his subjects is debatable. Certainly the two peace edicts of 1598 were crucially important in giving France some breathing space after 40 years of civil conflict. The Wars of the League in the 1580s and 1590s had been particularly ruinous and, with the economy in tatters and the third estate in revolt in the south-west, Henry recognised the need for peace. Both the Edict of Nantes and the Peace of Vervins were successful in the short term and served their purpose. The Edict of Nantes remained effective on paper for 87 years although tension was never far from the surface as can be seen in Louis XIII's assault on Protestant Béarn and the subsequent decision by the Reformed assembly at La Rochelle to divide France into eight circles. The Edict of Nantes did not end the Wars of Religion; it was the Peace of Alais in 1629 which fulfilled that role, although it was not until 1685 that the Edict of Nantes was revoked by Louis XIV in a bid to restore unity in France. Similarly, the Peace of Vervins sowed seeds of future discontent with regard to the marquisate of Saluzzo. Henry was bellicose by nature but recognised the need to buy time in order to restore royal finances. Yet his increasing aggression towards the end of his reign revealed his true intentions, and had he not been assassinated it is likely that he would have committed France to all-out war against Spain. Therefore, two important points must be made:

- The Edict of Nantes succeeded in maintaining peace because the population was ready to accept anything which offered a respite in the hostilities. In the long term, the problem of a Huguenot minority in the south still existed.
- Henry did not commit himself to an aggressive foreign policy until 1600 because he did not have the financial resources to do so, not because he did not want to. To argue that he had the welfare of his subjects at heart may be wide of the mark. Had he not been assassinated Henry may have been remembered as the king who took France into a ruinous and disastrous war against Spain.

Unquestionably the finest achievement of Henry's short reign was the restoration of royal finances. Thanks in large part to the ministry of Sully there was a budgetary surplus of 15 million livres by the end of Henry's reign. A shift towards indirect taxation, a liquidisation of past debts and innovative reforms limiting corruption all contributed to a steady financial base. Yet, while it was relatively straightforward to liquidate the past and write off old debts the actual economic rebuilding of France at grassroots level was a much more arduous and long-term task. In eastern France, local trade and agricultural had been heavily affected by the Wars of Religion and then Henry's preparations for the siege of Sedan. It was well into the seventeenth century before the industry and population of France saw recovery from the combined ravages of plague, war and famine which had so blighted the kingdom between 1562 and 1598. Moreover, the budgetary surplus of 15 million livres should be compared to the 10 million livres spent by the regent, Marie de Medici, between 1610 and 1614 on magnates such as Condé, Mayenne, Conti and Nevers in order to preserve peace. The purse-strings were certainly loosened after Henry's death and Sully's retirement. In short:

- Direct taxation remained high in several parts of the kingdom and economic recovery on the ground was slow. The people were still suffering the effects of war after Henry's death.

- The duration of Henry's reign was so short that we cannot expect too much in terms of long-term recovery. The simple recovery of royal finances was a remarkable achievement.

In terms of restoring royal authority and eroding provincial liberties Henry had mixed success. There can be little doubt that Henry did much to raise the prestige and status of the monarchy and he should be praised for the way in which he appeased leaguer nobles in the 1590s and unified the country in a war against Spain in 1595. Moreover, both the Edict of Nantes and the Peace of Vervins came at the right time and Henry skilfully played a middle line between Huguenot toleration and Catholic desires for unity which ultimately led to further conflict but which brought a sustained period of peace. Few unified aristocratic revolts occurred during Henry's reign, although the disloyal activities of Biron and Bouillon were a sign of things to come and the nobility proved more troublesome under the minority of Louis XIII culminating in the Fronde. Both for political and financial purposes Henry tried hard to penetrate local privileges and traditions. Tax farmers were regulated while the *paulette* served to bring in a predictable annual income and ensure loyalty from office holders. Royal lieutenants and *chambres de justice* were not really innovative ideas but in the context of the previous 40 years of warfare it was important that Henry set about re-enforcing the royal will in the countryside and in the towns. Again, given the duration of his reign could we really expect Henry to break down barriers that had existed for centuries? Provincial estates and urban councils remained thorns in the side of the monarchy and to an extent continued to undermine the authority of the crown. Henry wanted to tax the *pays d'états* more heavily, and through the creation of eight elections in Guyenne he did start to erode their privileges. However, Henry and Sully were never able to impose uniformity of tax collection on the kingdom and probably they never believed it possible. They were trying to restore royal authority and collect as much income as they could from the provinces. It seems clear that the brigandage and abuses carried out by lesser nobles during the Wars of Religion were much less serious during Henry's reign, and the king's idea to encourage royal governors to reside at court set a precedent for future kings. Therefore with regard to centralisation, Henry was able to:

- regulate corruption and increase the yield collected from the *taille*
- permeate the localities with royal agents who maintained law and order while enforcing the king's will.

However,

- Provincial estates and town councils still held much autonomous power and guarded their privileges fiercely.

- Too few royal commissioners existed to make a significant difference on the ground.

In conclusion, Henry's reputation has probably been inflated over time and in some respects he was fortunate that the people of France were ready for peace at any cost. Moreover, Henry was ably assisted by the very hard-working Sully to whom much credit should be directed. Henry may have been concerned for the welfare of his subjects and the general decrease in direct taxation must have been welcomed. Nevertheless, for the majority of the population life was still uncertain and hard. Henry himself was primarily interested in restoring the finances and maintaining order – the welfare of his subjects was a by-product rather than a priority. Henry restored royal authority, but such was the nature of French politics it was destined to be short-lived. On his death, Henry left a 9-year-old son to succeed him, namely Louis. The regent was Henry's widow Marie de Medici, ruling with a council dominated by Catholics many of whom were ex-leaguers. The situation mirrored that of 1559 and the fragility of Henry IV's years of stability was clear for all to see.

SECTION 3

The ascendancy of France, 1610–1715

WAS LOUIS XIV'S ABSOLUTISM A MYTH OR REALITY?

Absolutism as a concept revolves around the idea of kings being
appointed by God to rule as His representative on earth. As such they
were above the law and subject to no restraint on their authority. The
people over whom monarchs ruled could not resist them because kings
could be punished only by God. In theory, absolutism existed only in the
pamphlets written and disseminated by royal propagandists. In practice,
royal absolutism of a sort certainly developed in France throughout the
sixteenth and seventeenth centuries resulting in a more defined nation-
state and a more centralised government. At the heart of such
developments was the concept of monarchy. While restraints would
always exist on the power of French monarchs, Louis XIV's reign marked
the high point of royal authority: an authority based around the
traditional values of order, hierarchy and stability.

**Louix XIV as the
Sun King**

The zenith of French absolutism was supposedly reached during the
personal rule of Louis XIV (1661–1715). Throughout the course of the
sixteenth and early seventeenth centuries, French monarchs attempted to
enhance their own authority at the expense of traditional institutions such
as the *parlements* and the nobility. Indeed, we might argue that much of
the groundwork for Louis XIV's absolutism was laid by the centralising
policies of monarchs such as Francis I and Henry IV. A natural and
smooth progression from Louis XII through Francis I and Henry II, a
blip with the Wars of Religion, recovery under Henry IV, consolidation
and growth of royal authority overseen by Richelieu and Mazarin, with
absolutism hitting its peak under the personal rule of the Sun King is a
tempting one for historians to mark out. Such plans for French
absolutism did not of course exist. Yet we can see a gradual reduction in
the institutional restraints on the exercise of royal authority, and there is
little doubt that Louis XIV benefited from much of the work of his
predecessors.

The Estates General, for example, had long since lost any powers of
restraint on the French crown, while provincial estates had also seen their
political influence eroded throughout the late sixteenth and early
seventeenth centuries. The lack of authority from the estates gave the
crown increased powers in law-making and tax assessment and collection.
Royal intervention in the realm of municipal government under Sully,

Richelieu and Mazarin had weakened urban councils. Royal agents in the towns, such as the *intendants,* encroached upon urban finances while venality often served to alter the nature of previously elected offices into hereditary ones or ones that were up for sale. *Parlements* were perhaps the main institutions that curbed the full exercise of royal authority. Yet the *parlements* really only served northern and central France. Successive French monarchs had undermined the capacity of a *parlement* to interfere in politics and affairs of state, and even its pre-eminence as a law court had been threatened. Increasingly, the judgements of *parlements* were being annulled by royal law courts and its sphere of influence reduced by Richelieu's arbitrary commissions. The royal council was clearly becoming stronger at the expense of *parlements*. Perhaps we should not be surprised at this development under Louis XIV, as the reorganisation of the *grand conseil* had taken place over 100 years before under Francis I, a move intended to curb the influence of *parlements*. In short, Louis XIV was not doing anything new in terms of attempting to extend royal authority and erode local decision-making bodies. Yet we might argue that Louis XIV, more than any other French monarch, was able to project a more effective image of absolutism and centralise French government under the authority of the king more effectively.

At times of royal weakness in the sixteenth and seventeenth centuries political theories had emerged to challenge the divine right of kings. All French monarchs believed that it was God that established kings, and that it was the people's duty to accept this fact. The king could not be subject to himself; he was above the law. Only those to whom God gave responsibility for affairs of state could fully understand the full significance of statecraft and again it was the responsibility of the populace to accept this as politics were essentially beyond their comprehension. Yet, during the Wars of Religion both Catholic and Protestant resistance theories had emerged challenging the authority and right of the king to rule over his subjects in such a manner. Indeed, after the murder of the Guise brothers in 1588 on the authority of Henry III, the right to depose tyrannical kings had been forcibly expressed by Jean Boucher, in a tract that perhaps motivated the subsequent assassination of Henry III. The argument proposed by Boucher was that the contract between the people and God superseded that between king and subjects. The king had an obligation to God to rule justly and if he flouted this then he must face the consequences. Such radical ideas also surfaced during the Fronde where pamphlets stressed a constitutional argument emphasising the elective nature of the French monarchy and the importance of the nobility in the ancient assemblies of the Franks. Claude Joly picked up the mantle from Boucher arguing that French kings derived their power from the people and were subject to the laws of state like everyone else. Arbitrary law courts and the sidelining of *parlements* were wrong, while the Estates General should be called on a regular basis with the aim of re-establishing the ancient customs and liberties of France. Nevertheless, while such literature probably did represent the views of many of those who held office, it tended only to arise in times of crisis and royal weakness. In general, absolute reverence for the king and a firm belief that kings were divinely appointed and could only be removed by God's will prevailed.

Whereas in England the issues of arbitrary taxation without the consent of parliament and the use of star chamber as an arbitrary law court moved the commons to civil war and regicide, the story in France was a very different one. After the Wars of Religion, the emphasis on internal stability underpinned by a strong monarch, appointed by God, was heightened. The need for hierarchy and order was stressed again and again by royal propagandists. Absolutism did not emerge from the Wars of Religion; again that would be too simplistic. However, the traditional image of the French monarch as God's representative on earth, as the fulcrum of the traditional, natural order and hierarchy won increased support from the upper classes who were keen to win favour and status at Louis' court.

Therefore, in practice royal absolutism meant the erosion of provincial privileges, the intervention of royal authority through agents such as the *intendants*, the further weakening of institutions such as the *parlements*, arbitrary taxation and the projection of the king's image as a divine symbol of authority and father of the people. Such concepts and ideas were not new. Historians such as Knecht and Greengrass have argued persuasively that centralisation of government and the erosion of parochial traditions were key features of Renaissance monarchies. David Parker goes on to stress that, far from marking a break with the past, the concept of absolutism was very much enshrined in traditional values. Seventeenth-century royal propagandists appealed to the age-old values of hierarchy and stability. In some senses, the absolutism of Louis XIV was mythical in that restraints continued to exist and always would do: complete absolutism would probably result in a monarch who was little more than a murderous despot. Yet, in some ways, absolutism became a necessary myth for the subjects of Louis, particularly the nobility and office holders, who were attracted to the cult of the king and absolutist ideology.

HOW FAR DID LOUIS XIV OVERCOME THE OBSTACLES TO ABSOLUTIST POWER IN FRANCE?

Royal authority could not be limitless, and in the interests of security a certain balance had to be struck between the elevation of royal power and the continued existence of institutions that actually restrained absolutism.

The very foundations of the monarchy rested upon the existence of such institutions, and, while government could be made more effective by clearing away many of the overlapping royal offices that existed, it would have been virtually impossible to dissolve *parlements* and estates entirely. Nevertheless, royal power did increase and we might argue that Louis got as close to absolutism as was possible in an early modern western state without actually becoming tyrannical.

Moreover, Louis relied upon the sale of offices, just like his predecessors, for income. Venality could be seen as a further limitation on Louis XIV's absolutism, as it suggests a dependence of the crown upon its office holders. Venality, it could be argued, allowed leading families to monopolise leading positions at court and increase their political influence at the expense of the crown. The king's leading minister, Colbert, followed Richelieu's example in denouncing venality, but like his predecessor he soon saw little point in trying to make meaningful inroads into this practice. In theory, venality was a corrupt practice that undermined the power and authority of the crown. Yet, in reality, venality could be controlled and manipulated to suit the crown. The political interests of the monarchy could be advanced by venality as the crown essentially oversaw the whole process and decided who bought which offices. Louis could control the upward movement of power within court to suit his own interests and manage the system in his own favour. Far from being a constraint on royal power, venality actually enhanced Louis XIV's position, as nobles competed for royal favour and sought to advance their standing. Richelieu had reaped the benefits of a vast clientele network that was loyal to his interests and those of the crown. Similarly, Louis XIV benefited in the short term from the cash injection that venality brought as well as the control that it gave the king over royal office holders. The system was fluid and flexible. Initially, Colbert made attempts to root out corruption by placing minimum age requirements on those becoming judges and by preventing nepotism within the judicial system. However, to a great extent, and especially after 1670 when war loomed on the horizon, venality became a crucial part of Louis XIV's monarchy. For absolutism venality was a spur and a bridle for absolutism at the same time.

Regional traditions and privileges had long stood proudly independent of the crown and, despite attempts to unify the kingdom through language, law and communications, resistance to state intervention at a local level remained fierce. The *parlements* was unable to resist the return of the *intendants* into the provinces. One of the high points of the Fronde had been the removal of the *intendants*; however, Colbert redefined their duties and sent royal officials once again into the localities to investigate the machinery of government and tax collection. The *intendants* of justice, police and finance became regular royal agents under Colbert with the authority to override local officials if the need arose. The fact that the *intendants* effectively became resident administrators in the provinces demonstrates the scale of the task facing Louis and Colbert. Originally, the *intendants* were to have filed a brief report on how local government could be made more efficient and accountable to Paris. These royal agents were still resident in 1680, and to an extent their presence undermined the powers of local governors. Yet there was no attempt to restructure local government; *intendants* did not replace municipal officers and offices remained for sale in the provinces just as they did at court. Furthermore, it could not be expected that 30 royal officials with limited resources could transform the system: a system that had become an accepted part of French government. To many officials in the localities the *intendants* merely represented another layer of bureaucracy, and it is too easy to overestimate their significance. Indeed, it should be remembered that attempts to increase monarchical power in the localities were nothing new. *Généraux des finances* and *intendants* had been used before with similar results.

Taxation and, in particular, the efficient collection of taxation also suffered from inherent weaknesses within the system that had become so entrenched and part of everyday practice that the best Colbert could do was to manipulate them in the interests of the crown. Tax farming, venality, *rentes* were essentially corrupt practices but they had become indispensable elements of the royal income. The best Colbert could do was to control the system in the interests of the crown. *Intendants* were used to make more realistic assessments of taxation in the généralités, while indirect taxation targeted the wealthier sections of French society that were normally exempt from taxation. Colbert insisted on meticulous book-keeping and strove for balanced budgets. Yet, despite Colbert's best intentions, the structure and fabric of the fiscal system remained untouched. Inequalities and privileges such as clerical and noble exemption from direct taxation remained, and those who could afford to pay least bore the greatest burden. Naturally, the crown looked for ways to exploit the wealth of the upper classes. In 1695, the *capitation* was introduced as a form of poll tax from which only the clergy were exempted. Although noble opposition led to its brief abandonment it did become a regular feature of French taxation in the eighteenth century although predictably the assessment and collection of this tax was haphazard. Such developments were further built upon in 1710 with the *dixième* tax on income that once more required the nobility to contribute to the royal coffers. Yet on the whole it was the third estate that was viewed as the inexhaustible source of taxation. Louis XIV's absolutism must be tempered by the lack of uniformity and efficiency in tax collection, together with the continued malpractice in the localities. The fact that local customs tariffs still existed that made it easier for some outlying provinces to trade with foreign countries rather than with other provinces within France highlights the age-old problems that faced any attempts to reform. Louis XIV himself was wary of radical reform in the realms of finance because it may have provoked the nobility and upset the system of checks and balances on which the stability of the kingdom depended.

The *parlement* of Paris had long made claims to be the primary bulwark against growing royal authority. Indeed, given the infrequent meetings of the Estates General and the self-interests of provincial and municipal estates, this may well be true. Certainly, Louis XIII had discovered that there were elements within the *parlement* that would resist attempts to curtail their rights and privileges. Yet *parlement* was a venal institution rather than a representative one and Louis was able to use this to his advantage. Moreover, Louis made a concerted attempt to remind the *parlement* of its duties as a law court and to stay out of politics. Indeed, even in this legislative sphere, Louis was eager to make it clear where authority lay. The *conseil privé* increasingly heard cases that would normally have been dealt with by *parlement* and, frequently, decisions made by *parlement* were overturned in royal law courts. That there was little response to such arbitrary dispensation of justice demonstrated the lack of power that *parlement* wielded. While there was no radical change in the makeup of *parlement* or redefinition of its duties, Louis made clear in no uncertain terms that *parlement* did not share in the legislative process. He was the supreme law-maker and judge within the kingdom and *parlement* must defer to his decisions. In 1667 and 1673, letters patent forced the *parlement* of Paris to register edicts without discussion, thus reducing significantly powers of remonstrance. Again, we can draw similarities here with Richelieu's actions of 1641, and it should be noted that the *intendants* also encroached upon the judicial rights of *parlement*. Nevertheless, the institution itself was not abolished. Louis XIV did not dare risk such an act that might be viewed as despotic. Theoretical absolutism would call for the destruction of such institutions that attempted to curtail royal authority, yet Louis wisely had too much respect for established institutions that could not simply be shattered. Under his rule, the powers of *parlements* were significantly undermined to the benefit of the crown, thus paving the way for Maupeou's abolition of the *parlements* in 1771.

Similarly, the Estates General lay dormant, presenting no threat to the crown. At times of monarchical weakness, the Estates General had provided a forum for noble discontent and the presentation of grievances to the king. It had even pushed for royal taxation to be subject to its consent. Yet the last meeting in 1614 had demonstrated the ineffectiveness of this institution, as the majority of representatives were picked by the crown and few of their grievances were addressed. Provincial estates also declined in influence and status. Some representative assemblies remained in the provinces, most notably in Brittany and Languedoc where local privileges and traditions were fiercely guarded. Elsewhere, local estates were dissolved or were simply not called. David Parker writes that 1672 saw the last meeting of assemblies in Basse Auvergne, 1675 those of Quercy and Rouergue, 1683 those of Alsace and 1704 those of Franche-Comté. Political power and autonomy in the localities was thus reduced, although local fiscal and judicial systems on the ground were much harder to overturn, and efforts actually to extend royal authority in the localities met with mixed success. Moreover, provincial estates in the *pays d'états* continued to wield more political influence than those in the *pays d'élections*.

French law provided another limitation on royal absolutism. Codification had begun under Louis XII and continued through Francis I and Henry II, yet there was still a wide gap between Roman law in the south and customary law in the north. In the same way that internal customs and poor communications undermined attempts to centralise the kingdom, so a lack of legal uniformity highlighted the weaknesses of Louis XIV's absolutism. Colbert took on the huge task of attempting to codify French law, and with no little success. New legal codes were introduced between 1667 and 1685 including the civil ordinance (1667) or *Code Louis*, the criminal ordinance (1670), the ordinance of commerce (1673), the ordinance of marine (1681) and the *Code noir* (1685). Colbert also attempted to streamline police powers in Paris and place authority in the hands of a lieutenant-general. Colbert's aim was to enhance the upkeep of law and order within the capital and to make someone responsible and accountable for the rule of law. Yet once more the enormity of Colbert's task combined with Louis' wariness of reform resulted in little practical change. Louis generally got his way in the localities when it really mattered, but this was partly due to the personal strength of the monarch and his regime together with the fact that the king was operating within the existing political framework and not looking to abolish traditional institutions nor encroach too heavily upon local privileges. Colbert's genius was in making the existing system function so effectively in favour of the crown.

We have already asserted that venality created a vast clientele network among the new nobility, or nobility of the robe, who were largely loyal to the crown. Competition for status and favour at court had been used to the crown's advantage under Richelieu and Mazarin, and this was extended under Colbert. The old nobility or nobility of the sword offered little obstruction to royal absolutism as they were very much part of the established hierarchy and order that Louis was looking to preserve. In some ways, the political influence of the old nobility at court had waned slightly with the emergence of a new nobility created by venality and reward. Yet their social status remained untouched and Louis XIV, just like previous monarchs, depended upon his leading magnates to maintain order and to lead armies. As in other spheres, Louis was able to manage and control the nobility more effectively than many of his predecessors. In 1682, Louis XIV moved the court from the Louvre to Versailles and the cult of the Sun King was born. Louis did not force magnates to reside at court. Instead, as Parker argues, the great nobility wanted to be there, in an environment where they could enhance their political standing and position. Roger Lockyer writes that Versailles was consciously designed to tame the French aristocracy although in reality only a relatively small percentage of the nobility actually resided at Versailles. Nevertheless, it is true that the nobility of the robe dominated the *conseil d'en haut* although it must be remembered that the nobility of the robe did not emerge under Louis XIV, and venality had long been common practice. Many of the nobility of the robe had married into more established families and it was becoming more difficult to distinguish between new and old. The lack of noble revolts is viewed as evidence that a permanent court at Versailles kept the aristocracy under constant supervision and control, making Louis the fount of all patronage. However, this too created problems, as the French court increasingly became viewed as a separate entity by those outside it, and in times of economic hardship its extravagance and ostentation seemed out of place. The luxury and riches of Versailles were in stark contrast to the poverty of the third estate. The continual toil, poverty and hardships of the peasantry manifested themselves in frequent revolts. In Boulonnais in 1662, and Bordeaux and Brittany in 1675, peasants revolted against the financial impositions of the crown. The insurgents were harshly dealt with and conditions did not improve for the peasantry throughout Louis XIV's reign. Indeed, as war took its toll, life for the lower end of the third estate got worse. Absolutism promoted the interests of the aristocracy at the expense of the peasantry and it might be argued that such inequalities created long-term problems for the French crown.

The army constituted a crucial feature of an absolutist monarchy. The ability to mobilise a strong, professional army quickly and effectively underpinned royal power and control. Moreover, loyalty within the army was critical and Louis was well aware of past disloyalties such as that of the Duke of Bourbon in 1523. The man whom Louis entrusted with the task of reforming the army was Michel le Tellier. Le Tellier had already served as *intendant* of the army under Richelieu and had also worked under Mazarin as secretary of state for military affairs. He was the obvious man for the job in 1661, and over the next ten years he professionalised the army beyond recognition. His work was carried on by his son François-Michel le Tellier, marquis de Louvois. French armies were brought under central control and generals were made directly accountable to the king and his war secretary. Both father and son Le Tellier, but especially Louvois, issued regulations on recruiting, training and discipline. Corruption and abuses such as nepotism and the sale of important military offices were curbed. The projection of Louis XIV's image abroad and his pursuit of glory depended upon success on the battlefield. Le Tellier and Louvois ensured that France put out armies into the field that were unparalleled in terms of size and training. Louvois was a logistical master, ensuring that his troops were well fed and regularly paid. Both Le Telliers contributed to the establishment of *magazins*, which supplied armies with food and equipment. The key figure in the subordination of the army was, however, Louis himself. Officers were no longer distant aristocrats who theoretically answered to the king but in reality went their own way, using military resources often to advance their own cause. The officer class was no longer just a reward for loyalty or a status symbol; officers were expected to lead and fight, following their king's example in the process. War was a central feature of Louis' regime, and in many ways underpinned his absolutism. Centralisation of the army was not popular and Louvois in particular was an objectionable figure, but control of the military and the creation of an army answerable directly to the king was a success for absolutism.

François-Michel le Tellier, Marquis of Louvois

DOES COLBERT DESERVE HIS REPUTATION AS ONE OF THE MOST EFFECTIVE ADMINISTRATORS OF THE SEVENTEENTH CENTURY?

The career and achievements of Jean-Baptiste Colbert have split historical opinions. There is no doubt that, between 1661 and his death in 1683, Colbert committed himself to an enormous range of activities. Centralisation of government, law and order, the extension of royal authority, communications and overseas trade were all actively pursued by Colbert with single-minded determination. But it was in the realm of finance that Colbert really made his name, moving Geoffrey Treasure to write that if Colbert had done nothing more than bring order into the finances so that Louis could embark on his early wars with sufficient resources he would still have a prominent place in history. It is also tempting to place Colbert's achievements against those of Richelieu and indeed the man who succeeded him at court and his great rival, namely Louvois. Different interpretations exist of Colbert's achievements:

- **Robin Briggs** states that while no other minister to the end of the *ancien régime* achieved so much in terms of practical reform, it is clear that the changes he made were limited to making the existing system function more efficiently.
- **François Bluche** believes that Colbert was a compendium of talents; his advice indispensable upon matters of the economy, the navy, police and fine arts. He was the inheritor of the secrets of Mazarin and an admirer and imitator of Richelieu.

- **Geoffrey Treasure** thinks Colbert's vision to be comprehensive, his commitment total, his application heroic and his talent for administration prodigious.
- **D. H. Pennington** plays down Colbert's achievements, promoting the line that Colbert appears outstanding in the history of a state-sponsored economy more through the status his country achieved than through any unique success of his own; the notion that all Europe imitated a new French economic system known as Colbertism has long been discredited.
- Contemporary opinion also varied greatly after Colbert's death in 1683. The queen reported that such was the fury of the people that they wanted to tear his poor dead body from limb to limb. Conversely, the *New Abridged Chronology* stated that the prosperity and brilliance of this regime, the grandeur of the monarch, the well-being of the people would forever mourn the death of the greatest minister that France had ever had.

As with all great historical figures, Colbert's reputation has been derided, rehabilitated and revised many times throughout the centuries since his death. It seems important to view the achievements of Colbert in the context of the *ancien régime*: while it would be all too easy to highlight the limitations of his centralising reforms, we must look at the system and environment in which he was operating. Colbert was not embarking on reform with a clean slate; he was attempting to impose practical reform on regions that had entrenched traditions of autonomy. Parochialism and the rise of the Dutch economy are also important factors to consider when assessing Colbert's financial achievements. Nevertheless, whether one favours the more bellicose policies of Louvois or the measured stance of Colbert, it is evident that Colbert was a loyal and devoted servant of the crown for over two decades. In the final analysis it is critical to bear in mind that Colbert was devoted to serving the king and aiding him in his pursuit of glory. Colbert was therefore constricted by the values and ideology of that monarchy.

HOW DID COLBERT RISE TO PROMINENCE IN 1661?

Jean Baptiste Colbert's rise to power has often been viewed as a rags-to-riches story, indicative of the way in which Louis favoured a new administrative class rather than the established aristocracy. Colbert was from a banking family from Reims. One of nine children that survived out of eighteen in total, his upbringing was bourgeois and it was clear that his father, Nicolas, strove to better the Colbert family, using money and mercantile connections as well as marriage to extend their influence and social status. The Colberts were typical of that ambitious banking class who had struck rich through international trade and now sought to enhance their status through the purchase of office.

Nicolas Colbert had a financial office in Paris, and through his business contacts was able to push his son into the spotlight. Jean Baptiste was trained in law, and began his career as a clerk in the war department. Distantly related to what would become a great rival family, the Le Telliers, Colbert impressed both Le Tellier and Mazarin during the crisis of government, the Fronde. He soon entered Mazarin's household and worked hard on his master's behalf. It was here that he learned about French government; how to exploit loopholes in the system and how to manipulate patronage. He also experienced the peculiarities of the financial system and saw first hand how vast fortunes could be amassed at the expense of the crown. Mazarin left a fortune worth well over 35 million livres on his death, and Colbert had done much to administer and accumulate this fortune for the cardinal.

In the process, Colbert accumulated enough evidence to incriminate another individual who had made a quick and vast fortune out of royal service, Nicolas Fouquet. As Bluche points out, the heraldic crest of the Fouquets was a crimson squirrel while that of the Colberts was an azure snake. The image of the agile squirrel ensnared by the ruthless and cunning snake aptly portrays Colbert's pursuit of Fouquet. Fouquet as *surintendant des finances* had put great emphasis upon speculators, farming out royal assets often to the highest bidder in an attempt to raise money quickly to meet the demands of war. He played the system on behalf of the king, building up a complex clientele network in the process, not to mention a vast personal fortune. By the time Louis himself witnessed the extent of Fouquet's wealth at the *surintendant's* palatial Vaux le Vicomte in August 1661, he had already decided that he must be removed. Fouquet was imprisoned for three years before facing trial charged with what amounted to embezzlement and treason. Certainly, Fouquet was guilty of enriching himself at the expense of the crown, but Colbert himself was implicated in amassing Mazarin's fortune in a similar manner. Colbert managed the Fouquet trial carefully in order to prevent such allegations becoming public, but Fouquet put up a spirited defence even to the point of offering his estates to the royal accountants to undertake an audit of his supposed fortune. The additional charge that Fouquet was plotting in some way to defy the king forcefully was nonsensical and the evidence offered relating to the fortification of Belle-Isle was flimsy. Ultimately, the former *surintendant* was imprisoned for nearly twenty years at Pinerolo where he died in 1680.

Fouquet's fall paved the way for Colbert's rise and we should note the ruthless and vicious manner in which Colbert pursued Fouquet. Colbert now took his place on the royal council alongside Lionne and Le Tellier, and in 1665 he acquired the title of controller-general through which he undertook wide-scale financial reform of the system that both he and Fouquet had worked with in the past. Fouquet's fall also demonstrated the power of royal justice and sent out a strong message to those speculators who believed that easy money could be made at the expense of the crown.

WHAT WAS THE IMPORTANCE OF VERSAILLES?

Versailles was much more than an extravagant construction project. Rather it was a visual display of Louis XIV's power and glory. The palace bore his own stamp unlike the Louvre or Tuileries; Versailles was the king's creation and it reflected his needs and personality. Bluche writes that just as Le Nôtre's art disciplined nature, the art of Versailles served to discipline the court, the king's creation. Versailles was dominated by the quest for glory, and the scale and beauty of the palace reflected the majesty of the king. Above all else, the function of Versailles was to portray the image of an absolutist monarch appointed by God to rule. Versailles was a striking statement of the sacred nature of French monarchy. Images of Apollo abounded in the gardens, where visitors were invited to admire Apollo attended by nymphs, and on the ceiling of the throne room, emblazoned with Charles de La Fosse's masterpiece 'Apollo on his Chariot'. The architecture and artwork of men such as Rigaud and Le Brun showcased Louis XIV's France as a centre for culture and enlightenment. Moreover, the abundance of classical imagery portrayed Louis as a powerful and wise monarch, born to rule. The king's entire state apartment is dominated by the solar myth. Felibien writes that 'As the Sun is the emblem of the king, the seven planets have been chosen as the subject of the paintings in the seven rooms of this apartment so that in each of them those actions of the Heroes of Antiquity must be represented which relate to each of the planets and also to each of His Majesty's actions.' The symbolical motifs are seen in the carved ornaments of the cornices and on the ceilings. The walls of the state apartment are cased in marble from top to bottom, and, as Felibien observes, as one proceeds from one room to the next there is more and more wealth, not only in the marble but also in the sculptures and in the paintings embellishing the ceilings. Images of Hercules, Venus, Diana, Mars and Mercury stand alongside glorious episodes from the Dutch War and victories of the War of Devolution. Versailles became a symbol of unparalleled power and patronage. The myth of absolutism emerged from this fabulous palace.

Louis XIV is seen to have subjugated the aristocracy by luring them to Versailles with the prize of enhanced status but with little political authority. Louis maintained the nobility at Versailles in a state of dependence and luxury, sapping their resources and depriving them of their freedom. The political and administrative power was handed over to the new nobility of the robe, who owed their position to ability and loyalty to the king. Yet this interpretation, largely based on the memoirs of Saint-Simon, is too simplistic. In reality, only a fraction of French nobility resided at Versailles and even then very few were there all year round. Only 4000 could be accommodated at Versailles, leaving 96,000 nobles to account for in the rest of France. Moreover, while it is true that the majority of Louis XIV's ministers were not nobility of the sword, it would be wrong to assume that the old nobility were shorn of their responsibilities. On the contrary, the positions of royal governors, military leaders and leading clerics were still occupied by the old nobility. Importantly, ambassadorial posts to London or Vienna were often given to the nobility of the sword, thus extinguishing the notion that Louis deliberately sidelined the nobility of the sword. Louis did seem to favour the new nobility, those who had been rewarded for bureaucratic service or who had purchased ennoblement. The primary reason for this was that the new nobility had large amounts of disposable income that they were ready to spend on advancing their social position. The move towards war in the second half of Louis XIV's reign put a massive strain on the economy that could be eased slightly with the creation and sale of royal offices. Furthermore, there were more offices to go around because Colbert's centralising reforms created new layers of bureaucracy. At the highest political level, Louis perhaps favoured the nobility of the robe because they owed their status and position to him alone and they were his creatures. On another level, the new nobility provided Louis with an easy and reliable source of income. The old nobility were not discarded nor were they even sidelined. In the provinces and at court, their social status remained intact if politically they rather missed out. Above all else the nobility were left in no doubt that Louis XIV's regime would protect their interests. Versailles itself represented the orderly and hierarchical nature of Louis XIV's France; a France based around class rule. Whether at Versailles or in the provinces the nobility knew that collaboration and loyalty would be rewarded and the king's patronage was worth having.

The importance of Versailles lay in royal propaganda. Peter Burke, in *The Fabrication of Louis XIV* (1992), puts forward the idea that the imagery of Versailles was aimed at the aristocracy and foreign visitors. In the same way that the nobility demonstrated their admiration of Louis by imitating their king, so foreign princes looked to replicate the style and grandeur of Versailles. Ambassadors informed their governments about the splendour of Versailles. In 1685, the doge of Genoa was treated to a reception at Versailles. On seeing the interior he declared, '*A year ago it was Hell; now it is Paradise.*' To receive the Persian ambassador shortly before his death in 1715, Louis wore a black and gold outfit so heavily embroidered with diamonds that he had to change out of it before dinner. Saint Simon wrote gushingly that never had the king espoused such magnificence. The aim of such ostentation was to portray France as a nation to be feared; one that was strong and powerful.

Versailles also inevitably attracted the finest musicians, playwrights and artists, not by chance, but by design. Again, the aim was almost to promote a cult of the Sun King, using art, theatre and music to glorify France and flatter Louis himself. Colbert was at the forefront of this propaganda drive, linking the ongoing construction process to his economic policy of intervention and protection. He reopened the marble quarries, reorganised the former royal manufactories and created new ones such as the Gobelins tapestry works and the St Gobain crystal factory. Colbert required all artists and sculptors to join the Académie Royale de Peinture et de Sculpture (1663), with the intention of ensuring that Louis' image was promoted and enhanced by their work. The musician Lully, the comic playwright Molière and the painter Le Brun all served in the academy and all contributed to the glory of Louis XIV. The greatest spectacle took place in the gardens of Versailles in May 1664: the fête of the 'Pleasures of the Enchanted Isle' comprised a week of court spectacles, masques, ballets and fireworks. Bluche writes that Louis XIV's entertainments not only provoked amazement abroad, they also formulated taste, encouraged the chivalric spirit and contributed to public education.

Unquestionably there was an artificiality and falseness about Versailles fostered by courtly etiquette. For Louis, etiquette satisfied his sense of order, yet in some ways Versailles meant that the monarchy became even more remote from those in the provinces. Pennington sees the image of Louis change according to his mistresses. The first, Louise de la Vallière, represented a link to the nobility of the robe, while her replacement, Madame de Montespan, demonstrated the snobbish, superior attitude of those within the circle of the court at Versailles. Finally, Madame de Maintenon, secret wife of the king from 1683 following the death of the

The great fête of the 'Pleasures of the Enchanted Isle' at Versailles, May 1664

queen, attained great influence, reflected in the increasingly devout and pious nature of the court. Clearly such an outlook was in stark contrast to the beginning of the young Apollo's residence at Versailles. Censorship suppressed free thinking towards the end of Louis' reign and the Sun King became increasingly out of touch with new ideas and modern thought. Moreover, the cost in terms of construction and labour were shouldered by the third estate, made up of people who never stepped through the gates of Versailles. Yet Versailles was not meant for them; its purpose was to impress and in that context alone it was a success.

WHAT WAS THE BALANCE OF POWER IN EUROPE IN 1661?

The early seventeenth century had seen France adopt a relatively cautious foreign policy that had generally been anti-Habsburg in nature. Spain and the House of Austria had been the dominant forces in Europe and overseas where new markets and trade routes were beginning to be exploited in the new world. In its pursuit of secular objectives and material benefits, France had been prepared to ally with Protestant powers in order to undermine Habsburg authority. Aid and supplies were offered to the Dutch in their struggle for independence against the Spanish. In 1631, a treaty was signed with Protestant Sweden and its king, Gustavus Adolphus, in order to exploit the military might of that nation. Religious loyalties seemed to matter little in the realm of foreign policy as France looked to erode Habsburg strength and restore a balance of power in favour of France.

France declared outright war on Spain in 1635, and the French army was successful in defeating the Spanish at Rocroi in 1643, just as the infant Louis XIV succeeded his father. This crushing victory was followed by another at Lens in 1648, thus signalling the decline of Spain as a major power. France profited from the settlement of Westphalia in 1648, securing its eastern frontiers with the acquisition of Breisach and Philippsburg from Imperial hands. The war with Spain, however, went on until 1659 when Mazarin negotiated the Treaty of the Pyrenees. This treaty clearly marked a defeat for Spain. Not only did Spain cede Artois and Rousillon to France as well as Luxembourg and Hainault, but in doing so it implicitly recognised French superiority and primacy. A provision was also made in the treaty for Philip IV's daughter Maria Theresa to marry the young French king, Louis XIV. The bride had to renounce all claims to the Spanish throne and regular dowry payments were to be made from Madrid.

Therefore, Europe in 1661 was essentially one that had witnessed a shift in the balance of power from Spain to France. Virtually all of Europe had been involved at one time or another in the Thirty Years' War (1618–48) and economies had suffered as a consequence. General economic depression brought on by bad harvests and inflation had not helped matters. Germany in particular had been ravaged by the fighting and Spain had been forced to declare bankruptcy on several occasions. France was also exhausted by war although it had joined the conflict later and had used alliances and diplomacy carefully to avoid conflict until the odds were heavily in its favour. French resources were enormous although in 1661 the kingdom was in no position to fight. The navy constructed by Richelieu was in disrepair while the army was untrained and unequipped. More pressing was the state of the royal treasury that was heavily in debt.

Colbert restored royal finances and provided Louis with the economic security to wage war. Moreover, the growth in industry aided the production of cannon and iron gun fittings. Le Tellier and his son Louvois transformed the army into a disciplined and organised fighting force. Martinet, inspector-general of the infantry, instilled order into the troops, introducing marching in step and uniforms. Louvois was a logistical expert creating *magazins* which were food supply centres for troops on the move, negating the need for billeting which was deeply unpopular among local populations. Venality within the armed forces was significantly reduced, especially with regard to the top posts which were increasingly filled by men of ability such as Vauban. Sébastien Vauban became a master of siege warfare and fortifications, and he developed the modern bayonet. Louis himself was extremely interested in military affairs and oversaw the development of the French army and navy from the outset. The king commanded in the field although he preferred to leave strategic decisions to his generals and coordinate operations from behind the lines. The growth of the French navy stimulated by Colbert was also an important part of challenging Dutch commercial interests. The navy grew to become the biggest in the Mediterranean and naval arsenals were established at Brest and Rochefort.

In terms of diplomacy, Louis was assisted by a number of impressive secretaries of state including Lionne, Arnauld de Pomponne, Colbert de Croissy (brother of Colbert) and the Marquis of Torcy (son of Croissy). Louis, however, was the real master of French foreign policy and it was he who took the final decisions. In the early years of Louis' personal rule, the king was keen to assert himself in Europe and take advantage of the power vacuum left after the Thirty Years' War. A number of minor incidents gave Louis the opportunity to show off his authority and display aggressive intent. A major diplomatic incident arose in 1661 over precedence between French and Spanish ambassadors in London over which Louis threatened war. Philip IV inevitably gave way agreeing that in future French ambassadors would have precedence everywhere in Europe apart from Vienna.

Clearly the Peace of the Pyrenees had not put an end to Franco-Spanish rivalries, and Louis' desire to strengthen the north-western frontier between France and the Spanish Netherlands and even push French boundaries towards the Rhine was likely further to antagonise the Habsburgs. The Dutch were at first coveted as potentially important allies in a war against Spain, and it was for this reason that Louis declared war on England in 1666, a decision designed to neutralise the Dutch over French claims to the southern Netherlands. It was the traditional enemy of Spain that France targeted first in Louis' quest for glory.

A2 ASSESSMENT: FRANCE 1500–1715

QUESTIONS IN THE STYLE OF OCR AND EDEXCEL

Key theme: The Development of a Nation State: France 1498–1610

Key theme: The Ascendancy of France 1610–1715

Examples of questions on these themes

- How far did France develop as a nation-state 1498–1610?
- How important was religion to the development of France 1498–1610?
- How far did economic changes affect French society 1498–1610?
- To what extent did the power of the monarchy increase 1610–1715?
- How far did the monarch rule in the interests of his subjects 1610–1715?
- To what extent did Henry IV and Louis XIII lay the foundations of absolutism under Louis XIV?

How to answer these questions

Both of these themes focus on change and continuity over two centuries of French history. The emphasis in your answer should be on developing a broad overview of the period studied. There is no real requirement for detailed depth knowledge but rather candidates are expected to show breadth of historical understanding. With this in mind it is crucial to be able to deploy evidence from across the period and to use it skilfully. You must be able to demonstrate the major points of change and continuity that existed across the period using the material that you have learned. Try to identify significant turning points that will allow you to develop your argument effectively.

Style

- You must adapt your written style to cater for the broad sweep of history that you are studying. Avoid detailed analysis and in-depth analysis. Instead focus on more general issues concerning change and continuity, briefly using relevant examples in order to substantiate your argument.
- Select your evidence from across the period, demonstrating to the examiner that your knowledge is sufficiently wide-ranging.
- Organise your paragraphs analytically and thematically around general concepts and issues rather than specific events.
- Make a judgement at the end concerning levels of change and continuity.

Questions

1. How far did life change for the French nobility 1498–1610?

How to answer this question
Plan your answer thematically. The focus of this question is clearly the nobility. Think about areas in which their lives were affected and how other factors influenced their status within French society.

Key points might include:

- The emergence of a new noble class: the nobility of the robe. The reasons why this so-called *noblesse de robe* came to be, and the extent to which they impinged upon the standing of the old nobility will form a major part of your essay.
- The economic climate and the effects of both international and domestic wars on the financial security of the nobility will be important here. General peaks and troughs in the French economy were often exacerbated by events on the battlefield.
- Monarchical authority also had an effect on the lives of the nobility. How far certain monarchs were able to strengthen their own position at the expense of the nobility will form another strand of your argument. The financial pressures brought to bear upon the nobility during times of stress is also significant.
- Do not be afraid to demonstrate an appreciation of arguments between historians over certain issues, such as the extent to which the nobility were in crisis during this period, and make a judgement towards the end of your work.

2. How far were French monarchs absolutist rulers in the period 1610–1715?

How to answer this question
Here is a different question from a different period but the style remains the same. Once you have planned your answer around themes and issues look to select your evidence carefully from across the period. It would be easy here to concentrate on Louis XIV to the detriment of Louis XIII, Richelieu and Mazarin.

Key turning points might include:

- The Peace of Alais, 1629, signals the Huguenot defeat strengthening Louis XIII's kingship and confirming Richelieu's ability. This coincides with a general down-turn in Habsburg fortunes in Germany and the Netherlands.
- The Day of Dupes, 1630, confirms Richelieu as Louis XIII's chief minister. Richelieu soon develops a powerful clientele network with a power base in the inner council.
- Noble rebellions such as Cinq Mars (1641–42) and the Comte de Soissons (1641) ought also to be deployed to demonstrate opposition to Richelieu.

- Venality and the increased role of *intendants* in promoting royal authority would also be an important piece of evidence in your argument.
- The Fronde, 1648–52, highlights the weakness of the government whilst still demonstrating the strength of the monarchy as an institution. The long-term effect of the Fronde on Louis XIV should also not be forgotten.
- The remodelling of the army by Le Tellier between 1665–75 into a well-disciplined and effective fighting force.
- Colbert's restoration of financial security and codification of law.
- The role of Versailles as a means of projecting Louis XIV's image and controlling the nobility.
- Louis XIV's pursuit of glory abroad and the effects upon the economy highlighted by Nijmegen in 1679.

This list is by no means exhaustive but it does give some idea as to how to use material in order to reinforce points of analysis. The examiner does not expect to see a large amount of detail, but does expect you to demonstrate a range of knowledge.

3. How important was religion in the development of France 1498–1610?

How to answer this question
Be prepared to make some kind of balanced judgement towards the end of your essay. In this case an example might be:

Whilst religion potentially acted as a source of stability for the French crown and even strength under Francis I (Concordat of Bologna, 1516), it ultimately proved catastrophically divisive. The second half of the sixteenth century was plagued by religious war, and the emergence of Calvinism in France had done much to undermine the authority of the crown and the Gallican principles on which it rested. Although only 10 per cent of the population were Calvinist, their impact was enormous and the succession crisis of 1584 highlighted the fear of a potential Huguenot monarch.

BIBLIOGRAPHY

W. Beik, *Absolutism and Society in Seventeenth Century France*, Cambridge (1985)

P. Benedict, *Rouen during the Wars of Religion*, Cambridge (1981)

F. Bluche, *Louis XIV*, Oxford (1990)

R. Bonney (ed.), *Society and Government in France under Richelieu and Mazarin, 1624–1661*, London (1988)

R. Briggs, *Early Modern France 1560–1715*, Oxford (1977)

B. B. Diefendorf, *Beneath the Cross: Catholics and Huguenots in Sixteenth Century Paris*, Oxford (1991)

J. H Elliot, *Richelieu and Olivares*, Cambridge (1989)

M. Greengrass, *France in the Age of Henri IV*, London (1984)

M. Greengrass, *The French Reformation*, London (1987)

M. P. Holt, *The French Wars of Religion, 1562–1629*, Cambridge (1995)

M. P. Holt (ed.), *Renaissance and Reformation France*, Oxford (2002)

R. J. Knecht, *French Renaissance Monarchy: Francis I and Henry II*, London (1996)

R. J. Knecht, *The Rise and Fall of Renaissance France 1483–1610*, Oxford (2001)

R. J. Knecht, *Renaissance Warrior and Patron: The Reign of Francis I*, Cambridge (1994)

A. Levi, *Cardinal Richelieu and the Making of France*, London (2001)

A. Lossky, 'The absolutism of Louis XIV: reality or myth?' in *Canadian Journal of History*, 11 (1984)

J. Russel Major, *Representative Government in Early Modern France*, New Haven (1980)

D.H. Pennington, *Europe in the Seventeenth Century*, London (1989)

D. Potter, *A History of France, 1460–1560: The Emergence of a Nation State*, London (1995)

N. Zemon Davis, *Society and Culture in Early Modern France*, Stanford (1975)

INDEX

To help you get the grades you deserve at AS and A-level History you'll need up-to-date books that cover exactly the right topics and help you at exam time.

So that's precisely what we've written.

The Heinemann Advanced History Series

15th - 18th Century

Spain 1474-1700
0 435 32733 X

The English Reformation: Crown Power and Religous Change, 1485-1558
0 435 32712 7

The European Reformation: 1500-1610
0 435 32710 0

The Reign of Elizabeth
0 435 32735 6

The Coming of the Civil War: 1603-49
0 435 32713 5

England in Crisis: 1640-60
0 435 32714 3

France in Revolution: 1776-1830
0 435 32732 1

The Reign of Henry VII 1450-1509
0 435 32742 9

Oliver Cromwell
0 435 32756 9

France 1500-1715
0 435 32751 8

19th - 20th Century: British

Britain 1815-51: Protest and Reform
0 435 32716 X

Poverty & Public Health: 1815-1948
0 435 32715 1

The Extension of the Franchise: 1832-1931
0 435 32717 8

Liberalism and Conservatism 1846-1905
0 435 32737 2

European Diplomacy 1870-1939
0 435 32734 8

British Imperial and Foreign Policy 1846-1980
0 435 32753 4

Britain 1890-1939
0 435 32757 7

Britain 1929-1998
0 435 32738 0

19th - 20th Century: European

Russia 1848-1917
0 435 32718 6

Lenin and the Russian Revolution
0 435 32719 4

Stalinist Russia
0 435 32720 8

Germany 1848-1914
0 435 32711 9

Germany 1919-45
0 435 32721 6

Mussolini and Italy
0 435 32725 9

The Modernisation of Russia 1856-1985
0 435 32741 0

Italian Unification 1820-71
0 435 32754 2

European Diplomacy 1890-1939
0 435 32734 8

20th Century: American and World

Civil Rights in the USA 1863-1980
0 435 32722 4

The USA 1917-45
0 435 32723 2

The Cold War - Conflict in Europe and Asia
0 435 32736 4

Heinemann

Inspiring generations

01865 888080   01865 314029   orders@heinemann.co.uk   www.heinemann.co.uk

tel   fax   email   web

G769